The Future of Physical Education

Anthony Laker leads an outstanding international team of educational theorists in critically examining the theoretical underpinnings of physical education, and in challenging the rhetoric, the practices and the pedagogies that prevail in our schools. There has been a great deal of discussion surrounding the value of this subject in schools, particularly around the form that physical education should take. The domination of physical education teaching by the scientific/technical discourses is problematized and it is suggested that this domination limits the potential of the subject to be culturally and contextually relevant to students in schools. This edited collection aims to extend the worldwide academic debate on the future of physical education in schools by challenging the prevailing 'authorised curricula'.

Each contributor addresses a key contemporary issue in physical education bringing different perspectives as they relate to the evolving issues of the subject. They ask important questions about where we intend to take the knowledge we have gained from a legacy of positive research. These chapters tackle critical issues in modernist physical education and suggest how a re-evaluation could contribute to the continuing advancement of the subject for more diverse educational benefits. Laker draws this body of work together in a conclusion that describes a theoretically and pedagogically innovative physical education curriculum for the 21st century.

This book is a summary of the current state of research in physical education. It invites debate and discussions in the field and re-conceptualises physical education theory into inclusive practices located in the postmodern school world.

Anthony Laker is Degree Director, Physical Education, Department of Exercise and Sport Science, East Carolina University.

Routledge research in education

The Future of Physical Education

Building a new pedagogy

Edited by Anthony Laker

Foreword by George Sage

Routledge Research in Education

Routledge
Taylor & Francis Group

LONDON AND NEW YORK

First published 2003
by Routledge
11 New Fetter Lane, London EC4P 4EE

Simultaneously published in the USA and Canada
by Routledge
29 West 35th Street, New York, NY 10001

Routledge is an imprint of the Taylor & Francis Group

© 2003 Anthony Laker for selection and editorial matter;
individual chapters, the contributors

Typeset in Baskerville by Steven Gardiner Ltd, Cambridge
Printed and bound in Great Britain by
Antony Rowe Ltd, Chippenham, Wiltshire

British Library Cataloguing in Publication Data
A catalogue record for this book is available from the British Library

Library of Congress Cataloging in Publication Data
The future of physical education: building a new pedagogy / edited by
Anthony Laker; foreword by George Sage.
p. cm. – (Routledge research in education; 6)
Includes bibliographical references and index.
1. Physical education and training. 2. School sports. I. Laker, Anthony,
1951– . II. Series.
GV341.F88 2003
613.7'07 – dc21   2003046525

ISBN 0–415–28892–4

Contents

Contributors

Anthony Laker is the Degree Director in Physical Education in the Department of Exercise and Sport Science at East Carolina University. He has taught in primary and secondary schools, and has been involved in training teachers of both primary and secondary physical education. Anthony is the author of *Beyond the Boundaries of Physical Education: Educating Young People for Citizenship and Social Responsibility* and *Developing Personal, Social and Moral Education Through Physical Education: A Practical Guide for Teachers*, both published by RoutledgeFalmer. He has also edited *The Sociology of Sport and Physical Education: An Introductory Reader*. His current research interests include understanding and interpreting the physical education curriculum and sport experience from a global, cultural perspective. Anthony enjoys sailing, surfing and long-distance trekking.

Steve Estes recently served as Chair of the Department of Exercise and Sport Science at East Carolina University. He did his undergraduate and masters studies in physical education at San Diego State University and received his doctorate from Ohio State University. He is co-author of two books, both with Robert Mechikoff, *Knowing Human Movement* and *A History and Philosophy of Physical Education*. Dr Estes has studied history and philosophy of sport and physical education, the role of technology in physical education and the role of physical education in higher education.

Juan-Miguel Fernández-Balboa is a Professor of Education in the Department of Curriculum and Teaching at Montclair State University. Originally from Barcelona, Spain, he received his Doctorate in Education from the University of Massachusetts-Amherst. He currently teaches courses on 'critical thinking', 'curriculum change', and 'democratic educational theory and practice'. He has published widely, both in Spanish and English, in particular in the area of 'critical pedagogy'. Among his more salient publications is *Critical Postmodernism in Human Movement, Physical Education and Sport*, a book he edited and co-authored. Moreover, he is an editorial board member of journals such as *Sport, Education and Society*, *The Journal of Sport Pedagogy*, and *Ágora*.

Peter Hastie is an Associate Professor in the Department of Health and Human Performance at Auburn University. His area of specialty is sport education, having written numerous research papers examining the model. His latest text, *Teaching for Lifetime Physical Activity through Quality High School Physical Education* has been written for those who are preparing to teach in secondary schools. He has also contributed chapters to Silverman and Ennis' latest edition of *Student Learning in Physical Education: Applying Research to Enhance Instruction*. In his spare time, Peter enjoys adventure activities and travelling to remote places.

Doune Macdonald is an Associate Professor in the School of Human Movement Studies, the University of Queensland. She coordinates the health and physical education (HPE) teacher education programme and teaches the undergraduate curriculum studies courses. Prior to her university work she taught in primary and secondary schools and in 2000 returned to some part-time school teaching to be reminded of how challenging and complex teaching is. While she tries to critically reflect on her own practices, current demands of the tertiary sector seem to afford little space or opportunity. Her research interests include curriculum development and change, teacher education and the place of physical activity in the lives of young people. She lives with Steven, Erika and Sophie who constantly cause her to reflect.

G.S. Don Morris is a Professor of Kinesiology at Cal Poly-Pomona in California. Serving as the Pedagogy Coordinator, he has spent nearly a quarter of a century investigating what motivates children and students of all ages. Don has been engaged in comprehensive health research of elementary children for over a decade. Currently he is involved in a collaborative, comparative, cross-cultural youth study examining violent behaviour. His publications include *Becoming Responsible, Elementary Physical Education Program* now in its second edition, and *Changing Kids' Games* (with Jim Stiehl). He lives in the Sierra Nevada mountains and commutes to the Los Angeles area to his workplace. Don enjoys many outdoor activities such as skiing, hiking, fishing and just plain deck sitting and watching the mountains shift. Don also travels to and lives in Israel. He works with his colleagues at Zinman College as a pedagogy consultant and lecturer.

Stephen Silverman is a Professor of Education and Coordinator of the Movement Science and Education Program at Teachers College, Columbia University. Steve has published more than 75 papers and chapters and 10 books related to teaching and research methods. He previously served as chair of the AAHPERD Curriculum and Instruction Academy and president of the Research Consortium. He is a past editor of the *Journal of Teaching in Physical Education* and currently is serving as editor-in-chief of the *Research Quarterly for Exercise and Sport*. Steve is an Active Fellow in the American Academy of Kinesiology and Physical Education.

Richard Tinning is Professor of Pedagogy in the School of Human Movement Studies at the University of Queensland. Previously he was Professor of Physical Education at Deakin University where he pioneered the use of distance education and action research for inservice teachers of physical education. He has been involved in major Australian curriculum development projects, worked on large-scale professional development programmes for teachers and been a consultant to both schools and universities. He has published widely in scholarly and professional journals in physical education and authored or co-authored numerous books and monographs. Richard's research interests are informed by a socially critical perspective and include: physical education teacher education, physical education pedagogy, pedagogical work for the body and physical education and the healthy citizen. As a reflective practitioner he is currently involved in an embodied life history project in which he is both subject/object.

Foreword

The authors of this volume provide readers with a comprehensive and in-depth account of the past and present issues, controversies, and, yes, the accomplishments in physical education pedagogy. But they also take the additional step of speculating and proposing what the future will, or should, hold for this important endeavor. Each of the authors stake out a specific topic and then constructs a unique perspective from which to analyze that topic. They join a discussion and debate with deep historical roots.

All the authors discuss the antecedents of the particular topic they write about. This is commendable and useful. We must know backward to think forward. But the authors appropriately limit their historical commentary to their topic. So, as I thought about how I might use this Foreword to introduce readers to this book, I thought it would be helpful for me to more broadly locate the topics covered in this volume in a historical context. Although my account of the issues and trends in physical education pedagogy during the past century must necessarily be brief, hopefully it will give readers a better foundation for the topics about which the authors of this volume have written.

In much the same way that the search for the Holy Grail was one of the most enduring Medieval Christian quests by the legendary knights of King Arthur in Western European literature, the search for an appropriate and agreed upon pedagogy has occupied physical educators since the beginnings of modern physical education. From the physical education programs of Johann Basedow and Johann Guts Muths in late 18th century Germany, whose pedagogical practices were influenced by Jean-Jacques Rousseau's naturalistic education principles, to the gymnastics systems designed by Frederick Jahn in Germany and Per Hendrik Ling of Sweden in the early 19th century to strengthen the vitality of their respective nations, to the games and sports popularized by school boys in England in the mid-19th century, to the variety of physical education curricula and methods employed by physical educators through the 20th century, different visions of appropriate pedagogy have prevailed.

As a field of teaching and academic study in physical education emerged in the later nineteenth century, pedagogical issues and debate dominated the professional literature and conferences. In the United States, a variegated group of physical education pedagogy theories and practices competed for preeminence in what became known as 'The Battle of the Systems.' Several of the early influential college physical educators relied heavily upon the pedagogies employed in the German and Swedish gymnastic systems, others employed systems of calisthenics, while some of those who became the early leaders in physical education, such as Edward Hitchock at Amherst College, Dudley Allen Sargent at Harvard, Edward Hartwell at Johns Hopkins, and Delphine Hanna at Oberlin College, developed their own unique curricula and pedagogical approaches to physical education. Meanwhile, spirited debates in the literature and in conferences of physical educators continued over which of the pedagogical systems was the most appropriate for physical education students.

During the first two decades of the 20th century, physical educators became increasingly dissatisfied with the various 'systems of physical training,' as they were called, because all tended to ignore broad educational goals in their preoccupation with exercises that developed the physical body. Instead, physical educators increasingly embraced the educational developmentalism advocated by educational theorists. Under the leadership of Thomas Woods and Jesse Feiring Williams at Teachers' College, Columbia University, and Clark Hetherington at New York University, physical educators gradually adapted the theoretical orientation of educational developmentalism to physical education, formulating what became known as 'The New Physical Education.' This new physical education was grounded on the philosophy of education of American philosopher John Dewey, which emphasized learning-by-doing rather than rote learning and dogmatic instruction. Dewey also stressed that education must be an exploration of thinking and reflection, an interaction with and an environment for learning, and must be democratic where all share in a common life that provides associational settings.

Strongly influenced by the social and educational theories of John Dewey, Williams became the leading spokesman for the new physical education. Williams rejected the formal gymnastics pedagogies because he believed they thwarted personal development and the learning of moral and social values. He stressed that the mission of physical education was the development of the individual as well as the preparation of students to live in and contribute to a democratic society. Under Williams's direction, the pedagogy and curriculum theories of the new physical education dominated the profession from the 1920s through the 1950s, and he became the most renowned physical educator of the first half of the twentieth century.

The new physical education was firmly based on a belief that games and sport experiences develop qualities essential in personal and social living, such as self-sacrifice, self-discipline, individual responsibility, interpersonal cooperation, and teamwork, and that it also gives rise to ideals and practices of good sportsmanship and ethical conduct. All of these qualities, it was believed, promoted habits and attitudes conducive for the socialization of youth and the assimilation of American culture. With the new physical education, games and sports gradually became the major component of the physical education curriculum.

It is important to note that the notion that games and sports have the potential to achieve a variety of educational objectives, did not originate with the new physical education. During the early 19th century, student sports teams flourished in British private secondary boarding schools, although they were not a part of systematic programs of physical education. However, school sports won recognition by British educators as a medium for socialization, enculturation, and social control. By the latter decades of the 19th century, school sports were so popular that a moralistic ideology that became known as athleticism had evolved.

Borrowing the model of school sports in England, interscholastic and intercollegiate sports emerged in the United States, and by the early decades of the 20th century they had become a prominent extracurricular activity in American high schools and colleges. At the same time, the new physical education thrived with the growing public popularity of sports and the prodigious growth of public schools programs in physical education. Physical education teachers became the coaches of sports teams at both the high school and college levels. Thus, the curriculum and pedagogy of the new physical education became intertwined with the growing popularity of school and college sports.

Although the new physical education was the dominant paradigm during the 1920–1960 era, the curriculum and pedagogy of physical education was contested terrain, with dissenting voices and alternative paradigms. During the 1930s Charles McCloy at the University of Iowa was the leading critic of the new physical education. He was adamant about what he considered the lack of emphasis on physical development – strength, cardiovascular fitness, flexibility, etc. – in the new physical education. He did not favor a return to the old regimented, teacher-imposed, teacher-controlled pedagogy, but he argued for a physically demanding and vigorous curriculum along with more formalized instruction in his speeches and writings.

During the 1950s a major paradigm shift began in physical education as a response to two events. The first was a report claiming to show that American children were not as physically fit as children in other countries. The second was the emergence of the Cold War, the political and ideological struggle between the United States and the Soviet Union. One was linked to the other in that the Cold War held the threat of an impending war between the two world superpowers at a time that American youth appeared to be in a poor state of physical fitness – a bad sign, if war should actually occur.

Presidents Dwight D. Eisenhower and John F. Kennedy were both advocates of heightening physical fitness in the country at large, and both gave their full support to implementing physical education programs designed to maximize physical fitness. The American Association for Health, Physical Education, and Recreation (AAHPERD) immediately joined the drive for physical fitness by sponsoring various initiatives and conferences to motivate and encourage the implementation of curricula and instruction to promote physical fitness.

During the ensuing two decades a contentious debate transpired between those who advocated an emphasis on physical fitness for health and national preparedness and those who supported curricula and instruction accentuating games, sports, and dance, as well as movement educational activities borrowed from British educators. There were also creative efforts to combine the two approaches.

Overlapping the debate between those who were advocating physical fitness as physical education's unique contribution and those who were promoting updated versions of the new physical education, critical social thought began to make significant inroads into Western cultural attitudes and values. In parallel with critical social trends, scholarship in educational pedagogy and curriculum theory increasingly employed critical analyses during the late 1970s and 1980s. In sport pedagogy, critical social work regularly appeared in the literature. The past decade has witnessed an increasing amount of social critical inquiry and scholarship in physical education.

During the last half of the 20th century, the trends, issues, and debates in American physical education broadly corresponded with those throughout the English-speaking world. Post-World War II physical education in the United Kingdom was largely based on team games and competitive sports. More recently, there has been increasing apprehension about general public health and child-hood patterns of inactivity. This has led to the promotion of scientific and technical facets of fitness and wellness as well as contentious debates about the appropriateness of this trend. Australian and New Zealand physical education has advanced along similar lines, with health, fitness and the notion of 'body maintenance' assuming fairly dominant curricular positions.

Most of the socially critical scholarship in physical education pedagogy has been directed at sensitizing those aspiring to teach in physical education and those who are currently professionals in this field to the effects of their taken-for-granted assumptions and practices. These analyses and critiques have highlighted the oppression, inequality, and social injustices perpetuated by schools and teachers in the schools. They have emphasized and critiqued the dominant values that underlie school structure, teaching and administrative practices, approaches to learning, curricular approaches, and particular conceptions of subject matter. Most importantly, the socially critical scholarship has adamantly argued that both old (competitive team based) and new (fitness and wellness) curricula remain irrelevant and contextually barren for many students. Consequently, it has raised persuasive arguments in support of empowerment and emancipation as important goals for programs of physical education. Beyond that, critical analyses have given rise to novel concepts and terms that impart new insights to pedagogy in physical education, such as reflective teaching, social constructivism, postmodernism, post-structuralism – all of which are found in this volume – which serve as foundations for formulating creative changes in physical education curriculum and instruction.

Transformation in physical education curricula and instruction has been evolutionary in that new theories and trends inevitably retain some of the previous ideas and practices. For example, many of the ideas and practices central to the new physical education advanced by Jesse Feiring Williams are still embedded in contemporary physical education pedagogy, such as citizenship education, social responsibility through physical education, games for under-standing, and sport education – these too are all discussed in this volume.

Physical education pedagogy will likely remain a contested terrain, with a variety of principled positions, but what the authors of this volume convincingly illustrate is that creative physical educators continue to formulate new and imaginative ideas about how physical education pedagogy can be improved and how, as a consequence, human lives will be enriched. Like the increasingly diverse students that physical educators must teach – ethnic and racial minorities, at risk youth, underserved youth, mental and physically challenged youth, etc. – these authors propose diverse curricula and pedagogies to meet student needs.

By locating the topics covered in this volume in a historical context, I have attempted to illuminate how the persistent search for a better pedagogy for physical education has been ongoing. I believe aspiring teachers of physical education, experienced professional teachers, and even general readers will find this volume very beneficial for understanding how that quest continues.

I can summarize my views on the book by saying that anybody with even the slightest interest in physical education pedagogy should own and read this book. All of the authors are respected professionals and scholars; each has an impressive publication record, and the one impressive thing that each has in common with the others is a dedication to advancing the field of physical education pedagogy.

George H. Sage
Professor Emeritus
University of Northern Colorado

1 Physical education and educational sport

A philosophical justification

Steve Estes

Physical education is as old as education. Indeed, it is arguable that the first education attempted was physical education, and the justification for any education, whatever its form, was to facilitate the survival of the clan, be it family or extended. But when education became more than survival, arguments were probably presented as to exactly what should be learned, and when. It would seem that the more effective arguments stated why they were correct, and there were probably pragmatic observations that supported the claims of activities as effective physical education. Over time scholars found that the benefits that can be achieved through physical activity can be summarized in general categories, and arguments for physical education include discussions of health, skill development, character, and fun. How these arguments are used to philosophically justify the inclusion of physical education in education, where one hopes to educate a child, is the theme of this chapter. Also though, this chapter is about argumentation itself. The means of justifying physical education, rational argument, is changing before our eyes. If Stephen Toulmin (1990, 2001) and other critics of contemporary philosophy are right, and these arguments are persuasive, then we are entering a period where the certainty of correct methods of argumentation promised in the 17th century is an illusion, and a different understanding of how one settles arguments regarding philosophy, education, and right behavior is upon us. The certainty of the modern era, as in John Dewey's sense of the quest for certainty, appears to be passing, and along with it goes the support for conclusions that mitigated against many types of knowing that support physical education in education.

Just as the process of argumentation is moving toward some unknown future, so is the world of education. The arguments of the modern world, defined here as ways of thinking that became more commonplace after 1640, no longer justify physical education as well as we would like. Instead, arguments that may be more appropriate in our more fluid, dynamic times, appear to be taking hold, arguments that will better serve to include physical education in the 21st century curriculum.

Modernity and its assumptions

Critical to this chapter is the idea that during the late 16th and early 17th centuries a period now known as modernity developed out of the Renaissance, and that there is now evidence to argue that this modern period is evolving into something else in the late 20th and early 21st centuries. Postmodernity may be as good a title as anything else for this new period, and its characteristics are far from conclusive. Accompanying these modern developments in philosophy and culture during the 16th and 17th centuries were changes in education and physical education. The modern world view had an appropriately profound impact on how we study physical activity and justify physical education. So what are the characteristics of modernity, how did we get there, and why are some arguing that we are leaving this period?

Because this understanding of modernity has been expertly done by Stephen Toulmin,[1] I will summarize his argument as briefly as possible: the Western world moved from the skeptical humanism of Michelle de Montaigne, Rabelais, Shakespeare, and Erasmus to the rationalism of René Descartes, Galileo, and Newton through a complex series of historical and philosophical events. Once respected disciplines and processes of rhetoric, casuistry, ethnography, law and medicine gave way in prestige to the disciplines and processes of logic, abstract moral philosophy, geometry, and physics. It is arguable that physical education as an academic discipline suffers from this peculiarly modern perspective because the lived experience of movement can be as well understood through rhetorical, casuist, and ethnographic means as it can be understood through the methods of positive science. Toulmin explains why these Renaissance perspectives may have so much to say to us.

Modernity, as Toulmin defines it, is the complex set of attitudes, philosophies, and culture that has dominated Western thought since the late 16th century, and continues to organize contemporary intellectuals in the present day even as modernity suffers from attacks by practical philosophers in education, medicine, law, and a host of other disciplines.[2] To understand modernity as it existed at its peak, it is helpful to know something of the context in which it developed. Toulmin argues that modernity originated from Renaissance humanism and philosophers and philosophies such as Rabelais, Erasmus, Shakespeare, and Montaigne; and the reaction to these humanists and historical events by philosopher/scientists such as Descartes, Newton, and Galileo. The Renaissance was at its peak in the late 1500s and early 1600s when this shift occurred from Renaissance humanism to our modern rationality, and this shift evolved into our modern world view (cosmos) and an understanding of culture (polis). This change in attitude from Renaissance to modernity is captured in four phrases: from the oral to the written, from the particular to the universal, from the local to the general, and from the timely to the timeless (Toulmin 1990).

All of these areas have profound implications for how we study physical activity and justify its inclusion in education. Most powerfully, it is arguable that physical activity is oral, is particular, is local, and is timely, and a nuanced understanding of physical activity should include these perspectives. Certainly these perspectives on physicality should not be excluded for any philosophical reason. Viewed this way, it is arguable that one reason for the marginalization of physical activity studies in the academy, and the similarly marginal role of physical education in the K-12 curriculum, is that the very nature of physical activity defies the hegemony of modern, rational assumptions about knowledge prevalent since the time of Descartes to the extent that rationality excludes the oral, particular, local, and timely lived experience of physicality.

From the oral to the written

Plato's narratives of Socrates in Athens captured Western readers for centuries, but Western philosophy followed the logic of Artistotle, which held sway through the late 1500s. Plato's formalism was studied, but was not really practiced by philosophers, physicians, and lawyers in the secular world.[3] Toulmin's comparison of Plato's and Aristotle's reasoning captures the spirit of this difference. Plato was critical of the Sophists' use of rhetoric as, 'making the worse argument appear the better' (Toulmin 1990: 31). Aristotle, in contrast, treated rhetoric as an area that philosophers can address as an appropriate area of study. In the modern world, though, Plato's disdain for rhetoric (the oral) is so pervasive that the word rhetoric connotes the idea that one is being persuaded without any logic or truth behind the argument. Indeed, Toulmin notes that today those who study rhetoric 'have to explain that the term is not necessarily deprecatory,' indicating the extent to which this understanding of the process of persuasive speech has been affected by modern attitudes (Toulmin 1990: 31).

This characteristic of modernity affects physical activity to the extent that knowing physical activity is often transmitted orally in verbal and physical narrative. From narratives (Estes 1990; Polkinghorne 1988; Rosaldo 1989; Umphlett 1975) to pedagogy, knowing physical activity often occurs in the lived experience of movement, and this includes the oral expression of the activity. To limit knowing physical activity to the written, prescriptive, or technical is to eliminate an important aspect of physical education knowledge.

From the particular to the universal

Toulmin argues that modernity is characterized by the universal scope of philosophical reference. In contrast, prior to the time of Descartes it was common to refer to specific cases to make one's philosophical point. Known as casuistry, or the study of specific cases, this process is still practiced in law and medicine. The guiding principles were the procedures recommended in Aristotle's *Nichomachean Ethics*, and followed Aristotle's dictum, 'The Good has no universal form, regardless of the subject matter or situation: sound moral judgment always respects the detailed circumstances of specific kinds of cases' (Toulmin 1990: 31–32). Casuistry came under attack in the 1600s, though, and has never recovered; Toulmin notes that case ethics is now regarded with the same scorn as rhetoric is by logicians.

Kleinman (1979) discussed how human movement is best understood from the lived, subjective experience of the moment. Known as somatics, or the lived experience of movement, each movement experience achieves meaning as it is lived out in its own case. To the extent that casuistry is dismissed in the modern world, somatic experiences are relegated to the margins of knowledge in the modern world. There is also a significant body of science developing in exercise psychology that is supported by somatic awareness, where physical activity exertion is rated by the exerciser using a perceived rate of exertion. In summary, each instance of exercise can be understood as a case, and knowledge of physical activity is gained by the exerciser that is valued in and of itself.

From the local to the general

Disciplines of place such as history, ethnography, anthropology, and geography do not have the same status as those that transcend this limitation. Prior to the modern era, however, histories and essays carried with them a sense of credibility that was kept in balance by a studied human skepticism. At best, Descartes saw the inspiration behind history and ethnography as a pardonable human trait, and his philosophy clearly argued that knowledge that is true cannot come from the accumulation of sensed experiences. Philosophy in the modern sense is dedicated to finding the general principles lying behind local circumstances at all times and in all places, so issues of locality occupy a lower status on the hierarchy of knowledge.

Physical activity is always local in the sense that it must occupy place when it occurs. Consequently physical activity itself is philosophically less valued in modern thought than the theories that explain it. This low valuing of physical activity has been challenged by physical educators since the beginning of the discipline movement in the 1960s, but most of the arguments justifying physical activity studies accepted the modern notions of generalization, and argued that physical activity is academic because it is generalizable. Perhaps the most famous argument along these lines was Henry's (1964) argument that physical education is an academic discipline. Henry argued that

> An academic discipline is an organized body of knowledge collectively embraced in a formal course of learning. The acquisition of such knowledge is assumed to be an adequate and worthy objective as such, without any demonstration or requirement of practical application. The content is theoretical and scholarly as distinguished from technical and professional.
>
> (Henry 1964: 32)

Henry went on to argue that physical education (now frequently referred to as exercise and sport science or kinesiology) possesses a scholarly field of knowledge that included anatomy, physics, physiology, cultural anthropology, history, and sociology. In so doing Henry accepted the modern assumptions of academic disciplines, one of which is the generalizability of knowledge construction.

From the timely to the timeless

Prior to the modern era philosophers and medieval theologians dealt with the issues of everyday life with the same seriousness as they did abstract ideas and theory. As Toulmin argued, all problems of law and medicine are timely in that they refer to specific moments in time. With the acceptance of modern rationality, however, this valuing of the timely came to an end, and philosophers came to value more highly the timeless truths that can be generated with science. From the time of Descartes to the present, the emphasis of scientists was on principles that hold good at all times equally, and those truths that are specific to a particular moment became suspect.

Similarly, all physical activity experiences are timely. Like the arguments of Kleinman and other sport philosophers, the lived experience of physical activity is in the moment. Social scientists have tried to summarize these moments using social science techniques, and have developed a body of knowledge that explains, in part, experiences such as flow and peak experience (McInman and Grove 1991). These understandings of the experience of sport appear to transcend the timely experience of movement, and try to explain these phenomena in timeless terms. But it is also noted by these scholars that the experience of the movement is different in kind from the explanation of it, and forcing the timely experience of movement into the timeless world of modern thought distorts, and perhaps even perverts, the phenomenon itself.

The consequences of modernity for physical education

In sum, the explanations that served the Renaissance humanists so well in the 1580s became a luxury to those who followed them. The oral, the local, the timely, and the particular gave way to the written, the universal, the timeless, and the generalizable, and it was hoped by philosophers and leaders that this shift would help establish a body of knowledge that was more certain. But this change in orientation did not yield the results that Descartes and Galileo hoped for. John Dewey (1929) in the Gifford lectures called the change in orientation of philosophers, from the humane to the rational, the quest for certainty. In this modern framework of knowledge Toulmin argues that there are specific hierarchies that order our valuing of knowledge. The more certain a knowledge claim is, the more real and valued that knowledge should be:

> The intellectualism puts the different kinds of knowledge in an honor roll, with an understanding of pure mathematics, or *episteme*, at the head of the roll. The misguided priorities of social science, in trying to ape Newtonian astronomy, are a direct outcome of this choice. Close behind *episteme* comes *techne*: the kinds of instrumental knowledge that are typically presented as sets of printed rules having a theoretical *raison d'être* . . . Lower down the honor roll are the various kinds of practical knowledge that we master for reasons of survival and other human needs, such as the practical skills of *phronesis*

embodied in the arts of clinical medicine or sailing. The farther we go down the roll, the smaller is the part played by formal reasoning or language, and the larger part takes the form of those nonformal practical activities that Michael Polanyi has called the 'tacit dimension' of science.

(Toulmin 2001: 178)

The parallel between these generalizations and the study of physical activity in particular is striking. In short, the means by which we have argued for the inclusion of physical education in schools has been modern. Physical education scholars have sought to justify the inclusion in the schools and universities by arguing that what we do, study physical activity and get others to do physical activity, can be understood in modern terms. But Toulmin helps explain why this strategy is not particularly effective: physical activity is much better explained as possessing the characteristics of the oral, the local, the particular, and the timely.

Physical education scholars since the 1960s have argued for or against the discipline movement, and many of them rejected the scientizing of physical education as the field headed toward the 21st century. But none of the critics successfully explained why some disciplines fared better than others. Science fits the modern paradigm much better than do the social sciences, and the humanities barely fit at all. Those subdisciplines that rely on the social sciences (sport psychology, sport sociology) consequently have less academic prestige than do those that are closer to the most modern of disciplines, physics and geometry. And those subdisciplines that find their origins in the humanities find themselves at the bottom of this philosophical hierarchy.

From modernity to post 'something'

The idea that we are moving from one way of thinking about reality and knowledge is not new (Kuhn 1970; McIntyre 1981), and it is only in the 1990s in journals like *Quest* and *Sociology of Sport Journal* that scholars in physical education began to relate these arguments to our field. Toulmin notes that the modern method of argumentation, i.e. the type of thinking begun in the 1600s with respect to reality, knowledge, and values, has taken us as far as it can. Something better needs to supplant the modern world view of how we gather knowledge and impart it into children. Calling this new world view postmodern is as good as anything else; most importantly one should recognize that more diverse ways of thinking about physical education will benefit the field, and will better justify physical activity in the curriculum. In Toulmin's words, we are looking for a democracy of methods that can help us understand something about life that is not limited by a Cartesian/Newtonian view of reality:

The certainties that John Dewey found philosophers aiming at from 1600 on all took verbal forms, but these verbal 'foundations' added no security to our knowledge, as they rested on practical, non-verbal supports . . . the World-

View of Modernity thus stood knowledge on its head, like a tree painted by Baselitz: verbal superstructure replaced its substantive roots. Nor is this weakness overcome by substituting 'post-modernity' for 'modernity': all that does is to trade in an unhelpful verbal formula for the insistence that all such formulas are invalid, without exploring the practical foundation of our knowledge. Substituting . . . formal axioms for substantive experience . . . must finally give way to a less dogmatic point of view, which leaves the discovery of the preconditions for everyday 'certitude' – so different from mathematical 'certainty' to be achieved bit by bit, as we go along.

(Toulmin 2001: 207)

The task for physical activity scholars, then, is to argue for the democracy of methods that justifies activities of everyday certitude; those things we intuitively know that are oral, local, timely, and particular. And we must do so with what we have, that is by joining the modern traditions that have carried us this far and that all of us are familiar with, and by moving on from here. Consequently, the standard account for justifications of physical education should be reviewed. From there we can move on to the return to reason that Toulmin calls for.

Justifying physical education

The etymology of the word educate is the Latin word *educare*, which, depending on the translation, means to lead out, draw out, or to raise up one from some lesser state of being. It is understood that the acquisition of knowledge is central to this process, be it physical education knowledge or any other type. Implied in this ancient word, but still appropriate today, is the idea that a child moves from being a lesser person to a more complete one, and is able to ask at the conclusion of the educational experience, 'Who am I going to be?' (Wilshire 1990: 22). These arguments are evident today, and are reviewed in undergraduate courses to provide a foundation upon which the modern physical education curriculum rests. They are also a launching point for the positions taken by contemporary theorists who continue this ancient conversation; to justify the inclusion of physical education in a 21st century program of study. While the arguments change shape, sometimes subtly and sometimes not, the goal remains the same; to use physical education to help a child grow into an educated adult.

The standard account of the first arguments for physical education are better summarized by others, and I will focus here on only two: how ancient educators and philosophers justified the role of physical education in ancient Greece and ancient Rome.[4] Notably, accounts for these ancient arguments and justifications have remained fairly consistent in modern physical education histories, indicating the timelessness of these arguments and that they continue to be used in texts up to the present time (Van Dalen and Bennett 1971; Mechikoff and Estes 2002). Important to my argument is that contemporary modern arguments that justify physical education are quite similar to those that have been in existence for over 2,500 years, and that the necessity to be timeless limits, in an important sense, the possibility of more timely, particular, local, and oral justifications for physical education.

The arguments for having physical education began over three thousand years ago in the Western world, where, with the Greeks, the debate over what a human being is, and how one grows to be a complete human being, assumed the philosophical mantle peculiar to the Western world. While there were many arguments for physical education put forth by Greek philosophers and educators (these two roles were largely synonymous in the ancient Greek world), the most well known today would be Plato's argument that physical education provides for the development of character. Plato's justification provided the basis for future arguments that focus on the development of one's essence through physicality: soul, spirit, character, or however one wishes to define the non-material self (Plato 1987). As Plato and those who follow this line of thinking argue, physical activity in its many forms develops, or facilitates the development of, citizenship; that constellation of virtues that makes up one's character, and/or the moral self that guides one's behaviors in the material world. There are many variations on this theme, but all can be traced back to Plato and can be compared and contrasted with the original in order to gain perspective. Critical to all of these arguments is the idea that a human is composed of two categorically different essences; a non-material soul or mind, and a physical presence. What characterizes the Western intellectual tradition is the domination of the nonmaterial soul over the physical, and the characteristic of the soul most noteworthy is its immutability. Also, arguments for the inclusion of physicality in the curriculum are the ideas used to justify its existence. One does not, for example, do a handstand at a Board of Education meeting to justify physical education. Instead, one posits one set of ideas over others, and the effectiveness of these ideas justifies (or does not justify) the activity.

Physical education histories usually follow the Greeks with discussions of the Romans, who were less concerned with the development of character than they were with the pragmatic development of health and physical skill in the lived experiences of the Roman empire. Characterized by the Latin maxim *mens sana en corpore sano* (a strong mind in a healthy body), Romans observed that physicality was a critical component in the maintenance of health. The Romans also understood that physical skills, particularly martial arts, needed to be learned and perfected through an on-going education program, and that the successful learning of these arts was central to their military successes. The merger of these two goals, the healthful and the martial, was consummated in the arena. It is no accident that Galen and Hieronymous Mercurialis are understood to be among the first Western physicians, and that both were associated with Roman sport and gladiatorial combat. Just as important to Romans, though, was the understanding that physical training imparted on the learner certain moral lessons: obedience, discipline, and a sense of duty to the state. In sum, there was a philosophy behind physical training in Rome, and for the Romans this philosophy was coherent and effective.

Important to my argument here, Greek and Roman justifications for physical education are articulated in modern physical education histories and introductory texts (Van Dalen and Bennett 1971; Siedentop 1994; Wuest and Bucher 1999; Brown 2001; Mechikoff and Estes 2002). The point of these brief historical justifications of physical education is that they tend to use the arguments of modernity to justify physical education. The standard accounts that use history as a guide tend to look for themes that can be understood as being applied to all cultures. The idea that physicality can be used to develop the self or soul implies that all cultures can have this experience, and therefore this type of education justifies the activity to all cultures that believe in the soul. The contemporary version of Plato's argument that sport builds character started in England in the 1800s. Without going into whether or not sport really does build character, it is sufficient for this discussion to note that whenever this argument is put forth it relies on the timeless, generalizable nature of the human soul.

Similarly, the idea that physical education provides for instruction in the martial arts transcends cultures, time, lends itself to written histories, and is a generalization that explains and justifies physical education. Indeed, up until this point in time, the quality of this argument depended on the historical accuracy of the claims, and the ability to point out that all cultures have a militaristic bent that required some form of physical education.

Arguments that use physicality to promote health have a similar flavor. Historically, the argument has been that humans benefit from physical exertion of the proper intensity and duration. This understanding applies to humans regardless of historical period or ethnic background, and is documented in the medical literature. The recent concerns of the modern medical establishment regarding overweight and obese children rely on the methods of positivist science.

These arguments have been used for decades, and we use them when we look for similarities and differences between these ancient histories and our own times. These arguments are insightful, and provide context and perspective for what we do in the modern world with respect to physical education. It is easy to conclude that the arguments for physical education that persist are those that should continue to be used today. Primary (historical artifacts and records) and secondary (interpretations of contemporary historians) historical sources are available to support them. The texts of Greek and Roman philosophers, educators, and physical educators (paidotribes) are available for study. But while these ancient justifications and their contemporary interpretations explain what Greeks and Romans did and how they argued for the inclusion of physical education, they do not necessarily do the same for us in the 21st century.

These utilitarian arguments of citizenship, martial arts, and health were used to justify physical activity as educational for centuries, and as I note above these arguments worked in the 20th and 21st centuries as well. However, new arguments that justified physical education began to appear in the 20th century, and these arguments emphasized an entirely different approach. Specifically, characteristics of humans that appear to be much more friendly toward Toulmin's Renaissance, humanist science began to appear. Philosophers and cultural critic, Johann Huizinga, psychologist Mikhaly Csikszentmihalyi, and the physical educator

Sy Kleinman have taken an entirely different approach, which may indicate that a postmodern view of physical education may be approaching.

Humans have participated in ludic activities since the beginnings of civilization. Perhaps the best explanation for this phenomenon was put forth by Johann Huizinga, who argued that it is human nature to engage in playful activities (Huizinga 1950). This ludic impulse serves as the foundation of culture by developing the individual psyche in socially acceptable ways through shared play activities. Seen in this light, all that is creative in humanity is essentially play based, and physical education, as the vehicle through which play is most easily manipulated, is central to the curriculum and its contribution to culture. The more contemporary versions of this argument are found in educational psychology (beginning with Rousseau's *Emile* and running through Piaget's learning theories and beyond), the flow experience in psychology (Csikszentmihalyi 1990), and are now being promoted as somatics (Kleinman 1979, 2000).

Although the arguments for play, flow, and somatics can be viewed through the lens of modernity, all of these arguments possess a thread of something 'postmodern' in their justification of physical education, and, as we will see later, the more contemporary of them have a definite postmodern perspective.

Physical education and the postmodern

Arguments that explain physical activity from an entirely different perspective appeared in the 20th century. These arguments appeared in several different disciplines, but all of them have in common a characteristic of knowing that our Renaissance predecessors admired: humility. In these postmodern ways of knowing physicality the notion of humility caused the idea that we can know something with certainty to be dismissed, or considered irrelevant. Instead these arguments focus on what an individual person can know.

As noted earlier, Huizinga (1950) claimed that play is the central facet of culture, and this argument has existential roots that do not lend themselves well to modern, positivist assumptions:

> Summing up the formal characteristics of play we might call it a free activity standing quite consciously outside 'ordinary' life as being 'not serious,' but at the same time absorbing the player intensely and utterly. It is an activity connected with no material interest, and no profit can be gained by it. It proceeds within its own proper boundaries of time and space according to fixed rules and in an orderly manner. It promotes the formation of social groupings which tend to surround themselves with secrecy and to stress their difference from the common world by disguise or other means.
>
> (Huizinga 1950: 13)

Huizinga's definition of play focuses on an individual's experience of it. While his definition of play can be read as modern in that play's characteristics appear to be timeless, generalizable, and are written, they also focus on the individual experience of play which is oral, particular, timely, and local. Huizinga can be understood as transcending the modern and the postmodern, and his ideas are friendly to Toulmin's (2001) call for a democracy of methods in understanding human phenomena.

Similarly, Csikszentmihalyi (1990) argues that the ways of science have increased significantly the quality of our material lives, but have done little for the local, personal, timely, and particular facets of our existence:

> The answer seems clear: while humankind collectively has increased its material powers a thousand fold, it has not advanced very far in terms of improving the content of experience. . . . There is no way out of this predicament except for an individual to take things in hand personally. If values and institutions no longer provide as supportive a framework as they once did, each person must use whatever tools are available to carve out a meaningful, enjoyable life.
>
> (Csikszentmihalyi 1990: 16)

Indeed, Csikszentmihalyi argues that the ways of positive science have little to say with respect to justifying any personal experience, including physicality.

Closer to the field of physical education, Kleinman offered some basic principles for somatic education that values the local, oral, timely, and particular aspects of human existence:

> The pedagogical approach to the Movement Arts or Somatic Education . . . must be based on holistic principles. This may be accomplished by the development of what may be called a 'kinesthetic' phenomenology based on the following set of principles:
>
> • Life is a state of continuous creation and moving is a universal mani-festation of this creativity.
> • Thus, every act, every gesture, every thought contains all the elements we look for, and recognize in a 'work of art.'
> • Every behavior, gesture and thought, therefore, may be viewed as being 'artful.' These are, literally, creative acts.
> • Therefore, we function as artists at every moment.
> • Life and art become synonymous. Living becomes an artistic enterprise.
> • It becomes incumbent upon education, particularly, somatic education, to provide opportunities to create good art, to help us live our lives as good artists, both as theorists and practitioners.
>
> (Kleinman 2000: 98)

Kleinman comes closest to a postmodern or Renaissance experience of justifying physical education. His call for somatic education resonates nicely with contemporary criticisms of positivist physical education, and provides a model for how one can justify physical education in the 21st century.

Conclusion

Philosophical justifications for physical education appear to be changing, and these justifications appear to go hand in hand with the criticisms of modernity. One should be careful, though, in throwing the baby out with the bath water. The ways of positive, modern science were a reaction to limitations of Renaissance thinking that occurred over 300 years ago. And the modern way of viewing the world was seen as an improvement by those who lived in the 1600s. The benefits of positive science are all around us. Medicine, technology, and enlightenment politics are but three measures of the success of modernity. Furthermore, the standard accounts that have been used to justify physical education in education since 1885 have served the field fairly well. While most physical educators lament the loss of mandated physical education in many schools, the arguments of modernity worked for at least two centuries and arguably for much of the 20th century. While the modern arguments for physical education may not have been perfect, they were, to an extent, effective.

Yet postmodern theorists argue that limiting human existence and its manifold aspects, including physical education, to the positivism of modernity impoverishes the individual. To paraphrase Ray Bradbury (1962), 'Something "post" this way comes,' and there is not much any of us can do to stop it. Yet we can understand it, embrace and accept it. And if we are able to understand how cultural changes occur, then perhaps we can also understand how some of these changes may have an impact in, and on, physical education. If so, our ability to explain and predict how we study physical education and provide for students will be enhanced.

Notes

1 Toulmin's arguments regarding modernity, its pathos and solutions to it are actually in two works, *Cosmopolis: The Hidden Agenda of Modernity* (1990), and *Return to Reason* (2001). In the first case Toulmin describes how modernity developed just when it did, and why it developed so quickly and what its characteristics are. In the second, Toulmin argues for a return to reason instead of the physics and geometry standards of contemporary rational thought.
2 Modernization is discussed in a variety of disciplines, especially history, and this may lead to some confusion. I am concerned primarily with the philosophical perspective on modernization, as compared to the historical. Clearly the two overlap, and add to what we understand of how culture changes over time. For an excellent discussion of modernization in America, see Brown, R. (1976).
3 Philosophers have noted the similarities of Platonic thought and Western Christianity; this argument is focused, though, on the secular activities of philosophy and education.
4 There are numerous histories of physical education available, both in academic journal articles and as undergraduate textbooks. Two of the best scholarly works that summarize Greek and Roman attitudes toward physical education are Forbes's (1972) essay on 5th century BC Athenian physical education, and Lindsay's (1967) masters thesis and subsequent publications on Roman attitudes toward physical education.

References

Bradbury, R. (1962) *Something Wicked this Way Comes*, New York: Simon and Schuster.

Brown, S. (2001) *Introduction to Exercise Science*, Baltimore, MD: Lippincott Williams & Wilkins.

Brown, R. (1976) *Modernization: The Transformation of American Life, 1600–1865*, New York: Hill and Wang.

Csikszentmihalyi, M. (1990) *Flow: The Psychology of Optimal Experience*, New York: Harper and Rowe.

Dewey, J. (1929) *The Quest for Certainty: A Study of the Relation of Knowledge and Action*, New York: Minton, Balch.

Estes, S. (1990) 'Sport myth as lived experience', unpublished doctoral dissertation, Ohio State University.

Forbes, C. (1972) 'Athenian physical education in the fifth century, BC', in B. Bennett (ed.), *History of Physical Education and Sport*, Chicago, IL: The Athletic Institute, 151–160.

Henry, F. (1964) 'Physical education as an academic discipline', *Journal of Health, Physical Education, and Recreation*, 35(7): 32–33, 69.

Huizinga, J. (1950) *Homo Ludens*, London: Routledge & Kegan Paul.

Kleinman, S. (1979) 'The significance of human movement: A phenomenological approach', in E. Gerber and W. Morgan (eds), *Sport and the Body: A Philosophical Symposium*, Philadelphia, PA: Lea & Febiger, 2nd edn, 177–180.

——(2000) 'Summing Up: A chronological retrospective or dancing the body electric', *Quest*, 52(1): 89–101.

Kuhn, T. (1970) *The Structure of Scientific Revolutions*, Chicago, IL: University of Chicago Press.

Lindsay, P. (1967) 'Literary evidence of physical education among the ancient Romans', unpublished masters thesis, University of Alberta, 1967.

McInman, A. and Grove, J.R. (1991) 'Peak moments in sport: A literature review', *Quest*, 43(3): 333–351.

MacIntyre, A. (1981) *After Virtue: a Study in Moral Theory*, Notre Dame, IN: University of Notre Dame Press.

Mechikoff, R. and Estes, S. (2002) *A History and Philosophy of Sport and Physical Education*, New York: McGraw-Hill Higher Education, 3rd edn.

Phaedo and *The Republic*. All references are to *The Dialogues of Plato*, translated by B. Jowett, New York: Washington Square Press, 1966.

Plato (1987) *The Republic*, Desmond Lee (trans.), London: Penguin Books.

Polkinghorne, D. (1988) *Narrative Knowing and the Human Sciences*, Albany, NY: State University of New York Press.

Rosaldo, R. (1989) *Culture and Truth: The Remaking of Social Analysis*, Boston, MA: Beacon Press.

Siedentop, D. (1994) *Introduction to Physical Education, Fitness, and Sport*, Mountain View, CA: Mayfield Publishing Company.

Toulmin, S. (1990) *Cosmopolis: The Hidden Agenda of Modernity*, Chicago, IL: University of Chicago Press.

——(2001) *Return to Reason*, Cambridge, MA: Harvard University Press.

Umphlett, W. (1975) *The Sporting Myth and the American Experience*, Cranbury, NJ: Associated University Presses.

Van Dalen, D. and Bennett, B. (1971) *A World History of Physical Education: Cultural, Philosophical, Comparative*, Englewood Cliffs, NJ: Prentice Hall, 2nd edn.

Wilshire, B. (1990) *The Moral Collapse of the University: Professionalism, Purity, and Alienation*, Albany, NY: State University of New York Press.

Wuest, D. and Bucher, C. (1999) *Foundations of Physical Education and Sport*, New York: McGraw-Hill Higher Education.

2 Sport in culture

Anthony Laker

Not only does sport pervade our culture, but it has an important place in a multitude of other cultures. In this way, sport provides a commonality of experience on a global scale that is extremely rare in any other field of human experience, except perhaps religion. It is because of this commonality that sport has the potential to provide a common language which could be used to communicate within, and between, a variety of cultures. This shared experience has a number of operational contexts. First, there is the small-scale, sometimes sub-cultural, context. Here sport is conducted locally and in community settings. This has often been referred to as the grass roots of sport. At this level, sport represents, among other experiences, a chance to share a social occasion with one's fellow sports participants. Sport contributes to the development of local history and tradition and many events are as a result of historical and traditional considerations. The cricket match on the village green or the darts match in the pub are examples of this level of engagement. Second, there is the national scale. This aspect of sports participation and involvement includes national leagues, such as soccer's Premiership, and national sporting characteristics and contributes to a national sporting identity. Sport at this level is a far more serious venture, usually highly competitive and often professional. It serves a variety of purposes, not the least of which is providing a spectator spectacle. Third, there is the international, or global context. This provides an interface for the meeting of a variety of local and national sporting endeavours. This ranges from the village rugby team on tour abroad to major international sporting events such as the World Cup or the Olympic Games. These major events are sometimes the site of political actions and of vested national interest. Again, spectatorship and the public consumption of sport is important. As such, the media play a large part in the operation of international sport. The major purpose of this chapter is to look at the place and importance of sport in this variety of operational, and essentially social, contexts.

Sporting acculturation is enhanced by such diversity and extends the boundaries of personal development and cultural awareness. Young people, or indeed any informed, rational and educated people, need to know about the society and the culture of which they are a part. Thus, knowing about academic subjects (at least while one is involved in education), taking part effectively in the democratic process, knowing about current affairs, and knowing about the place that sport holds in culture are some of the disparate elements of the informed, rational and educated person. A further purpose of this chapter is to investigate and elaborate on how and why this sporting component of acculturation occurs.

Education plays a major role in the socialisation of young people. It certainly has a responsibility to educate youngsters about a society's sporting culture, history and tradition. In this way education has a contribution to make to the process of sporting acculturation. Therefore, I intend to take the ideas expressed in the main analysis of this chapter and suggest how they can be built into an effective curriculum component. This will enable the educational establishment to take advantage of sport's pervasive nature and build a pedagogy, at least in physical education, that has the potential to make a major contribution to the cultural development of young people. It is hoped that the resulting enlightened sports citizens will be able to use the medium of sport in an expanded manner to enhance, and perhaps in some cases establish, communication and discourse in local, national and global environments.

Culture

In its simplest form, a culture is a system of values, meanings and symbols that are shared within a society. This mechanism enables societies and individuals to operate without having to continually redefine these values, meanings, symbols and points of reference (Humberstone 2002). It would be impossible to communicate effectively if we had to say what we meant by religion, for example, every time we used the word or, in this case what we understood by the word sport. A shared system of social and cultural understanding makes that communication possible. However, some symbols have different meanings in different cultures. A good example is the symbol of the cross. In one cultural context it indicates religion. In another cultural context, as a traffic sign, it indicates that we are approaching two roads that intersect. A cross on its side, in yet another context, indicates that something is wrong, incorrect and possibly needs to be done again. However, in a mathematical context, that same cross on its side means 'multiply'. The various meanings of symbols are clearly dependent upon the context in which those symbols are placed.

Symbols do not have to have physical substance, they can be found in actions and language. Gestures, expressions, body language and movements can have very specific meanings in different cultural contexts. In Western society, we commonly throw paper and small pieces of household rubbish on a fire. However, in Hindu and Buddhist communities the household gods live in the hearth and it is an insult to throw rubbish at them. A further example of common practice in one culture being offensive in another is the giving or receiving items with one's left hand. This is poorly regarded in some Asian and Eastern cultures because of the sanitary function for which the left hand is used. It is expected that people offer and receive with both hands. Although we, as foreigners, have to learn these customs to ease our progress in others' cultures, the customs, or symbolic actions and gestures, are part of everyday existence in those cultures. The local population does not have to think about how they should act. Becoming an accepted part of a culture involves learning the values, meanings and symbols that are representative of the culture. Ethnographers and anthropologists investigating other cultures have commonly immersed themselves in those cultures to live the experience of the people they are researching. In a similar way, becoming a member of the community of sport is partly to do with learning the 'language', the ways of doing and being, the ways of dressing, as well as learning and practising the physical skills necessary to take part in the sport. Only by immersing oneself in the sub-culture can one become part of the group, or even truly understand the group. As Butts (2001) pointed out in his study of surfers as a sub-culture, it is not enough to learn the language, have the clothes and equipment, one must live the life. One can superficially 'talk the talk' but to be truly acculturated one must 'walk the walk'.

More recently, the concept of culture, and what constitutes culture have been subjected to a critical broadening. Humberstone (2002: 63–64) suggests that we need to look at the ways in which 'ideologies and practices are constructed through systems of meanings, by webs of power and through organisations and institutions that produce and legitimate them'. This implies a political component to the notion of culture that exposes previously hidden interests and motivations. Thus, the dominant cultural features are representative of the hegemonic process that itself perpetuates the overarching meaning of what any culture actually is. In the same way, the sports world has processes and practices that make up its culture. It also has power structures that dominate its interpretation. This privileging of certain aspects of physical activity is exemplified by John Major's (a British Conservative Prime Minister from 1990 to 1997) statements that promised to put sport (as opposed to dance, gymnastics, health-related fitness, outdoor pursuits, etc.) back at the heart of school life (DNH 1995). Clearly then, a culture of sport is created by many factors, not just the sharing of meanings, symbols and values. It is created by the hegemonic propagation of those meanings, symbols and values that serve and promote the interests of the organisations and institutions that produce them.

Sport as part of culture

The word culture has connotations of high class, quality, refined tastes and good manners. This view holds that culture is art; paintings, sculptures, drama and the like. This is an elitist view of culture and is limited by its narrowness of application, for it is only one aspect of culture. It is also exclusionary in that it restricts the abilities of a large proportion of the population to have any part in the defining aspects of their own culture.

Given the nature of the way a culture is characterised and defined, it might not be entirely accidental that the word culture carries this attendant baggage. It is in the best interests of the institutions and structures of power to have ownership of notions of what constitutes culture. This allows control of membership to authoritative groups thus supporting a hierarchical view that culture is only appropriate for certain (selected) segments of society. The culture represented by this limited view also excludes many sporting activities, unless they are acceptable to the organisational power-broking institutions. Acceptable activities would include tennis, cricket, possibly some horse racing and shooting. We could easily create a stereotype of what this culture includes but it serves no real analytical function; what we create is merely a small sub-cultural part of the parent culture. We create a particular aspect of culture that has been referred to as 'high' culture. The converse of this is naturally that a 'low' culture also exists. Stereotypically this would refer to the tabloid press, pop music and TV. Sports that are acceptable in a 'low' culture would include football, darts and NASCAR racing. This elitist division has little appeal, or indeed use, in the arena of academic debate and, as the boundaries between these two opposing cultural dichotomies have become ever more blurred, the currency of this framework is devalued.

This blurring has occurred to a large degree because of the immense popularity of sport. This has led to sport having a large role in the definition and character-isation of many cultures, particularly Western cultures. As an example of this blurring, it would be easy to stereotype the crowd at a football match as lower or working class consumers of low culture sports. However, the reality of the composition of the crowd would be somewhat different. It is entirely possible, and in some locations probable, that there would be many segments of society represented, with some notable celebrities, politicians and representatives of high socio-economic groups. Similarly, participants in cricket, skiing and squash cannot be easily defined and stereotyped any more; there are participants from a large number of social groups. As George Sage documents (Sage 2002), media attention given to sport has grown very rapidly in recent years. Sport now has global appeal and the media has almost global coverage. As a result, sport is far more accessible now than ever before and more segments of society are becoming interested in the phenomenon of sport, at least from a spectator point of view.

The number of pages in newspapers, the number of minutes on TV, even the number of sport-dedicated radio and TV channels is continuing to grow. Is this merely indicative of the increase in information available worldwide because of the developments in information technology, or is it a real increase in interest in sport pointing to a growing place and importance in culture? The answer lies in the large growth in companies involved in recreation provision, leisure travel, adventure travel, sportswear manufacture, increased viewing figures for the majority of televised sporting events, increased attendance at sports events such as Premiership football matches and more university degree courses devoted to sport, leisure and recreation. In fact, almost anything that is connected to sport, leisure and recreation is experiencing growth.

The importance of sport in any Western culture is not really a point of debate any more. However, the huge increase in sport associated business as mentioned above is only part of the story. Sport impinges on many facets of everyday life. This ranges from conversations at work and at home to national interest during events like the World Cup and Wimbledon. To have nothing to say about sport or to have no knowledge of the sporting world is to isolate oneself from a large part of the cultural flow of one's society. Given that sport *is* part of a community, it is incumbent upon society to ensure that individuals are educated into that community. This means that knowing sport, about sport and doing sport should be an objective of the educational process. To cite Gardner's multiple intelligences theory (Gardner 1983), kinesthetic intelligence is one of seven intelligences (the others are linguistic-verbal, mathematical-logical, visual-spatial, musical, inter-personal and intrapersonal) and therefore part of each individual's potential. If we ignore that aspect of personal development we are limiting the possibilities for individuals to take a full part in the cultural life of their community. The other intelligences tend to have more privileged positions in our educational system anyway, but the development of a complete person requires that we address all aspects of that person. Gardner's intelligences tend to match the qualities necessary to understand one's own culture. Language skills and mathematical abilities are obviously vital in one's education, but it is also desirable to have a knowledge of literature, music and art as they are important in enhancing cultural richness. A knowledge of sports and their histories and traditions has a place as well. Thus, an argument can be made for the potential of any of Gardner's intelligences to significantly contribute to one's knowledge of one's own culture. Just as education in Renaissance times was partly concerned with equipping people to take a place in polite, cultured society, so education today should take account of sport's important place in culture and offer people the chance to take a full part in every aspect of their culture.

Sub-cultures

The preceding sections have shown how the defining characteristics of any one particular culture come into being, how they are privileged and how institutional power structures within that society seek to maintain them. This is a social hegemonic process that self-perpetuates and attempts to maintain the *status quo*. This is the case for all levels of culture, from local to global. However, it also works on a smaller scale, the microlevel of sub-cultures.

Within cultures there are sub-cultures. These are groupings of individuals within a larger culture. These individuals share specific systems of values and meanings and this develops their clear and separate identities. Sub-cultures often have very distinctive ways of dressing, talking and behaving that are clearly identified as being peculiar to the group. The distinct, and separate, nature of their language, appearance and actions is what binds individuals within a sub-culture together. This separateness is what makes them strong and sometimes closed. Their shared differences (from the parent culture) are cherished and guarded so that they become the characteristic that not only defines them to themselves, but allows and aids the identification of the sub-culture to others. Some of the most obvious examples of sub-cultures are groups that have a sporting or recreational interest as their unifying characteristic. Climbers are a sub-culture. For the climbing sub-culture, the unique characteristic of that community is that they go to the mountains, the hills, the cliffs and the crags and try to climb them. These behaviours are supported by beliefs and values that set climbers apart. There is also an exclusionary nature to sub-cultures which means that without possessing the unique characteristic one could never join the sub-culture. So one could never be included in the climbing sub-culture if one did not climb. Joe Simpson writes about climbing in *The Beckoning Silence* (Simpson 2002). Part of the book describes other groups connected in some way to climbing. There are undoubtedly privileged groups who enjoy limited membership of the sub-culture. In the case of climbing, these are clothing and hardware manufacturers, journalists, photographers and the like and these groups will be allowed some access, but they will not be part of the central group; they will not be part of the climbers' sub-culture.

The culture of sport and the place of sub-cultures within that culture is a convenient mechanism to use when conducting a sociological analysis sport. However, there are drawbacks to this approach. The defining characteristics, the particular attraction that makes sport so powerful to many people, also allow it to be separated from mainstream social, cultural and political life (Dyck 2000). By assigning the world of sport and physical activity to sub-cultural groupings which in themselves constitute a larger sub-cultural group, we could be assisting the notion that sport is separate and irrelevant to most people's everyday life and also separate from a truly rigorous and intellectual examination. It is not my intention to make a case for the recognition of sport as a central part of social and cultural life, the wealth of mass media exposure does that for me, but let us be aware that our study of sport should not be isolated from other social phenomena. The world of sport, the culture of sport, is a dynamic part of a larger culture and has an ecological relationship with, and within, that culture. On an individual level participants aspire to be members of the sporting community, but they are also inevitably part of many other communities.

The roles of sport

Sport has different meanings in a variety of cultural settings; and we have noted that there has been a vast expansion in all aspects of the sports world. It has also been suggested that sport, as a part of education, should lead to the development of complete citizen/individuals ready to take a full part in the cultural (including sporting) life of their communities. But what, apart from providing a distraction, does sport do within, and for, a community; what is the social and cultural function of sport? I have previously suggested that there are a variety of functions for sport including those of social interaction, provision of tradition and myth, the experiencing of emotion and cultural reproduction including functional social replication, social conformity and as a cultural strand (Laker 2002a).

Social interaction

As already indicated, sport pervades many areas of culture. The media, the language and not least our everyday interactions. It provides a common topic of conversation, a safe ground for a social encounter. It is the stereotypical topic of conversation. To pass the time of day with 'What do you think of England's chances, then?', is as natural as saying 'Hello, how are you?' Such a simple conversation is the product of years of acculturation. The amount of media coverage assists this interaction by providing the material for discussion. Television, newspapers, magazines and radio all add to the interactive milieu that can be used in social settings. Sporting terms have also become embedded in our language. One can be 'for the high jump' or 'out in left field' (United States) and most people will know what is meant by the terms. These shared meanings allow the speakers to maintain a discourse without resorting to continual redefinition of terms. In these ways, among others, sport eases the social interaction of our society.

Tradition and myth

Sport loves tradition. That is why Wimbledon is still played on grass and Manchester United's 'theatre of dreams' stadium has such powerful imagery. However, sport contributes greatly to the tradition and social mythology of a culture. Many of these stories of sporting events are told repeatedly until they become part of the common culture, i.e. the culture that is recognisable to the majority of a society (Inglis 1977). Virtually everyone in England knows that the English football team won the World Cup in 1966, and that the racehorse Red Rum once opened supermarkets! These events hold important places in our social and cultural history and, as such, are an important part of the social and cultural function of sport. Learning the tradition and myth that relates to any particular activity is a vital function of becoming part of the sub-culture of that activity. This cannot be done quickly, one learns these aspects as one becomes part of the community of practice through legitimate peripheral participation (see Chapter 3 for further discussion).

Expression and release of emotion

The experience of sport can provide an extreme range of emotions, from high elation to deepest despair. Winning a crucial game or exceeding one's expectations in sport can provide the highs; whereas losing unexpectedly or letting oneself down with a poor performance can provide the lows. These emotions can also be felt vicariously through another team's or individual's performance. Parents often experience these emotions through their children, sometimes painfully! Some sporting or recreational endeavours can provide spiritual experiences. Completing a first triathlon, or a marathon, perhaps seeing the sun rise on a mountain pass are events that can be almost religious in intensity. They are not religious, in that they have nothing to do with the concept of an afterlife, but they can certainly be spiritual. The juxtaposition of success and failure enables joy and sadness to be experienced in a relatively safe way. Sport provides our culture with an acceptable avenue for that particular celebration of human physical endeavour and I believe this to be one of sport's most attractive features. The sadness and joy felt in sport have none of the consequences, sometimes very serious, that occur in other areas of our existence. Sport is not a matter of life and death, in spite of ex-Liverpool football manager Bill Shankley's somewhat facetious claim that it (football) is more important than that! Sport almost encourages a polarisation of emotions; the joy of winning is sweeter because of the sadness of losing. Of course, that does not make losing any easier to bare or any less real to the sportsperson experiencing it, but it does give a relative value to the emotion by weighing it against the feeling of winning.

Cultural reproduction

Structural functionalists would claim that play, sport and recreation serve to promote economic exploitation, patriarchy, hegemony and an outdated work ethic that supports a capitalist *status quo*. Sportsmen and women are viewed as factors of production. Their performances are for public consumption, and the expenditure of those who use sport for recreational purposes supports a booming sports industry. By playing sport, we learn to conform to rules and regulations, submit our individuality to the will of the team and respect the authority of governing bodies and referees and umpires. As we progress in our sporting lives, the impetuosity and irrelevance of youthful play is extinguished and young athletes are increasingly trained, coached and moulded into socially acceptable versions of what sportspeople should look like, not only in terms of appearance but also in terms of behaviour and public demeanour. The eccentric is always viewed suspiciously. Just as geniuses have a mystique that cannot be quantified or qualified, so those who express too much individuality in sports are not regarded as ideal role models. By definition, the eccentric and the genius are away from the centre, apart from the norm, in terms of skill, and often from a social behaviour standpoint. Huizinga (1955) suggests that the so-called civilising process works to eliminate play as humans progress through their lives. Therefore those who are perceived to 'play' while taking part in sport, i.e. not take it seriously, are frowned upon. In a similar way, the sporting establishment is wary of the characteristics that set geniuses apart. There is no coaching theory that accounts for genius, but the very best coaches allow it to flourish unhindered. From a sociological stance, eccentricity is viewed by structural functionalists as a form of deviance; genius is similarly viewed in sport. So, very few sports participants can resist, or want to resist, these pressures to conform. Becoming part of a community of practice, a sports sub-culture, is dependent on the adoption of commonly held traits and behaviours. Most sports people want to conform to these norms because sport culture has conditioned them to believe that these are appropriate, correct, reasonable and legitimate.

The converse argument is that sport participation is voluntary and we therefore take part of our own free will. Sport contributes many things to our everyday lives; joy, fitness, self-expression, excitement and release from stress. The tradition of sport in culture and the important place it holds in many lives make it worthwhile.

The mythology and tradition of sport, referred to earlier, are not part of a capitalist plot; they enrich our existence and provide a thread that runs through our social history. Without sport, leisure and recreation our lives would be of lesser quality. Whichever argument you hold to is determined by your political persuasion and your sports experiences. However, it is recognised that the world of sport is noticeably conservative and resistant to change. This may be because those traditions are so dearly valued, or it may just be that we like things the way they are and so we support the *status quo*.

It has already been shown that sport is an important strand that runs through cultures both historically and in the present. One needs to know about sport if one is to fully understand one's culture. Ethnic diversity is increasing in Western cultures and this enriches the experience within a culture. This has much to offer in promoting a culturally diverse appreciation. The cultural contribution of sport is enhanced by such diversity and extends the boundaries of personal development and cultural awareness. The variety of this sporting cultural strand is unlimited ranging from mass acknowledgement of the Olympic Games to a village cricket team or an ethnic group maintaining their sporting rituals in local communities.

Global sport

In common with an increasing number of aspects of life in the 21st century, sport has 'gone global'. This does not only apply to the major sports festivals such as the Olympic Games and the World Cup, but it applies to any number of lesser events. The obvious reasons for this are the rapid developments in information technology and the relatively recent ability to communicate instantly from almost anywhere on the planet to almost anywhere else (Sage 2002). Results are instantly accessible, viewing is constantly available and information about sport, both live reporting and archival data, is growing at a frightening rate. If I cannot remember who won the World Cup in 1970, I look it up on the internet instead of going to my bookshelf (it was Brazil, they beat Italy 4–1, and it took me 20 seconds). What this means is that, in countries that have the technology, there are no sports unknowns any more. The sporting culture of France, say, is as accessible to me as is the sporting culture of the United States. I can view it, I can read about it, I can know about it.

However, it is not possible to live the experience via the internet, the newspaper or the radio. Those varieties of modern media cannot tell us what it feels like to be a part of that sporting culture. What we are provided with, as sport consumers, is a method of vicariously experiencing the moment. I cannot experience what it is truly like to be a fan of an American football team watching the Superbowl in the company of other fans; or what it feels like for the local cyclist hero from a French village to be leading in the Tour de France as he speeds through his village. Only by thoroughly immersing oneself in a culture can one really experience and understand the true nuances of that culture. Anthropologists researching 'in the field' attempt to immerse themselves in the culture to provide their readers with the deep ethnographic description of that culture. Some writers have attempted to do the same with sport. *Football Against the Enemy* (Kuper 1996) – a discussion of the relationship between football, politics and culture in a number of countries, *In the Red Corner* (Duncan 2001) – the place of boxing in Cuban life, *Beyond a Boundary* (James 1963), a study of West Indian society as epitomised by cricket, and *Brilliant Orange* (Winner 2001), how one country's (Holland's) culture and history shape the way it plays football, are all examples of this type of writing. We might not have the experience, but we have a wealth of knowledge.

There are other reasons for the globalisation of sport. As sport reaches new markets and populations, there is an increased possibility of generating profit from any number of products. The sport itself is not only a product to be sold, as in TV rights, but shirts, magazines and caps also become saleable products. Capitalist sporting imperialism has truly arrived. Historically, all empires that have occupied other countries have exported their sports and pastimes, as well as other aspects of their cultures. After all, that is one of the reasons for encroaching imperialism: the promotion of one set of ideals over another, be these of a political, social or sporting nature. Although generally based around economic exploitation, cultural imperialism seeks to derive wealth from, and control of the dependent nations. The British exported cricket, rugby and football when the British Empire was at its height, but this was only a small part of the process of hegemonic power and domination. In economic and sporting terms, these dependent countries become deskilled and harvested (Maguire 1999). This means that natural resources are exploited, cheap labour is employed and the most highly skilled are attracted away from third world countries to first world countries. As an example of this, African athletes have traditionally been recruited to American universities, and African football players are increasingly attracted to European football clubs. This combination of deskilling and economic control is a powerful mechanism that is hard to resist. This mechanism was, and is, reinforced by some of the functions of these games, which were partially to condition and define a set of behaviours in the participants. Players played to the rules, worked hard to achieve success and respected the rule of authority. These conforming behaviours were very desirable in colonial peoples who were expected to work for the benefit of a business and a society half a world away. Not only was a sport being exported and played, a political and social ideology was being promoted (James 1963). Although there was certainly a commercial aspect to imperial colonisation, there was no commercial aspect of this sporting imperialism. Nowadays there is an entirely different reason for globalising sport. The global market for sport allows capitalist business to 'colonise' the accessible world with its products. A set of ideals is promoted and advertised and sport is commodified in an attempt to increase profits for a business, again perhaps half a world away. In many cases the vehicle for this promotion is now sport. It would appear from this brief discussion that the use of sport has changed, from supporting a political ideology to supporting a commercial ideology. This may be the case and perhaps this tells us more about a changing world order than it does about sport. Empires based on nations and geography have been replaced by empires based on information technology and commerce. Sport has been used, and continues to be used, by the empire builders.

The experience of sport

I began this chapter by suggesting that there was a commonality of sports experience that might be built upon and utilised as a common language. I have argued above that although we can 'know' sport we cannot really share the same experiences as peoples in different cultures. For example, I can know that horse riding competitions are important in Mongolia (Lhagvasuren 2002), but I cannot experience those competitions unless I actually take part in them. Similarly, sailing is a popular sport in south-west England. I have experienced it and I know about it. However, although Mongolians can know about sailing it is very unlikely that they will fully understand the experience of the activity because they have not done it. Does this mean then that we are doomed to remain in our limited cocoons of personal and direct experience? This is the argument that says that one cannot be a paediatrician or a teacher until one has been a parent because only then can one understand children. There is common ground; the common ground is that both the Mongolian horsemen and the sailors in south-west England have shared an experience of sport and physical activity. It will not have been exactly the same experience, but it will be recognisable as a mostly pleasurable experience brought about by sport and physical activity participation. Experience is such a personal thing that even the same event can be experienced differently by different people, different perceptions of what happened will be held and the retelling is mediated by that experience. The passage below illustrates the argument:

> Cricket has a long tradition in English private schools. The game is played on manicured lawns with impeccable etiquette. The uniform is 'whites' without exception. The crowd, if there is any, applauds politely and the players accept their fortune, good or bad, with dignity and grace. The game lasts all day with breaks for drinks and lunch, and can quite often end in a tie. Contrast this with the same sport being played on a West Indian beach, although some argue that this pastime has been somewhat replaced by basketball because of TV exposure to the NBA! The participants are exuberant, anyone can play, the pitch is the uneven sand and the ball often lands in the sea. The uniform is beach shorts and there are no umpires. Therefore, there are many friendly disagreements concerning whether the batsman was in or out! The game ends when the top is lifted off the first Red Stripe. The sport is the same sport – cricket; but is the experience the same, is the meaning of playing the same? Certainly not, however, if students from Eton met West Indians, a game could be played. There is enough commonality of experience to allow an inter-change in a common language that would result in an intercultural discourse, i.e. a game of cricket would happen. That would result in an experience shared by both groups.
>
> (Laker 2002b: 6–7)

What is being described above is a hypothetical situation that suggested that there is an essential essence to sport and sport participation. Physical activity and sport has a common structure, an underlying framework that binds all sports and physical activities together. This essence consists of the physicality of sport, the rules, and the basic playlike nature of the experience. Much of the experience of game playing and sports is socially constructed and for this reason it may be that a post-structural view needs some consideration (Sarup 1993). This claims that each individual experience is arrived at by a combination of prior exposure, constructivist learning and current involvement; in other words the experience of playing the game is developed in a specific context and is thus contextually dependent. So where is the common ground, the common language, that facilitates this unspoken communication. The language is the game, or sport, or activity itself. The physical form of striking a ball, or walking long distances, or catching an object is the same in any culture, no matter where or when it is practised. The activity, that Huizinga (1955) tells us is derived from play, provides us with a means of intercultural discourse; a means of communication unlike any other. In addition, this medium of interaction is free from notions of class, elitism, sexism, ageism and racism. Those characteristics are allocated by different cultures. There are other forms of communication that have this ability to cross cultural and national boundaries, music and painting for example, but unfortunately they are not as widely available to mass audiences as sport.

Acculturation and socialisation into this common experience

Becoming part of a community and being a member of a social system involves learning how to act, speak, dress and generally conduct oneself. Eitzen and Sage (1997: 77) say that it is a 'process of learning and adapting to a given social system'. The use of the word, adapting, suggests that the process is an interactive one whereby one acts, witnesses response and then reacts, perhaps modifying, changing or in some way altering one's first action. All the while one is developing a growing knowledge and vocabulary of socially acceptable behaviours that allows one to work, live and exist in the parent society. Although in this example this process is commonly referred to as socialisation, the mechanism is the same as the one that operates when one is acculturated into a community of practice, in this case the sporting community or any particular sporting sub-culture.

Acculturation and socialisation occur into, during and also out of a set of practices, in this case the set of practices is characterised as a sporting sub-culture. The agencies that enable the process are many and varied, and there are a number of factors that affect one's level of involvement and degree of access to the community. The family, including siblings as well as parents, is the first and obvious agency but this is later followed by friends, or peers, teachers and coaches, role models and, of course, the media. The community agencies most effective during participation are fellow participants, peers and those whose behaviour one aspires to follow. The main reasons for children and young adults to want to continue in sport is to socialise with their peers, to have fun and to learn new skills (Stroot 2002). All of these are key elements in the acculturation process. So, having decided to try to join the community of practice, the experiences that maintain interest and socialise are the factors that participants seek anyway. This is a very powerful combination of circumstances. The culture of the sport begins to exert a hegemonic influence and participants will maintain the customs, traditions and *status quo* of the activity as their participation continues. This public display of sub-cultural identity is an obvious statement of commitment and connection.

Degree of access and level of involvement depend on a number of factors. Degree of access refers to the amount of a sub-culture one is granted access to. For example, some women are only granted access on certain days and times at a few golf clubs. This naturally limits the degree to which they can become a full member of that community of practice. (However, it should be suggested that they may not want to become a full member of such a community!) The amount of the sub-culture to which they have access is limited by the factor of gender. Level of involvement refers to the time one spends engaged in the activities of the sub-culture. As an example, a skier who has a low income may only be able to afford skiing on dry ski slopes in the UK, whereas more wealthy community members would probably travel to the European Alps or the American Rockies to ski each year. The level of involvement is thus limited by socio-economic factors. One could also cite examples using race and ethnicity, religion and level of education as well as the two examples of gender and socio-economic status used here.

It can be seen that acculturation, which includes degree of access and level of involvement in a community of practice, is dependent on a dynamic mix of factors. What one experiences in sport and how one perceives those experiences, the meanings attached to them and the importance attributed to the experiences are determined by the acculturation process. There is a certain amount of knowledge that participants need to acquire before they can aspire to full membership of a sporting culture and before they can become full participants in that community of practice. What this knowledge is will depend on the specific culture, but some general principles are discussed next.

What do our children need to know, and how will they come to know it?

Kirk and Tinning (1990) made the point 13 years ago that physical education has come to be dominated by scientific functionalism. Positivist science has hijacked the subject and seeks to educate, or produce, healthy bodies that demonstrate all the characteristics of efficient machines. The recent adoption of health as a dominating rationale for physical education in schools, particularly in the United States, is an example of this (Corbin 2002). Physical education is in danger of being reduced to the teaching of a series of bio-systems (Kirk 1995). This reductionist approach depersonalises the body and the body's abilities in activity, it only addresses the psychomotor and ignores the fact that humans are thinking, feeling entities who must have social and cultural features as part of their existence. Being a sports citizen is not only about being an efficient, healthy and skilful mover, it also requires that participants know about the world of sport and activity, what it means in and to their society, and that they appreciate the various benefits that participation can provide. What constitutes physical education is the result of political and structural factors that bring vested interests into the decision-making process. Scientific functionalism has held a privileged position in this process for too long and the result has been a physical education that is perceived by students as being irrelevant and uncontextual. Of course students need to be educated in the psychomotor domain but this is only part of what is desirable. Young people need to know the cultural significance of sport, they need to learn the language of sport and to be skilful participants naturally, but also to be critically aware of the importance and potential of sport and physical activity.

Kirk (1995) suggests that physical education also needs to equip students to counter the pernicious claims of popular physical culture that promotes only one type of body as being acceptable; the slim, toned body of many advertising campaigns. He champions a move away from a steady stream of team sports that have resulted in much disillusion among young people. Many students consider this type of curriculum to be boring and irrelevant. A brief review of his plan indicates secondary level students being able to choose from a wide range of activities and agreeing/contracting to complete a number of hours of participation to gain the required credit. Such activities might even be carried on out of school time and away from school grounds. This would force physical education teachers to tailor their offerings much more to the students' interests. Students would also need to be taught to cast a critical eye on the claim of popular physical culture. It is this aspect that makes the curriculum educational as opposed to just recreational; students would be educated to evaluate what they see and what they do. Of course Kirk's ideas presuppose that students at primary/elementary level develop a whole range of physical competencies and 'a physical literacy of skills and knowledge' (Kirk 1995: 372) to enable them to take advantage of such a curriculum. I will later suggest what such a continuous curriculum might look like.

Another curriculum proposal that partially addresses the cultural aspects of physical education and sports activity is Siedentop's (1994) sport education proposal. He suggests that this curriculum goes some way to meeting the needs of future sport citizens. This model provides a curriculum designed to help young people become literate, competent and enthusiastic participants and consumers of sport. This curriculum model is described elsewhere in this book (p. 41), but suffice it to say here that sport education incorporates the defining characteristics of sport in the real world, i.e. sport as a community of practice, as opposed to the skill-based, linear version of sport commonly found in school physical education. Of course, this also means that sport education has many of the characteristics that are problematic for sport such as elitism and exaggerated competition (see Chapter 7 for further discussion on this issue). However, this serves to make the subject far more relevant to the students' experiences of what sport is really like. It also has the potential to address sport in other cultures. Kinchin and O'Sullivan report on a project that adopted this approach. A Cultural Studies unit of work was developed and incorporated into the physical education curriculum. The objectives were to 'encompass an integrated, sustained, practical and intellectual involvement in sport and physical activity' (Kinchin and O'Sullivan 1999: 41). The students were presented with the historical and geographical background of volleyball and encouraged to engage in a theoretical investigation of sport in society. The findings suggest that the majority of students enjoyed their physical education lessons more than ever and acknowledged the long-term relevance and importance of the learning experience. This type of approach openly acknowledges that the psychomotor domain is only one of a number of domains within school sport and physical education, the others being the cognitive, social and affective domains. Each of these needs to be adequately considered in planning any curriculum, especially one that purports to have a socially critical and a culturally aware agenda.

How these proposals can be built into an operational curriculum is discussed in the concluding chapters. There are other initiatives that will also be incorporated into that concluding proposal. Those examples used above are examples that indicate the first steps towards a socially and culturally relevant physical education curriculum. They go some way to answering the question: what do our children need to know and how will they come to know it?

Summary

This chapter has attempted to illustrate that sport and all its variants – physical education, activity, recreation and so on – have a central and developing place as a cultural institution. This is not only true of Western cultures, but also of many cultures worldwide. The degree of importance attached to sport will vary, but media coverage and popular interest indicate that, for many people, and peoples, sport is a central part of their daily lives.

The suggestion that sport is part of a common cultural language is examined by reference to sporting sub-cultures and the ease with which sporting metaphors are accepted into daily use. In essence, sport serves a number of functions that enhance the socialisation process, social interaction, a site of tradition and myth, expression of emotion and acculturation being but a few of these functions.

Even though big-time sport has become a global phenomenon with instant viewing and vast resources generated from it, the experience of sport itself can differ greatly, dependent on a number of factors. Global location, socio-economic status, level of participation and degree of expertise will play a role in determining our experience of sport – what it means to us. While these experiences will necessarily differ there remains a common factor in all of them; that is, the essence of the game which transcends all these other boundaries. This is the common language, the similarity, the binding force that prompts me to propose the inclusion of the study of sport in programmes aimed at developing global citizens.

Study of this type is needed to equip students to deal with all the elements of popular culture that assault them from all sides. They need to be adequately educated in their information processing and decision-making abilities. Students also need to be aware of the cultural significance of sport in their own community and in the wider communities of practice. A curriculum that takes this approach could certainly be more relevant and contextual to the students' own experience than many of the curricular models that are used currently.

The area of study that supports this notion is growing. In recent years Armstrong and Giulianotti have edited two books (1997 and 2001) studying football from an anthropological and cultural perspective, and MacClancy (1996) examines sport in cultural and social locations while discussing meanings and interpretations of the experience. These are just samples of the increasing academic study of sport as a social and cultural institution. This is an indication of the growing awareness that sport is not a trivial pursuit. It is an extremely important, and sometimes all-consuming, aspect of the human condition. It is no longer too precious to say that sport is not just about playing games, it also has a contribution to make to the quality of our lives and to the knowledge we bring to the understanding of other cultures. That is why sport and its educational manifestation, physical education, have a vital role to play in educating young people, not only about sport itself, but also about cultural differences, understanding and even tolerance.

References

Armstrong, G. and Giulianotti, R. (1997) *Entering the Field: New Perspectives on World Football*, Oxford/New York: Berg.
——(2001) *Fear and Loathing in World Football*, Oxford/New York: Berg.
Butts, S.L. (2001) ' "Good to the last drop": Understanding surfers' motivations', *Sociology of Sport Online*, 4(1).
Corbin, C.B. (2002) 'Physical education as an agent of change', *Quest*, 54(3): 182–195.
DNH (1995) *Sport: Raising the Game*, London: Department of National Heritage.
Duncan, J. (2001) *In the Red Corner: A Journey into Cuban Boxing*, London: Yellow Jersey Press.
Dyck, N. (ed.) (2000) *Games, Sports and Cultures*, Oxford/New York: Berg.
Eitzen, D.S. and Sage, G.H. (1997) *Sociology of North American Sport*, Chicago, IL: Brown & Benchmark.
Gardner, H. (1983) *Frames of Mind: The Theory of Multiple Intelligences*, New York: Basic Books.
Huizinga, J. (1955) *Homo Ludens*, London: Routledge & Kegan Paul.
Humberstone, B. (2002) 'Femininity, masculinity and difference: what's wrong with a sarong?', in A. Laker (ed.), *The Sociology of Sport and Physical Education: An Introductory Reader*, London: RoutledgeFalmer, 58–78.
Inglis, F. (1977) *The Name of the Game: Sport and Society*, London: Heinemann.
James, C.L.R. (1963) *Beyond a Boundary*, London: Serpent's Tail, 1994 edn.
Kinchin, G.D. and O'Sullivan, M. (1999) 'Making physical education meaningful for high school students', *Journal of Physical Education, Recreation and Dance*, 70(5): 40–44.
Kirk, D. (1995) 'Physical education and cultural relevance: A personal statement', in A.E. Jewett, L.L. Bain and C.D. Ennis, *The Curriculum Process in Physical Education*, Boston, MA: McGraw-Hill, 2nd edn, 369–373.
Kirk, D. and Tinning, R. (1990) 'Introduction: Physical education, curriculum and culture', in D. Kirk and R. Tinning (eds), *Physical Education, Curriculum and Culture: Critical Issues in the Contemporary Crisis*, London: Falmer, 1–22.
Kuper, S. (1996) *Football Against the Enemy*, London: Phoenix.

Laker, A. (ed.) (2002a) *The Sociology of Sport and Physical Education: An Introductory Reader*, London: RoutledgeFalmer.

——(2002b) 'Volleyball in the shadow of Annapurna', *The Chronicle of Physical Education in Higher Education*, 13(2): 6–7.

Lhagvasuren, G. (2002) 'Historical contributions of Mongolians to world physical culture and sport', *Journal of the International Council for Health, Physical Education, Recreation, Sport and Dance*, 37(2): 10–12.

MacClancy, J. (ed.) (1996) *Sport, Identity and Ethnicity*, Oxford: Berg.

Maguire, J. (1999) *Global Sport: Identities, Societies, Civilizations*, Cambridge: Polity Press.

Sage, G. (2002) 'Global sport and global mass media', in A. Laker (ed.), *The Sociology of Sport and Physical Education: An Introductory Reader*, London: RoutledgeFalmer, 211–233.

Sarup, M. (1993) *An Introductory Guide to Post-Structuralism and Postmodernism*, Athens, GA: University of Georgia Press, 2nd edn.

Siedentop, D. (1994) *Sport Education: Quality PE Through Positive Sport Experience*, Champaigne, IL: Human Kinetics.

Simpson, J (2002) *The Beckoning Silence*, London: Jonathan Cape.

Stroot, S.A. (2002) 'Socialisation and participation in sport', in A. Laker (ed.), *The Sociology of Sport and Physical Education: An Introductory Reader*, London: RoutledgeFalmer, 129–147.

Winner, D. (2001) *Brilliant Orange*, London: Bloomsbury.

3 Citizenship, sport and physical education

Anthony Laker

Citizenship, as an aim of education, has a long history. Citizenship has been a topic of debate in education provision from the days of the Greek city states to the present day. Apart from providing the military with fit young men, the main rationale for education in Greek times was to educate the populace for citizenship, i.e. so that they, the people, could show involvement in public affairs (Van Dalen and Bennett 1971). Nearer the present day, John Dewey's (1916) work showed a more philosophical approach. *Democracy and Education*, for example, is a world renowned classic in the philosophy of education for citizenship in a democratic society. This idea that education can have citizenship as an outcome has been revitalised over the last few years. This denotes a trend to a more holistic sense of education, which Dewey advocated, in which students are not merely equipped with knowledge, but they are also exposed to the characteristics, abilities and talents necessary to help them live a full life in a social community. It is no longer acceptable just to teach facts, dates and equations. How people deal with facts, dates and equations and, more importantly, interact with each other, is now seen to be crucial in developing a society of rational, educated, caring individuals, i.e. citizens. This appreciation has resulted in technical and scientific types of knowledge being supplemented with more humanistic, philanthropic aspects of the educational process. Constructivists claim that knowledge is socially constructed. In fact the whole of one's social persona is socially constructed because we develop our ideas of who we are and what we are worth partly as a result of what others think of us. How we view ourselves as components of a much larger community is also socially constructed by our interaction with others. This social developmental process cannot exist in isolation. It is affected by, and it affects, many other aspects of an individual's development. The argument continues that because of this interactive process, citizenship cannot be taught in isolation; it must be shown to be relative to other arenas of social and educational activity. This chapter is concerned with how citizenship is incorporated into some of these arenas of social and educational activity; namely, physical education and sport.

Any subsequent discussion first needs to address a certain number of questions directed at clarifying the issues and terms being used. We need to have a good understanding of what citizenship really is, what are its components and what kind of contributions can school sport and physical education make to the development of citizenship. In addition, a historical and global perspective would help to conceptualise our ideas of the curricular incorporation and adoption of citizenship. There have been a number of initiatives in curriculum development that have recently demonstrated an assumption that education has a responsibility for promoting citizenship in students. The investigation of the origin and development of this process would be fruitful to the deeper analysis. As well as a historical and global perspective, any meaningful analysis must have a strong connection with a theoretical framework. Constructivism has already been mentioned as an effective framework for analysis. More specifically, situated learning theory (Lave and Wenger 1991) has become the educational offshoot of constructivism. This theory focuses on learning as a social process and has a number of attractive component concepts; namely, *legitimate peripheral participation* and *communities of practice*. These concepts will be explained later and further analysis will be based on the adoption of these concepts and how they relate to school sport, physical education and the development of citizenlike characteristics in students. Lastly, this chapter will examine exactly how physical education and school sport can make a contribution to the effective teaching of citizenship. As well as using school sport and physical education as a vehicle for this teaching, they can also be used to encourage the development of citizens of sport. These would be participants who take a full and active part in their sport, not only by being participants but also by being rational, educated and caring individuals within the sporting context. Individuals meeting this description would be participants who were involved in, or at least aware and concerned about, the governance of their sports; they would be advocates for their own sport, and for sports in general, and they would be actively involved in promoting their sport and the many benefits of the world of sport. They would recognise the extensive relationships that exist within the sporting world, and also between the institution of sport and other societal institutions, such as politics, education, and cultural, ethnic and sub-cultural groups within any given society.

Citizenship defined

Any attempted definition of citizenship must necessarily be context specific. So, definitions of citizenship in first world, democratic nations would be different from definitions of citizenship for nations emerging from totalitarian regimes towards a more democratic government. Because of the problematic nature of specific, political definitions, we will only attempt a working definition that is appropriate for use in educational, sporting and social communities. Nevertheless, there are some commonalities in all definitions.

One of these commonalities is the concept of rights and responsibilities. Allen (1997), suggested that the rights of citizens cannot be exercised without the acceptance of some responsibilities. In this way, citizens become accountable to themselves and their communities. Freedom of speech and access to justice are regarded as basic human (citizen) rights and citizens must be willing to defend, exercise and promote those rights, both for themselves and for others. It becomes a symbiotic relationship whereby individuals are granted rights by the state, or community, in return for compliance with social values and group norms and the acceptance of responsibility in the defence of those values and norms. This *status quo* can only exist if those who are granted the rights, value the existence and exercise of those rights. This is particularly pertinent at this time. The recent worries in the United Kingdom, about 'levels of apathy, ignorance and cynicism about political and public life and also involvement in neighbourhood and community affairs' (QCA 1998: 4) hastened the introduction of Citizenship into the National Curriculum in England and Wales and thus into the mainstream of educational life. As will be shown later in this chapter, this concern has also been seen in a number of other countries, for example in the United States (Bennett and Wughalter 1999; Hellison *et al.* 2000; Putman 2000), and seems to be a reoccurring factor in social commentary.

In reaching a working definition of citizenship, the characteristics that represent effective citizenship in our young people, and in our young sportspeople, are social and moral responsibility, community involvement and political literacy. These components are suggested for use in an educational capacity by the Crick Report (QCA 1998) and expanded on by Laker (2000) in a physical education and sporting context. In addition to these components, citizenship allows people to operate effectively and in a responsible manner, exercising and defending their rights, and protecting those less able or less fortunate. This definition will suffice for now in that it gives us a basis from which to begin a more detailed and closer examination of the concept of citizenship, not only in an educational context, but also in a sport-related context; and perhaps reach a more refined interpretation of what it is to be a citizen. The term *sport-related context* will be used to include school sport, formal physical education and also the much larger field of recreational sport indulged in by a segment of the population at large. Where differentiations in application need to be made between physical education, school sport and community recreational sport, this will be made clear in the text.

Social and moral responsibility

Crick's (QCA 1998) explanation/definition of this component of citizenship is somewhat limited because of the application for which the report was designated. The work is closely related to the National Curriculum framework in England and Wales and I want to expand considerably on that framework, thus bringing in an international contextual relevance. The definition expanded here will be applicable to any number of educational, sporting and community settings.

Social and moral aspects of the curriculum are closely linked to the notion of citizenship. The social and moral responsibility suggested as a first component of citizenship fits very well with what the school curriculum is required to deliver now, and will be required to deliver in the future. There are complete models of the curriculum based upon the notion of social responsibility (Hellison 1985, 1996; Morris and Stiehl 1999; Laker, 2001).

Hellison (1985,1996) proposes a hierarchical system of levels of responsibility. They progress from irresponsibility through respect, participation and effort, self-responsibility, sensitivity and responsiveness to the well-being of others, to the final level of community responsibility. The level beyond the one students are operating at is called a goal until they reach that level and then the level after that becomes the next goal and so on.

Morris and Stiehl (1999) suggest that children's games possess a variety of benefits of which character building, reduction of delinquency and development of socially desirable behaviours are just a few. Their programme of games which are changed to achieve this variety of benefits is aimed mainly at the primary/elementary level and also claims benefits such as fun, fitness and encouraging a sense of community. This rationale is supported in a special feature in the *Journal of Physical Education, Recreation and Dance* (Morris 1993) which deals exclusively with issues of responsibility in physical education settings, self-responsibility and social responsibility being key components of the propositions.

Laker (2001) takes a curriculum planning and development approach to including responsibility and personal, social and moral education (PSME) into the physical curriculum. He deals with planning, implementing, assessing and reflecting on programme development. At each stage of the curriculum process there are practical suggestions for the inclusion of elements of responsibility and PSME. This practical guide for teachers has an array of activities and strategies that can be implemented in class that promote characteristics such as fair play, sportsmanship, moral decision making and responsible behaviour.

This is not the place for further explanations of these models; interested readers will go to the original sources, but these models do indicate that some importance is now being placed on this aspect of the citizenship debate. But why is moral and social responsibility a component of citizenship, what does it have to offer our young people? Any society wants its young people to know right from wrong, to behave in a moral way (whatever that means in the social context), and to support a moral code that enables large numbers of people to live effectively and harmoniously together. Sport, as a cultural component of society, and physical education, its educational counterpart, can help with these aspects of social and moral acculturation. It has often been stated that playing team games, or any other games, teaches people to play by the rules and to adopt the conventions of fair play. One only has to watch the large number of professional sports on television to know that this is not always so. However, in most educational circumstances, the context is much more controllable. Children can easily be taught the fair way, in society's view, the right way to play games. They can be taught that playing by the rules allows the game to take place for everyone's benefit. When this is applied in a more global context, this transfers to the vast majority of people obeying the law of the land to allow society to function.

Some people cheat and are devious in their dealings with others, but generally most people 'play the game' and are fair and law abiding. Can this be attributed to sport and physical education? The answer has to be no, not solely. But, school sport and physical education play a large part in this process as a part of the whole educational package. There is compelling evidence suggesting that what is consciously promoted in physical education carries over to other areas of the curriculum (Sharpe, Brown and Crider 1995). This evidence encourages a holistic approach to learning.

Moral responsibility and moral behaviour can occasionally become confused with the concepts of right and wrong in a religious sense. After all, some behaviours are morally acceptable in some religions and morally wrong in others. The ongoing debate on the rights and wrongs of abortion, including the rights of the parents, especially the mother, is a prime example of this difference of religious opinion on moral matters. There is also a spiritual aspect to sport and activity that sometimes gets confused with feelings of a religious nature. Sport is not a religion but it can promote spiritual experiences. Euphoric feelings produced by sporting experience are few and far between for the majority of us, but a modified version of such elation can be experienced by many students in an educational setting. The festive and celebratory nature of sport can certainly be highlighted in physical education. So, although sport can promote feelings similar to those associated with religious practice, school sport and physical education must deal with experiences that manifest themselves in physical ways. Therefore any spirituality in sport is preceded by some kind physical activity, moral judgements and behaviour are promoted in physical activity contexts and responsible behaviours are encouraged and developed using sport and activity as a means to that end.

Social and moral responsibility are crucial components of the education process. As will be shown later, a number of countries have instituted a call for education to take on more responsibility itself in these areas of social experience. Whatever the reason for this – the supposed breakdown of the family unit, lack of respect for people and property, easy access to violent and frivolous entertainments, and so on – the fact remains that education is now charged with instilling the fundamentals of moral and social responsibility in our young people. School sport and physical education are able to play a major role in this. The sporting experience itself depends on the application and exercise of moral and social responsibility by its participants, its spectators, its officials and all its constituents. Sometimes those groups are found wanting; participants cheat, officials act outside of the rules and spectators fight. However, in school sport these happenings are rare and should not detract from the possibilities available to interested educators. A number of authors have shown how this can be achieved and some of these examples will be reviewed later in the chapter.

Community involvement

The second part of the citizenship definition is community involvement. Students should learn about their communities and become involved in the everyday life of these communities. Ideally, this would include some aspect of service learning in the community.

The community within which schools exist inevitably represents their physical and socio-economic surroundings. Schools are part of the larger community because they are physically in the community. Schools are also communities in themselves, and within these school communities there are smaller community units such as teams, classes, the student body, the teachers and various clubs and interest groups that have certain sub-culture features that are also identifiable as community features. These features include a common interest, some uniquely identifying factor such as a sport or a uniform, and a responsibility to others in the community or sub-culture. Lave and Wenger's (1991) situated learning theory refers to *communities of practice*. Although not clearly defined in the original, Kirk and Macdonald (1998) use the term to mean a collective or group who share practices. This definition suits the application in educational settings and also the existing social structure within a school. There are already communities in existence; there is no need to construct and impose a new structure of communities. Learning about community involvement can begin in very small ways, e.g. a learning community (a class or a few students involved in groupwork in physical education or any other subject), a team community (a sports team with a common purpose; the enjoyment of sport in a competitive environment) and a social team (perhaps a recreational school club intent on experiencing the social side of sport).

These communities of practice can obviously be any size and in the school sporting hierarchy, the next level would be groups who are representative of their larger populations, such as house (intramural) teams or school teams. These communities have an element of exclusivity that restricts entry and membership and can create elitist barriers between them and the larger student community. This does not have to be the case. In the United States, school teams are a major source of community pride. Local newspapers carry reports of their games and the feelgood factor of a community can be greatly affected by the performance of its school teams. Even though membership to these communities is limited, membership of a sporting community of some sort is available to all students.

Students live in the community that the school serves. Even though they are already part of that community, students can begin to be taught the value of that community demonstrated by the school's active involvement within the community. It is a challenge for many people to view the school as an integrated part of the greater community and not a separate place where children go to receive an education. Schools that establish real links with their communities are much more successful at changing this view than those that exist in isolation. In some ways we can all be teachers and learners. Many people in communities have much to offer children. Many schools welcome an educated, concerned group of individuals into their classrooms. These people are a welcome addition to the ability of schools to provide an inclusive and well-rounded education. Helping with sports teams, specialist skills in the arts and extending foreign language offerings are just some of the areas that can use expertise from outside school.

Although it is important for the community to go into the school for a school and its students to become a true part of the community, they also need to go outside the school gates and into the community itself. In physical activity terms, students will benefit from contact with clubs, teams and recreational opportunities within the community. It will make what they do at school more relevant to their real lives as part of the greater community. It will also expose them to the wider array of options for pursuing an active lifestyle when they leave school. Links with sports centres, local clubs (of all ability levels) and various recreational organisations can produce rich experiences for the students.

Conversely, many schools have extensive community education programmes and meet many of the educational needs of some parts of their communities. Sometimes it seems that the majority of community education programmes are for the middle classes, for whom the value of education has already been demonstrated and for whom school was a rewarding experience. It is worth remembering, however, that for a large segment of the population, when they leave the school premises for the last time as a student, there is little intention of ever returning. Unfortunately, this suggests that the education they received as a school student had very little relevance to their lives as adults, or it may be that the schools have very little vested interest in encouraging continued involvement. Maybe the community education programme does not offer what they want or need. Perhaps the emphasis on lifelong learning is mistaken, or maybe school has so many negative connotations for many people that they can never break away from those images of years long gone.

One of the ways that schools can serve the greater community is to instil in their students the concept that they are part of a global community of learners. In physical activity terms, there is a global community of sport. Sportspeople from whatever background have a common means of communication, a common foundation of interest and a sharing of the sport experience that joins them and links them into a sports community. Part of the role of physical education and school sport is to teach children this common language, to instil this interest and to provide opportunities for this sport experience to take place. The learning and mastery of skills, knowledges and values is needed to facilitate students becoming legitimate participants in this global community of sport. Just as a school working effectively in a community to establish new links and enrich those that are present can promote a sense of belonging within a community, so physical education and school sport can help develop a sense of belonging in the global sporting context. This empathetic and communal sport experience is born of the knowledge that there is a sharing of the essence of the sporting experience in whatever social context the experience inhabits. One hopes that this can provide an association missing from the lives of many young people. Jim Stiehl (1993) proposes a model of responsibility development that progresses from personal responsibility through social responsibility to environmental responsibility. It is within these second and third domains of responsibility that young people can be provided with a sense of place and a feeling of belonging. They can begin to establish their own sporting identities which will hopefully locate them in the sporting and recreational context which constitutes part of our global community.

Many schools have service learning programmes which allow students to volunteer and help in their locality. There are also schools that have exchange arrangements and links with schools in other countries, both in Europe and worldwide. These arrangements often include sporting events and this aspect is considered to be a valuable part of such relationships although probably not the most important. The power of sport was illustrated when there was a football match between Afghan players and a team from the peacekeeping force in a stadium that had been used for public executions by the Taliban. Laurie McMenemy, who was coach to one of the teams, was quoted as saying, 'Sport is the common denominator. It puts everyone together and a football match here is a victory before the game even kicks off' (George 2002). This event did not make major changes in the world but it did encourage a return to normality in that strife-torn region. The fact that there was a language of common experience, i.e. football, allowed the event to take place and that is a tribute to the power of sport. What better social function could there be than helping a community to heal and encouraging that community to have faith in its own future.

Political literacy

Perhaps a better title for this component of citizenship would be democratic awareness. The word *political* has connotations of strident doctrine and forceful ideology which are not so strongly prevalent in *democracy*. The word *democracy* has kinder associations. Whichever phrase is chosen, there are similarities in the associated characteristics. A politically literate, or democratically aware, person is free to choose to participate in public life because they have a desire to do so, not out of a sense of duty. By acting in such a way they can become active in the life of their community. As Allen (1997) suggests, young people need to know how the political becomes personal, and how their lives are affected by the actions of councils and governments, and also sometimes by events on a global, as well as a local scale. This suggests that just having knowledge about democracy is inadequate on its own, students need to be able to practice democracy if they are to have the freedom to choose involvement in political life.

What this means in practical terms is that students should have an under-standing of how our societies, communities and nations function at all levels of operation, from city or town council to European and international agencies. Part of a student's education would expose them to political, legal and social systems and the intricacies of governance that structural functionalists say maintain the *status quo* in any given society. Implicit in this, is that students will be able to critically appreciate how these systems work, whose interests they serve and how the implementation of power is achieved in a supposedly democratic environment. This development of young people with an ability for critical analysis is one sign of a mature democracy that can afford the luxury of being questioned and challenged. Not all societies can afford to grant such liberal possibilities to their citizens. A truly democratic society has an obligation, or responsibility, to educate a free, rational and knowledgeable population. The population then has a responsibility to function in a politically literate and democratic way, either supporting or challenging, but always within a framework that recognises the rights and responsibilities of all citizens within that community.

How can school sport and physical education help in this aspect of education, or should school sport and physical education even attempt to become a part of this wider educational aim? A superficial examination suggests that sport has little to offer in the way of democratic awareness and political literacy. Sports governing bodies are not known to be the most democratic entities in terms of governance. There is also the stereotypical coach/player relationship that has had military and draconian overtones. The bullying coach of a losing team or a weary athlete is an image much used by Hollywood. As an institution, sport is fairly autocratic, both in the way it is run and also in the way teams, sportsmen and women, and coaches operate. The position of coach is almost always viewed as that of a dominant leader rather than a facilitator. This varies with different sports and ability levels. Some sports such as American football and gymnastics are very coach dominated, while others such as orienteering and cricket are less so. A coach in a recreational setting operates with the agreement of the players, whereas a coach of a professional football team, for example, has complete control over all playing matters and sometimes control over other aspects of their players lives. In this way the coach can sometimes represent an imposing and repressive management structure that treats players as components of the production process. The product is a sporting event to be consumed by the fans and the outcome is a profit for the owner/management.

Coaches of school sports are almost invariably also teachers at the school. This dual role can be problematic in a number of ways. A coach works with athletes who are essentially volunteers, whereas a teacher works with students in physical education who are required to attend. The didactic and command style used in the teaching of most physical education lessons is not always the most appropriate style of coaching for use with a group present by choice. Coaches must adjust their style to reflect their changing role, just as students must adapt to their roles which change from student to athlete. It would be impossible for teachers to completely step outside their teacher role, even when they are coaching. This is one of the reasons why school sport and physical education are not natural arenas where one can witness democracy at work.

There are many examples of political involvement in sport and of the politics of sport. By taking a global view of the world of sport, students could be made aware of a number of political issues. There are examples where sports have been used for political ends and this demonstrates that the use of sport is far from politically democratic, the boycotts of the 1980 and 1984 Olympics being cases in point. An example of the politics within sport would be the Bosman ruling that allowed football players to change clubs with far more freedom at the end of their contracts. Perhaps current events in the field of sport could be used to illustrate the notions of politics and democracy as they apply to, and within sport. Although physical education and school sport may not contribute directly to political literacy and democratic awareness, they could definitely provide examples of democracy and how it works in real contexts, e.g. local clubs, community funding for sport and election of students to advisory councils within school. For students who enjoy physical activity, these examples that are more relevant to their interests could provoke an understanding that the exercise of democracy as a part of the political process is not that remote from their lives, in fact it impacts in very real terms on the things that they enjoy the most, i.e. sport and recreation.

The section on social and moral responsibility highlighted a number of curriculum models that privileged responsibility as a major outcome of physical education. Some schools are structured in a way that actively promotes citizenship development in the students. The United World Colleges, for example, 'encourage young people to become responsible citizens, politically and environmentally aware, committed to the ideals of peace, justice, understanding and cooperation, and to the implementation of these ideals through action and personal example' (United World Colleges 2002). Although political literacy and democratic awareness can be promoted by using school sport and physical education, there are no physical education curriculum models that have this objective as their main function. The most easily adaptable model that already includes concepts of team membership, community responsibility and some elements of the decision-making process, is sport education (Grant 1992; Siedentop 1994; Hastie 1996, 1998). Sport education was developed in response to increasing dissatisfaction with traditional physical education. It was felt that although sporting activities made up much of the content of physical education, the essential characteristics that make sport such an important cultural institution were missing from school physical education. The curriculum model was designed to educate young people who would be competent at sports, literate in the understanding of sport and enthusiastic in their participation in sporting activities. The major characteristics of sport were built into the curriculum: sports in seasons, team affiliation, formal competition, a culminating event, record keeping and festivity. Having been assigned to teams, students then adopt a variety of roles such as coaches and captains, referees, record keepers and governing committee members. These roles can be changed throughout the season as the teacher sees fit. Essentially, the students take ownership of their programme and run the sport for the season after the teacher has provided the all-important initial input of teaching the sport's skills, planning and organising the majority of the programme. By running the programme and assuming the responsibilities of the different roles, the students can experience at first hand the democratic process at work in a sports context. Some programmes have devolved responsibility by allowing students to select activities, teams and roles within those teams. Although, to date there has been no research that evaluates the sport education model in its potential or ability to develop and promote citizenship in participating students, this model seems to lend itself to this development. Obviously, further research is needed to support the contentions made here.

Citizenship in education: examples from pre-modern times to the present day

One of the main purposes of education is to support the society or community in which it is provided. In very early times, education, or what passed for education, would have been to ensure the survival of the community. In many ways this community survival and society support is still prevalent, and a function of education, today. The sociological notion of hegemony (i.e. the process that maintains the social *status quo* and perpetuates power structures) and the theory of structural functionalism (i.e. the institutions of society work together in mutually supportive ways) provide ample frameworks for these ideas of cultural support and reproduction (Sage 1990; Coakley 2000). If this cultural support and reproduction mechanism were not important, why should there be such a prominence attached to the development of citizenship? Why should societies want good citizens if not to play a major role in supporting those societies? This is not to argue that such a motive is wrong, merely to point out that the culturally reproductive role of education is as old as education itself, we merely have a new emphasis placed on it at this time.

As examples of pre-modern cultures, ancient Greece and Rome were two that had identifiable aspects of citizenship in their education systems. Dualism, the idea that humans had two components, academic and physical, formed the foundation of Greek educational thinking. In each of two philosophical positions both body and mind held positions of importance, for different reasons. In the first philosophy, the body needed to function adequately in order for the mind to operate effectively. In the second philosophy, humans were dualist in nature, composed of body and mind and it was desirable to develop each element to its full potential. Dualism was further exemplified by the Greek curriculum, which featured two components: gymnastics and academics. In either philosophy, the education of the body was considered a critical part of developing a complete citizen. Training to achieve a good physique was one way in which men could be more like their gods, who were viewed as superhumans. Education had different goals in different city-states (Mechikoff and Estes 1998). For example, Sparta required its citizens to be prepared for military activity. This was the mark of a good citizen. Naturally, the physical (gymnastic) component of education predominated and the academic was secondary. Athens, on the other hand, sought to develop citizens who were liberally educated and well-rounded individuals. Athenian education used a broad curriculum to instil values and attitudes acceptable to the state. Fitness in both city-states was important. Lack of fitness denoted poor citizenship; in Sparta because it was socially irresponsible to be unfit for military service, and in Athens because it was a sign of a poor education. Thus, the definition of good citizenship in many of Greece's city-states included an element of physical development through physical education.

The Romans also included physical education and prowess at sports as part of their citizenship ideal, at least in the earlier days of the Roman empire. In these early times the populace were trained to be useful citizens and soldiers. Students were educated to become strong and skilful for fighting and living efficiently. The natural focus of education was preparation for service to society. Part of being a good citizen was to be educated to protect society if necessary, to live without being a burden on society, and to be a useful member of that society. There are many parallels with this focus nowadays. Taking responsibility for one's own health suggests that one hopes not to be a burden on the health system. Perhaps the critical theorists could take a look at the current emphasis on health in the physical education curriculum and conclude that the motivation behind the initiative is not entirely altruistic but includes a vested interest in reducing health care system stress. Being a useful and productive member of society is also used as a rationale for parts of the educational process. Again, critical theorists would claim that education is partly to do with being trained to be an efficient part of the production process to serve the seats of capitalist power. As the Roman empire became more financially successful, the necessity for an efficient citizenry gradually decreased. Similarly, the need for physically educated citizens decreased and Romans became spectators of increasingly brutal spectacles instead of participants in healthy activity.

Towards citizenship education: an example from England and Wales

Towards the end of the capitalist eccentricities of the Thatcher era (1979–90), there were growing concerns that years of individual wealth promotion had eroded the altruistic nature of British society (even though Margaret Thatcher herself famously claimed that there was no such thing as society). Definitions of freedom had changed so that people were not free to be dissident, but were now free to be significant wealth producers. The theory was that wealth created by these individuals would trickle down to those with less disposable income. In fact the rich got richer and the poor got poorer! They were also free to be an unprivileged underclass with very little in the way of a social support structure (Allen 1997). The notion of Active Citizens began to be promoted by the government. These were individuals who should take responsibility for their own actions and conditions thus enabling, or validating the rolling back of the welfare state. The extensive use of volunteering was encouraged as a way of giving to the underprivileged. This was critically viewed as a free substitute for the gaps that had appeared in the welfare state. 'Care in the community', a slogan of Thatcher's, was really, free-of-cost care in the community. Doctors, teachers and the police were respectively charged with encouraging individual health responsibility, taking responsibility for one's own learning and behaving in a morally acceptable way.

The government sent mixed messages in terms of being responsible for one's own education. A National Curriculum was introduced in 1992 that prescribed subject content and choice. So students were expected to be responsible for their own education as long as it matched what was acceptable and viewed as legitimate by the authorities. It has been suggested (Kirk 1992) that this was a political move by the waning Conservative government to marshal public opinion against a supposedly liberal educational establishment, thus demonstrating a willingness by the government to act on behalf of the people in maintaining (the government's) social values. Citizenship education was not included in the National Curriculum at this stage, but the seeds had been sown for later initiatives. The government's view was that young people needed to be trained in duties and responsibilities and respect for the law; very much a conformist approach.

The work of Crick and Lister in the 1970s (Crick and Lister 1978) was picked up following the Active Citizen initiative and resulted in a report, authored by Crick (QCA 1998) on education for citizenship and the teaching of democracy. This was the report that laid the groundwork for defining citizenship for educational purposes and outlining the nature and practices of the democracy as they could be applied within and outside the formal curriculum in England and Wales. It was recommended that the teaching of citizenship and democracy was so important 'for schools and the life of the nation that there should be a statutory requirement on schools to ensure that it is part of the entitlement of all pupils' (QCA 1998: 2). Because the reporting group believed that cross-curricular attempts at such teaching had failed, the subject was elevated to full subject status within the National Curriculum in England and Wales in 2002. It would be included in the programmes of study for all students aged 5 to 16. Crucially for school sport and physical education, the report suggested that the whole ethos of the school should reflect the aims of active citizenship. This was to be conducted within the school and in its relationships with local communities. Such a statement offers an open door to sport and physical education to contribute in a very real way to effective citizenship education.

Citizenship in the National Curriculum (QCA/DfEE, 2002)

It could easily be argued that the main elements of what constitutes citizenship have always been promoted in schools and other educational settings. Up until recently, it was the hidden curriculum that privileged a set of values and attitudes about what was important in society and the way people should behave in communities of various sizes. After all, these are the essential characteristics of the hidden curriculum. The difference now is that the curriculum is overt and visible to all. It has been formalised and now represents official policy. In some ways this is to be welcomed because it foregrounds what society holds as important and allows schools to legitimise their curricula. We must also recognise that what is presented in the formal curriculum version of citizenship now serves the same function as the hidden curriculum version used to serve. One set of values and attitudes is being privileged at the expense of other variations. No matter how good, equitable and tolerant the content appears to be, it remains the authorised version that has been approved for consumption by the students and for delivery by the teachers. While individual teachers might not have much input in decisions of curricular content, subject teachers, such as physical educators, can interpret their contributions to the cross-curricular effort in ways that they deem appropriate. Before we get to that point, we will briefly review some of the content of citizenship in the National Curriculum as an example of one structured curriculum package.

Up to age 11, personal, social and health education (PSHE) and citizenship are combined together. Students should:

(a)   develop confidence and responsibility and make the most of their abilities;
(b)   prepare to play an active role as citizens;
(c)   develop a healthy, safer lifestyle;
(d)   develop good relationships and respect the differences between people.

Among the learning experiences that should be provided are opportunities to feel positive about themselves, take and share responsibility, and consider social and moral dilemmas. Within these parameters, there are a series of recommendations that teachers could use in planning their delivery. Some of these lend themselves particularly well to physical education and school sport. Very young students, i.e. up to age 7, should be taught what is fair and unfair, that they belong to a variety of communities, that they can improve their health and well-being and that they should play and work cooperatively. Later, i.e. up to age 11, students should be taught about topical issues, problems and events, why and how rules are made, how the media present information, the benefits of exercise and to challenge stereotypes. While these were not planned with physical education or school sport in mind, it can be seen that these topics could easily be incorporated into the subject's curriculum. This would allow sport and physical education to make an early contribution to PSHE and citizenship thus establishing a cross-curricular relationship that could be used to advantage in the later school years.

When students move on to secondary education at age 11, citizenship becomes a subject in its own right in the National Curriculum. As a result, the requirements, learning experiences and suggested range of topics become more refined and specific. Students should:

(a)   understand about becoming informed citizens;
(b)   develop skills of enquiry and communication;
(c)   develop skills of participation and responsible action.

Under these broad headings, students should have learning opportunities about such topics as the work of community groups, the role of the media, the world as a global community, social and cultural issues and be able to take responsibility in school and community-based activities. There is also a range of other suggestions based on rights and responsibilities and understanding other viewpoints through discussion and debate. While these components of the curriculum do not specify that physical education should be used to develop these learning activities, it is not difficult to visualise how this could be done. At this age, and to take some of the above ideas, sport in community groups, sport and the media and global sport are certainly topics that would be ways of using a cross-curricular approach to include sport and physical education in citizenship education.

So far this chapter has considered what citizenship is and how it has become an important concept for schools to accommodate within the curriculum. The final sections of this chapter look at a theoretical framework that supports the use of school sport and physical education in teaching about citizenship and some suggestions about how this might be accomplished.

Physical education and school sport defined

Physical education and community recreational sport are fairly self-explanatory. Physical education is taught in formal, timetabled lessons that take place in school settings, although sometimes these school settings are located off campus. Community recreational sport is recreation of a sporting nature provided within, and by, a community for its constituents. School sport, however, needs a brief explanation. School sport will be taken to mean any activity of a sporting nature organised by a school, or educational institution, outside of the regular timetabled, curriculum physical education lessons. This could take the form of intramural or house sports, varsity matches and competitions where participants represent their school, and regional, state, national and international events where participants compete against other school athletes in their sport at a more advanced level of competition. A huge range of abilities is covered in this array of competitions from supposedly recreational, at the intramural level, to elite performer at the international level. The underlying factor that unites all aspects of school sport is that there should be some element of educational value attached. The type, and possibly the amount, of educational value will change dependent upon the level of competition, the manner in which it is presented and conducted and the outcomes, both intended and unintended. However, the argument that supports school sport in all its forms claims that the educational experience of participants is enhanced by taking part in school sport. It is the level of enhancement that may vary.

Situated learning theory and citizenship

The situated learning theory of Lave and Wenger (1991) has much to commend it when looking at the rationale for the application of a concept such as citizenship in educational settings. This theory is based in the constructivist theory of learning. This states that learning is not done in isolation. It is a social and active process. Prior knowledge, situational constraints, the ecology of the gym and the instructional climate are all factors influencing learning. Learning cannot be separated out from its social and cultural context and will proceed at a varying pace dependent upon any number of interrelated factors. In short, learning, the acquisition of new knowledge, both cognitive and psychomotor, is socially constructed. We are exposed to a new skill, we combine that with already existing knowledge (skill) and reform it into a package that incorporates the old and the new into an amalgam that reflects ourselves, other learners and the environment. Much of the criticism of physical education is that it is not relevant to the everyday lives of the young people who are supposed to benefit from it. Constructivist theory in the form of situated learning acknowledges this irrelevance and seeks to conceptualise what happens in physical activity pedagogy thus providing an understanding of how to bring relevance and context to learning. How this works in physical education will be explained later.

The twin concepts of *legitimate peripheral participation* and *communities of practice* are central to situated learning theory. *Legitimate peripheral participation* means that active involvement in meaningful physical activity is real or authentic, and begins with novitiate status before moving towards full membership of the activity community as participants develop the characteristics and relationships that signify sub-culture membership. Meaningful physical activity is that which is relevant to the lives and interests of young people. It might not be traditional physical education as we know it, indeed, what constitutes traditional physical education is questionable (Kirk 1992). Meaningful physical activity could easily have more of a recreational, lifetime sport component to it.

For such an experience to be real and authentic it must assume some importance to its participants. Much of what students do in physical education is unimportant to them. It becomes important if it is meaningful. *Communities of practice* are similar to sub-cultures. As with a sub-culture, this means a group of participants who share certain defining characteristics. In this case the major defining characteristic is participation in a physical activity setting. Each member of the group contributes to the values and shared symbols and meanings of the group, thus constructing a shared definition of meaningful participation. Within educational physical activity settings there are a number of communities of practice. Teachers are a sub-group, as are students, club members and so on. A community of practice could be as large as the global sporting community or as small as a group of students playing doubles badminton. The smaller groups/communities are constituent parts of the larger community. This notion of varying communities enables us to locate behaviour in a variety of social and cultural settings, thus adopting the constructivist framework of social learning theory.

Other authors have applied the situated learning theory to various aspects of physical education. Kirk and Macdonald (1998) used situated learning theory, particularly the idea of communities of practice, to present new ways of thinking about physical activity pedagogy. Their claim was that physical educators needed a new way of thinking to enable them to face challenges such as the alienation of many young people from physical education. They argue that many of the communities of practice within which school physical education is practised, and which are actively promoted by physical education, no longer exist outside the school. For example, coaches and facilitators of recreational sport very rarely, if ever, use the command style of teaching still commonly used in physical education. Because these communities do not exist, the participation in school physical education is not legitimate, nor does it allow students to progress from peripheral to full membership. Kirk and Macdonald suggest that new forms of physical education would better model the new communities of practice. These forms include social and moral responsibility, health-related fitness and sport education. I have already argued that social and moral responsibility and sport education are well placed to promote citizenship through educational physical activity. I would also suggest that responsibility to oneself that health-related fitness represents is also an appropriate vehicle for citizenship promotion.

In a more recent article, Kirk and MacPhail (2002) use similar arguments to adapt the Teaching Games for Understanding (TGfU) framework to take into account situated learning theory and to promote the TGfU as a vehicle for a more relevant physical education. Some of the criticisms levelled at the traditional method of games teaching are that it uses uncontextual skill practices before allowing students to play large-sided games that only allow minimal participation by the majority of the players. Each game is taught separately, with little transfer of skill between similar games, and the skill application used in games is not of a very high standard. With a limited amount of time available for games teaching within the physical education curriculum, this traditional method has been viewed as inefficient and lacking in educational benefit for a majority of the students. By contrast, the TGfU attempts to help the learner understand the tactical nature of games categories and appreciate the need for tactical awareness to effectively play the game. Modified game forms are used to help learners make sense of games and use decision-making skills in implementing skill usage. Skills are taught when the learners ask for them, or demonstrate a need to master new skills that will facilitate better tactical decision making. In this way, the performance and teaching of the game is situated in a relevant location, that is, in the playing of the game itself. The TGfU makes use of the constructivist approach by applying situated learning theory in a community of practice. The students develop and learn new knowledge as a response to situational challenges (tactical games problems) within a group of sports players (the team or class of students). It is hoped that by learning to play games in this way, students will become socialized into communities of practice, i.e. they will become full members of those communities.

It can now be seen how certain ways of teaching, in this case the TGfU, can be used to encourage students to adopt characteristics of citizenship. In the case of the TGfU, players are encouraged to adopt situational identities within a community of learners (sports players). They learn various roles within sports and how to relate to other players in the community of learners, while developing their abilities as games players. Further examples and suggestions of how school sport and physical education can be used to promote and develop citizenship appear below.

Practical implementation

Social and moral responsibility

There are two points of view that epitomise the debate on social and moral education. First, social and moral education is the responsibility of parents, family and, in some cases, the church and should not be included within the domain of school expectations. The reason being that our education system represents only one ideology and this set of values would be promoted at the expense of other ideologies. These neglected sets of values could well be those embraced by some segments of our society. The second view is that schools cannot be ethical bystanders and ignore the problems of society and the call for citizenship education from the community (Stoll 1995). The reasons that instigated the citizenship initiatives are enough to carry the argument in favour of inclusion. Increasing political apathy, social exclusion, lack of a sense of community and the disaffection of young people are persuasive in the case for social and moral responsibility education.

Laker (2001) proposes a curriculum model for developing these affective areas in students. The model advocates implementation in the areas of cooperative behaviours, individual traits and sportsmanship and fair play. Sports, games and most physical activities have something of the concept of morality in them. Most sports cannot be played effectively if players do not adopt the relevant sporting morality. This usually takes the form of playing fairly and doing the right thing. Sportsmanship and moral behaviour are an integral part of the sports-related context, particularly at school. Using the structuralist learning approach it is possible to construct learning situations that emphasise moral behaviour. Points for fair play which lead to awards, fair play scenarios posed by the teachers such as letting students referee their own games, and fair play games which require self-scoring and self-report are a few strategies that can be used. The *Fair Play for Kids* manual (Commission for Fair Play 1990) has a wealth of games and activities of a similar nature such as fair play agreements, invent a game and compliments charts.

Older students might become more engaged by discussions of situations that have occurred on TV or in the newspaper. With video-replay and a multitude of analysis there is a continual flow of controversial situations that could be used to elicit comment and group discussion of the various merits of the event. Questions such as 'Was it fair?', 'Was it right?' (a different question), 'Does that happen in school matches?' can all be used to generate discussion and debate. Use of these real world examples greatly enhances the relevance of the attempt at situated moral education.

Another concept that might be useful with older students is that of *respect for the game* (Butcher and Schneider 1998). This concept promotes the game, or sport, or activity as the most important thing. Winners and losers are merely components of making a game and therefore less important than the game. It can be pointed out that without losers there are no winners, and without both winners and losers there is no game. To play by the rules for the sake of the game demonstrates a high level of morality because participants submit their own desires to win at all costs for the benefit of completing a game/sporting/activity encounter.

Physical education lessons and many sports environments are social situations. Students come to these events with a social agenda; if this does not interfere with the teacher's instructional agenda then the subsequent social process can be productive in developing affective characteristics. Many activities have a cooperative component built into them, particularly team activities. Players must work together to be successful, or at least to be effective as a team. Activities can be structured to exaggerate their cooperative nature in promoting social development. Games such as volleyball and tennis can be structured so that the length of the rally is the criteria for success, not whether one side manages to win a point. Students can also be used by the teacher in assisting with instruction. Reciprocal and small group teaching can be useful in giving students a small amount of responsibility at the same time as encouraging students to work together in a social setting.

Arnold (2001) suggests that the teacher has four major functions in promoting moral behaviour, but these roles are equally applicable to social development. The teacher should be an initiator into the practice of sport, including its rules, values, ethical traditions and conventions of play. The teacher should be a knowledgeable leader of discussion with a personal viewpoint and a commitment to hearing argument from all sides. The teacher should act as a role model, an exemplar of the values embodied in sport. And finally, the teacher should be a counsellor to those who have difficulty choosing the moral and social sporting path and instead choose to do what is wrong. As students are educated into acceptable moral and social behaviours, they will be able to behave in ways that are beneficial to them and also to a larger community, whether that be sporting or social or both.

Community involvement

Schools are already part of the communities in which they are located. The students are also part of that community. There is a multitude of other communities that can be used to increase student involvement. The class is a community of learners, or a community of practice to use the phraseology of situated learning theory. Sports clubs, school teams and intramural groups are all types of communities. Students are inevitably involved in many of these communities. In suggesting ways in which schools can advocate increased community involvement, we will consider the local and the global.

Sport education has much to commend it and some of this has been discussed earlier. On a local scale, i.e. school-based, students become affiliated to a community/team and fulfil a variety of functions for that community/team. They could be officials, players, coaches and so on. Each role is crucial to the success of the community/team, that success being measured by whether the team takes an effective part in the sporting activities of the curriculum. Social development, self-responsibility and responsibility to, and for, others are key elements of being members of a team. By being involved in a viable team situation where success is dependent on each student doing their part, these personality traits can be practised and hopefully developed and improved (Hastie and Buchanan 2000). Sport education used in this way matches in very closely with the first two stages, self and social responsibility, of Stiehl's (1993) responsibility model.

The third stage of Stiehl's model, environmental responsibility, is suited to the global view of community that can also be examined in school sporting contexts. A sense of place and a feeling of belonging are affiliations missing from the lives of many young people. This can be addressed somewhat by adopting sport as a common ground or a common language shared by a variety of cultures world-wide. School sports and physical education can teach students the skills, values and attitudes that will help them take their place in the global community of sport. Teachers should point out the commonalities of the sporting experience, instil interest and provide opportunities for this sports experience to take place. School travel, exchange programmes and cultural events often include sports-related activities. This is not possible for all, or even for a majority, but teachers can still teach about sport in other countries and the place that sport holds in other cultures. In this way, students can be encouraged to become citizens of the sporting world. Citizens of this world still have rights and responsibilities that must be exercised in a sporting activity context. They must also have cognitive, psychomotor and affective knowledge of activity, about activity and in activity. In essence, they have an obligation to be active, legitimate participants in a global community of practice.

Political literacy

There have already been a number of suggestions for the use of physical education and school sports in the teaching of democratic awareness. Sport education can be a vehicle for this and the use of examples from the world of professional sport would certainly hold the interest of the students. Students will become knowledgeable about how sport has a political side and also how sport and politics are inextricably entwined at the local, national and international level.

However, the world of sport and activity can do more than just offer examples. Teachers can get their students to actually engage in the political process in a sports-related context. Election of officers in school sports clubs, campaigns for student elections, debates, intramural rules and appeals committees, and physical education and a sport representative on a student council are all opportunities that could be taken to enhance political literacy of students. Students could become involved in rule setting, establishing guidelines for appropriate behaviour, equipment use and club membership criteria. All of these are political actions and functions, albeit in a very localised and secure environment. Nevertheless, some democratic principles prevail and are relevant to a variety of contexts. When combined with the former awareness of the relationship between politics and sport, this practical exposure to political actions will provide a kind of situated political literacy education.

Summary

This chapter has examined what is commonly meant by citizenship and defined that concept for further discussion. The historical background to today's growing emphasis on citizenship and personal, social and moral education culminated in reviewing the Thatcher era and how education deals with the issue as a curriculum initiative. It was suggested that situated learning theory provides a valid theoretical framework for attempts at practical implementation in a physical education and school sport location. The concluding ideas for practical implementation show that much can be done to accommodate education for citizenship in the school sport and physical education. This is very much 'on the agenda' for a variety of social and political reasons. Sport cannot be a panacea for all the world's ills, but there is growing realisation that a real contribution can be made. In the future of physical education, this contribution needs to be part of the new pedagogy.

References

Allen, G. (1997) *Education at Risk*, London: Cassell.

Arnold, P.J. (2001) 'Sport, moral development and the role of the teacher: Implications for research and moral education', *Quest*, 53(2): 135–150.

Bennett, R.S. and Wughalter, E.H. (1999) 'Social justice and diversity' (monograph), *Quest*, 51: 4.

Butcher, R. and Schneider, A. (1998) 'Fair play as respect for the game', *Journal of the Philosophy of Sport*, XXV: 1–22.

Coakley, J.J. (2000) *Sport in Society: Issues and Controversies*. Boston, MA: McGraw-Hill, 7th edn.

Commission for Fair Play (1990) *Fair Play for Kids*, Gloucester, Ontario: Commission for Fair Play.

Crick, B. and Lister, I. (1978) 'Political literacy. The centrality of the concept', in B. Crick and A. Porter (eds), *Political Education and Political Literacy*, London: Longman.

Dewey, J. (1916) *Democracy and Education: An Introduction to the Philosophy of Education*, New York: The Macmillan Company.

George, M. (2002) *Football Fever Returns to Kabul*, (online) available: http://news.bbc.co.uk/hi/english/world/south_asia/newsid_1818000/1818521.stm (13 February 2002).

Grant, B.C. (1992) 'Integrating sport into the physical education curriculum in New Zealand secondary schools', *Quest*, 44: 304–316.

Hastie, P.A. (1996) 'Student role involvement during a unit of sport education', *Journal of Teaching in Physical Education*, 16: 88–103.

——(1998) 'Skill and tactical development during a sport education season', *Research Quarterly for Exercise and Sport*, 69: 368–379.

Hastie, P.A. and Buchanan, A.M. (2000) 'Teaching responsibility through sport education: prospects of a coalition', *Research Quarterly for Exercise and Sport*, 71: 25–35.

Hellison, D.R. (1985) *Goals and Strategies for Teaching Physical Education*, Champaigne, IL: Human Kinetics.

Hellison, D.R. (1996) 'Teaching personal and social responsibility in physical education', in S.J. Silverman and C.D. Ennis (eds), *Student Learning in Physical Education: Applying Research to Enhance Instruction*, Champaigne, IL: Human Kinetics, 269–286.

Hellison, D., Cutforth, N., Kallusky, J., Martinek, T., Parker, M. and Stiehl, J. (2000) *Youth Development and Physical Activity: Linking Universities and Communities*, Champaigne, IL: Human Kinetics.

Kirk, D. (1992) *Defining Physical Education: The Social Construction of a School Subject in Postwar Britain*, London: Falmer.

Kirk, D. and Macdonald, D. (1998) 'Situated learning in physical education', *Journal of Teaching in Physical Education*, 17(3): 376–387.

Kirk, D. and MacPhail, A. (2002) 'Teaching games and situated learning: rethinking the Bunker-Thorpe model', *Journal of Teaching in Physical Education*, 21(2): 177–192

Laker, A. (2000) *Beyond the Boundaries of Physical Education: Educating Young People for Citizenship and Social Responsibility*, London: RoutledgeFalmer.

——(2001) *Developing Personal, Social and Moral Education through Physical Education: A Practical Guide for Teachers*, London: RoutledgeFalmer.

Lave, J. and Wenger, E. (1991) *Situated Learning: Legitimate Peripheral Participation*, New York: Cambridge University Press.

Mechikoff, R. and Estes, S. (1998) *A History and Philosophy of Sport and Physical Education. From the Ancient Civilizations to the Modern World*, Boston, MA: McGraw-Hill, 2nd edn.

Morris, G.S.D. (ed.) (1993) 'Becoming responsible for our actions: what's possible in physical education?' (special feature), *Journal of Physical Education, Recreation and Dance*, 64(5): 36–37.

Morris, G.S.D. and Stiehl, J. (1999) *Changing Kid's Games*, Champaigne, IL: Human Kinetics, 2nd edn.

Putman, R.D. (2000) *Bowling Along: The Collapse and Revival of American Community*, New York, NY: Simon & Schuster.

QCA (1998) *Final Report of the Advisory Group on Education for Citizenship and the Teaching of Democracy in Schools*, London: Qualifications and Curriculum Authority.

QCA/DfEE (2002) (online) available: http://www.nc.uk.net/home.html

Sage, G. (1990) *Power and Ideology in American Sport: A Critical Perspective*, Champaigne, IL: Human Kinetics.

Sharpe, T.L., Brown, M. and Crider, K. (1995) 'The effects of a sportsmanship curriculum intervention on generalized positive social behavior of urban elementary school students', *Journal of Applied Behavior Analysis*, 28(4): 401–416.

Siedentop, D. (1994) *Sport Education: Quality PE through Positive Sport Experience*, Champaigne, IL: Human Kinetics.

Stiehl, J. (1993) 'Becoming responsible – theoretical and practical implications', *Journal of Physical Education, Recreation and Dance*, 64(5): 38–71.

Stoll, S.K. (1995) 'Should we teach morality? The issue of moral education', in A.E. Jewett, L.L. Bain and C.D. Ennis (eds), *The Curriculum Process in Physical Education*, Madison, WI: Brown & Benchmark, 333–336.

United World Colleges (2002) (online) available: http://www.uwc.org/uwchome.html

Van Dalen, D.B. and Bennett, B.L. (1971) *A World History of Physical Education: Cultural, Philosophical, Comparative*, Englewood Cliffs, NJ: Prentice Hall, 2nd edn.

4 Social responsibility through physical activity

G.S. Don Morris

In the world of today's children, many have asked, what's worth doing? Perhaps an examination of the conditions in which many children nowadays must function can suggest a direction we might consider (Morris and Stiehl 2002). It seems obvious to us that we cannot expect to have successful, broadly supported educational programs if they do not operate in concert with the larger cultural and social context. However, if we adopt this approach it is easy to be lured into a current cultural paradigm, the frame of reference from which we view the events unfolding in our world, which suggests an epidemic of urgent societal problems, terrible conditions in our schools, and an ominous future. We hear that in our cities, for example, kids kill kids and some sleep in the streets. More and more children are unhealthy, both physically and mentally. More suffer from child abuse, substance abuse, inadequate childcare, and family breakdown. Many are embittered and hurt. They live amidst violence and rejection, in broken streets, broken glass, broken sidewalks, broken families, broken hearts. Their music, their rap, their video, their art reflects their broken world (Morris and Stiehl 2002).

In what kind of world do children live today?

The world is changing. Childhood is changing and schools must change as well.

> Johnny can't read because he needs glasses and breakfast and encouragement from his absent father; Maria doesn't pay attention in class because she can't understand English very well and she's worried about her mother's drinking and she's tired from trying to sleep in the car. Dick is flunking because he's frequently absent. His mother doesn't get him to school because she's depressed because she lost her job. She missed too much work because she was sick and could not afford medical care.
>
> (Kirst 1991: 615)

As recently as 1991 we see that the facts in the USA are appalling:

25% of youngsters are from families living in poverty;
33% of youngsters are living with a single parent (usually a working mother);

40% have parents who will divorce before the child reaches age 18;

14% are born to teenage mothers;

15% will become teenage parents themselves;

25% probably will not finish high school (10% of whites; 30% of Afro-Americans; 40% of Latinos; 50% of Native Americans);

5% of high school seniors drink alcohol daily;

56% of seniors began using alcohol prior to high school;

54% of seniors have used illegal drugs;

And 270,000 boys carried handguns to school at least once; 135,000 did so each day.

(Patterson and Kim 1991)

Things have not improved in the past decade. Have you heard any of the following?

- 'My mom forgot to wash my PE clothes, that's why I can't dress out today.'
- 'It's not my fault.'
- 'He made me so angry I had to throw the ball at his face.'

Are these examples of individuals answering for their behavior, actions or decisions? Are they representative of individuals willing to be held accountable for their actions? It seems that we live in a world in which responsible behavior is the exception: blaming, whining and finding fault is the norm. The behavioral consequence is visible daily in our homes, schools and classes.

Furthermore, the adult value system into which these children will grow is not promising. We live in a nation where nine out of ten citizens lie regularly (36% intentionally lie to hurt others, violate trusts, and their lies have legal consequences, 66% of us believe that there is nothing wrong with telling a lie), where only 13% of us believe in all of the Ten Commandments, where 20% of women are assaulted by their dates, and where 83% of us believe that our parents' generation was much more ethical than our own (Patterson and Kim 1991). These statistics characterize a value system in serious trouble. Youth today are exposed on a regular basis to less than empowering messages presented as news stories by all facets of the media. These messages that identify dismaying messages can reinforce a mentality that, in turn, can foster a mood of resignation. Sample some of the stories anyone can read, hear about or see daily:

In Los Angeles, at least three police officers that witnessed the notorious videotaped beating of a black motorist have filed for workers' compensation, claiming that they suffered anxiety and stress.

Josephson Institute for Ethics released its report on the state of ethics among American youth: 33% of high school, 16% of college students admit to shop lifting last year; one in eight college students admits to fraud; 61% of high school, 32% of college students admit to cheating on an exam at least once; and one-third of students say they are willing to lie to get a job.

The American Psychological Association recently reported that the average child watches 3 hours of TV a day, sees 100,000 acts of violence and 8,000 murders by the end of elementary school and spends more time watching TV than they spend in school.

A local school paper recently provided this quote from a high school student, 'Why not steal? It's easy, exciting, saves money, and it's not hurting anyone.' This comment uttered by a student seems to reflect the attitude of students who steal food from the lunch lines.

The Associated Press ran a story about Security Pacific Bank indicating that its trust department routinely overcharged thousands of clients by millions of dollars during the past 20 years. 'The over billings were not isolated mistakes but represented a pattern of abuse.'

These stories and countless others like them are beamed into our homes or dropped off during the early morning hours in our driveways in the form of newspapers for all of us to review daily. The focus is upon that which is not working rather than on that which is working. Why create a climate of dismay? Why not inspire ourselves with dreams instead of scaring ourselves with gloomy pronouncements?

So for us, it is necessary to ask what is worth doing in education? This time framing it in terms of what might be and what we might do about it. The preceding statistics and stories are the sum total of individual choices and individual behavior, and only changes in behavior by each of us will turn this situation around.

Thus, this is the context in which many youngsters are growing up today. It is a context that can affect children's lives in ways that are very predictable. However, the outcome is not necessarily inevitable. As teachers, we each have a unique opportunity to construct an educational climate that causes a shift from what is probable to what is possible.

In what kind of world do we want children to live?

Can you imagine what might be possible for Johnny if he did learn to read; and for Maria if she was not afraid of making mistakes and she paid attention in class; and for Dick if he not only attended school, but also spearheaded a war against absenteeism? Can you imagine further what might be possible in a school where every child is healthy, creative, self-disciplined, curious, caring of others, able to work with others, concerned about the community and environment, and possessing a playful spirit? Is this type of environment probable, no? Is it possible? Absolutely, yes! Might it be possible to help children become socially responsible?

For the last decade or so there has been a thoughtful examina
ization process in education. There is a belief and perhaps empi
schools operating within a social responsibility framework mig
today's children. This in turn may help shift a society toward i
of life. This chapter will examine the concept of social responsil
cation within a sport and physical education environment. Addit
will share some personal thoughts regarding programs that se
a difference in children's lives.

Let us begin with some common language. Socialization is the process by which
children and adults learn from one another. We humans seem to do this naturally
as we play and discover the social world around us. Likewise, we experience
planned socialization when other individuals take specific actions that are designed
to teach us certain values, behaviors, and attitudes. One can argue that the socialization process is a powerful tool to enable individual human development.
According to Thomas Lickona (1997) responsibility incorporates healthy personal
development and caring interpersonal relationships. Responsibility means that
one should show regard for the worth of someone or something and then
emphasizes a positive obligation to act on that regard (Morris and Stiehl 2002).
Becoming socially responsible allows for a culture and a society to function in a
positive manner.

Do sport and physical activity build appropriate social behaviors?

This has been a question asked by many people for many years. Everyone has his
or her own opinions and experiences. I have heard that participation in sport and
physical activity builds such social behaviors as character, teaches young people to
persist, to overcome obstacles, to stand firm, to learn about self-control, to learn
how to cooperate with others and much more. However, do we really know if any
of this is true? During the last 20 years researchers have been investigating these
and other questions related to a variety of socialization issues. The early work was
done within a sporting environment and within the last 10 years or so we find
researchers carefully examining other physical activity programs as possible
promoters for appropriate social responsibility behavior. As one studies the
empirical research in this arena, you notice that several different approaches have
been identified.

Much of the initial research surrounding sport and social behavior addressed
the notion of character building. For an extensive review of this topic Shields and
Bredemeier (1995) are useful. They concluded that the existing research did not
support the idea that sport enhanced the development of character or moral
development. It is important to note that these authors also suggested that much
of the early research in this area was methodologically flawed. Poor sampling,
no matched samples and cross-sectional design employing the use of varying
psychological inventories were some of the additional problems with the early
research.

Much has been written suggesting that participation in sport and physical activity promotes pro-social behavior among students. This debate has been with us for many years. As long ago as 1956 it was perceived by Little League parents that their sons' participation in baseball actually enabled their sons' cooperative behaviors (Skubic 1956). Throughout the late 20th century the debate continued with Raush (1965) finding contradictory results. During the 1970s several researchers demonstrated that there was not necessarily a strong relationship between sport participation and the concepts of altruism, fair play and positive attitudes toward others (Burchard 1979). However, Armstrong (1984) indicated that sports participation did indeed positively contribute to pro-social behaviors of teamwork, fair play and the like.

An interesting inquiry into this age-old question presented itself in the 1980s. Might modified games that focus upon cooperation promote pro-social behavior? Some interesting work by several different individuals yielded support for this suggestion (Orlick 1981; Grineski 1989a, 1989b).

The research in this pro-social behavior arena during the mid-1970s through the 1990s was substantial. A great deal of research was centered on the following topics: Does sports participation diminish delinquent behavior? Might aggressive behavior be reduced through sports activities? Can a case be made that sport produces positive moral development and moral reasoning? Do participants become good sports? It is not the purpose of this chapter to review the research; I again recommend Shields and Bredemeier's (1995) work for details.

It is useful to note that a great deal of the work in the area of pro-social behavior has engaged youth at risk, special needs youth, and some regular education students. In the early 1990s the youth serving 'industry' was in full operation. Any numbers of programs had been developed and were in some form of operational stage. Joy Dryfoos (1991) examined the programs aimed specifically toward youth-at-risk students. She wrote a most enlightening article that attempted to review the programs that worked. She identified some 100 diverse programs that seemed to offer the potential for changing high-risk behaviors. The programs were designed for four entirely different categories of prevention: early substance abuse, reducing acting out behavior, sexual activity, and improving school performance or attendance. She identified two common themes that seem to have existed among these programs: individual attention and multi-component multi-agency community-wide programs. An analysis of these programs is presented and although an older article now I recommend it. It provides a historical perspective and analysis as an explanation for what many of us are doing today. Successful programs focus primarily on the antecedents of high-risk behavior rather than the exact behavior. Thus a need for early intervention, identification of basic social skills, parental and community support formed the basis for successful programs.

With this as a background let us examine sport and/or physical activity programs of the 1990s that truly focused upon social responsibility concepts as the primary intervention or prevention strategies. Without a doubt, Don Hellison's work fostered renewed enthusiasm for this approach. Hellison has spent many years formulating a self-responsibility program, implementing the programs and sharing with us his trials and tribulations. He reported his initial foray into this arena with his classic *Beyond Bats and Balls* (1978). The focus early on in his work was the development of a physical education model for teaching self-responsibility to delinquency-prone youth. Fortunately for our field he has written extensively about this approach (Hellison 1983, 1985, 1986). This model was recognized 'by curriculum and instruction scholars as an exemplar of teaching social development through physical education' (Jewett and Bain 1985 as reported in DeBusk and Hellison 1989). In the DeBusk and Hellison article the entire program is outlined for the reader – I recommend it for a brief introduction into the model's components. Hellison's program model consists of six self-responsibility goals presented as developmental levels. Since the late 1980s, Hellison's model has served as a foundation for many other individuals interested in teaching social responsibility through physical activity.

Hellison, together with Nikos Georgiadis (Hellison and Georgiadis 1992), taught social values through participation in an after-school basketball program. The original model was modified and shared with at-risk youths in urban Chicago. Its purpose was to promote empowerment and values through sport skills. The program had concrete and measurable self-esteem levels of progression. This approach produced good results among the participants and prompted further inquiry into the model's use.

In an edited feature (Morris 1993), I introduced a variety of responsibility themes in a feature entitled: 'Becoming Responsible for Our Actions: What's Possible in Physical Education?' Several authors contributed their experiences implementing social skill development within a physical education setting. Jim Stiehl discussed the specifics of a program he and I created, entitled 'Becoming Responsible'. Rita Mercier discussed student-centered strategies for teaching social skills; Rae Pica shared her responsibility program designed for young children. Along with graduate students, faculty, and majors, Hellison (1993) developed several different kinds of before and after school clubs that used physical activity as an intervention medium to teach social responsibility behaviors within Chicago's inner city. He coined the term, coaching club, for each of these experiences. His target audience was at-risk inner city youth. Sports activities of martial arts and basketball served as the movement medium. As the students arrived at the club, they were reminded of the club's goals and then moved into the day's sport activity. Specific responsibility objectives were infused within each day's lesson. They spent time daily reflecting with one another what they had experienced and even entered their thoughts into journals. They determined what responsibility level they had operated within, they decided if they had met individual goals regarding self-control, team work, self-coaching, and personal coaching. When necessary the students put in corrections. They also worked on generalizing these behaviors outside the gym. Yet another use for teachers was developed and made available for teachers.

James Kallusky (1996) reported how he taught secondary school at-risk students in East Los Angeles, California, social responsibility skills, knowledge, and behaviors. He used Hellison's emerging self- and social responsibility model (Hellison 1985) as the framework for his program. Kallusky recognized the need to expand Hellison's model and separated self-control from other Level One – Respect components. The results were promising and he has produced significant positive social results.

Tom Martinek and Don Hellison (1997) continued to uncover the role physical activity could play with increasing students' resiliency to undesirable behavior. Their work particularly wanted to determine if social responsibility programs could improve at-risk students' resiliency against the high-risk conditions of their neighborhoods. To be resilient meant that children had the ability to rebound successfully from an exposure to severe risks found in the neighborhoods in which they lived. This requires that a student be able to negotiate confrontation and challenge from other individuals. Both Tom and Don realized that resilient students are autonomous – that is to say, they have clarity with respect to who they are and thus can act independently. They take back control over their environment. Furthermore, resilient students have a sense of optimism and hope. This allows students to set goals, persist, and get into action regarding their future. Their major premise was simply this: develop a social responsibility program that promoted and cultivated the traits associated with resiliency. They offer excellent program design strategies for those working with under-served youth.

Tom Martinek (1997) reported on programs working with under-served youth in the United States. He was an editor for a five-article feature in *Quest*. This is an especially informative series for those educators serving at-risk youth. Topics include sport psychology, fitness, sport sociology, teacher education preparation programs and an elementary physical education program as critical in the life of youth. Hal Lawson (1997) made an eloquent argument for universities to address the plight of children in the United States. His arguments were sound in 1997 and are applicable in 2003. He gave us a call to arms, to begin helping our nation's children – it is our social responsibility.

Tom Lickona (1997) offered the nation another look at the development of character education as a primary responsibility of our public schools. He provided a cogent argument for such a program emphasis and he shared a model for implementation. He, along with several colleagues, has created a center for the 4th and 5th Rs (Respect and Responsibility) at the State University of New York, Cortland. The program consists of the following components:

- the teacher as caregiver, moral model and moral mentor;
- creating a caring classroom community;
- moral discipline;
- creating a democratic classroom environment;
- teaching values through the curriculum;
- cooperative learning;
- the conscience of craft;
- ethical reflection;
- teaching conflict resolution.

This model expands the social responsibility work beyond youth at risk. The concepts, knowledge and skills became part of all classrooms, thus enlarging the service arena.

The mid- to late 1990s was a time of expanding social responsibility programs around the United States. There was a perceived need to examine how educational programs, and particularly physical education programs, could respond to crucial social conditions, e.g. 50% of American children had large amounts of unsupervised discretionary time, growing pressures to experiment with drugs, sex, and use violence as a primary conflict resolution mode. Nicholas Cutforth (1997) shared how he began one of his after-school programs. He provided the blueprint for beginning a program designed to enhance at-risk youth's social responsibility development. Of particular note are his personal reflections about adopting an ethic of service. This alone should be mandatory reading for all future physical educators.

Teaching under-served populations social responsibility skills has moved toward the forefront of a school's physical education curriculum. Several new programs have been developed and shared. Martinek and Hellison (1998) identified how one might begin to teach values and goal setting to young students in a physical education setting. Their insights have helped many individuals around the country to begin programs focusing upon a variety of different responsibility aspects.

Parker, Kallusky and Hellison (1999) offer a very practical series of strategies for working with students utilizing a responsibility model. The strategies are low-risk for teachers and at the same time provide high impact for students. Some of the strategies include giving students decisions to make with respect to equipment distribution, using a variety of teaching methods and teaching self-management skills.

Martinek, McLaughlin and Schilling (1999) have created a most interesting program entitled 'Project Effort: Teaching Responsibility Beyond the Gym'. The project responded to local school needs for alternative programs to help their students learn about personal and social behaviors in elementary-aged students. The focus was on at-risk children in local communities. The essence of the program was to provide after-school physical activity programs coupled with an in-school mentoring program. They have reported significant success with this program and are especially interested in the behaviors generalizing away from the school.

Don Hellison (1999) wrote a most interesting article that addressed the question of whether character development through sport is rhetoric or reality. Much had been written about social responsibility programs in physical education or physical activity programs. The questions now are, what works, what to avoid, and might this work elsewhere with other types of students? This is a labor-intensive, context-specific approach to classroom design. One should remain cautiously optimistic. This work requires the ability to adjust, to think on one's feet, and to be willing to change the way one interacts with students.

Anthony Laker (2000) not only celebrates the nature of physical education and sport but looks at the theoretical background to claims of affective development through physical activity participation. His analysis demonstrates that such claims are by no means new, but have a long history behind them. One of his other works (1996) describes a teacher education program designed to help teachers promote personal characteristics in their students, while his practical guide (2001) provides teachers with a wealth of ideas for incorporation into physical education lessons. This guide is set in a curriculum planning context and covers planning, implementation, assessment, and reflection.

Jeffrey Beedy and Tom Zierk (2000) also have offered the potential social responsibility program designer some sound thoughts. Their collective work has primarily focused upon character development through sports activities and yet their insights are valuable to those of us engaged in the entire spectrum of social responsibility programming. Their work has concluded that sports do have value as an educational medium for students.

Gatz, Messner, and Ball-Rokeach (2002) share varying points of view regarding the role of sport in developing students' lives. This is an edited book that addresses many issues surrounding the impact sport has upon our youth. Suffice it to say that the authors challenge some of the benefits attributed to youth sports participation. They address the idea that sports participation may or may not positively impact on youth's fitness, well-being social competence, self-esteem, and moral development. They raise some critical questions that certainly challenge any thinking person's perspective with regard to youth sports participation. Therefore, it is worth considering that youth development through sports may depend on the quality of the youth sports program and its leadership.

Whatever you do with sport and physical activity programs, it is imperative to first develop your philosophical belief structure and then ensure that all activities are consistent with the structure.

In summary, do these programs work? Yes! How one defines work is, of course, critical to the affirmative response. If we think it is important to provide students with knowledge, skills and behaviors that support effective interaction among one another, then, yes, some form of the aforementioned programs work. By this I mean they promote positive change in overt actions by students. As you have read the previous pages you have noticed that the primary target audience has been at-risk students. The question that begs to be asked is: does this make sense for other student populations?

There are multiple reasons for including social responsibility concepts in programs that encompass all students. First, the world in which we all live is similar to the one described at the beginning of this chapter – it is indeed an equal opportunity context. Second, for groups to successfully interact it is necessary to possess and then act upon social skills. Third, there seems to be a relationship between school climate and overall school performance. Fourth, many physical education programs have recognized the importance of addressing these ideas and have included social responsibility goals into their core philosophy.

The remainder of this chapter will be spent identifying strategies for inclusion of social responsibility concepts across different curricula models, i.e. sport education, fitness, and wellness. I shall demonstrate how this can be accomplished by using 'Becoming Responsible', a program I developed with Jim Stiehl (2002). I shall also infuse other individuals' ideas that have proven successful.

What will it take for social responsibility to be included?

Simply put, students must acquire certain skills and knowledge, and then take appropriate day-to-day actions. Teachers must create an environment that will facilitate the occurrence of those things. In other words, we need to teach in such a way that students get what they need to get, and do what they need to do. In that regard, we have found it helpful to keep the following question in mind: what is possible with my students, and what is my responsibility in creating the opportunities for that to occur?

Fundamentally we can create an environment that consistently supports the development of responsible behavior among our students regardless of curriculum model employed. Naturally we will need to make decisions. Each day we make decisions about what we are going to teach (content/activities) and how we are going to teach (instructional methodology). We contend that children can and should accept responsibility for their actions. For this to occur, we need to make some conscious decisions about the following:

- Do I want to try new possibilities? You may have to think thoughts that you have never thought, and take risks that you have never before taken.
- Am I willing to devote some time to activities that can promote responsibility? Change, however, will not occur overnight, because many children already believe 'I am not capable, not important, not responsible,' and so on.
- Can I commit to persevering over an extended time period? These activities are presented over time throughout one's curriculum.
- Will I attempt some language if it appears new or different? There is a connection between words we use, beliefs we hold, and actions we take. Accompanying the activities are some suggested ways of speaking with children that can facilitate becoming responsible.

What do we mean by becoming responsible?

Responsibility means taking care of others, our surroundings, and ourselves. This includes fulfilling our obligations, keeping our commitments, and striving to do and be our personal and moral best, and nurturing and supporting one another. Other characteristics can be viewed as specific forms of responsibility (e.g. compassion, cooperation, risk-taking, self-discipline, honesty, and helpfulness, to name a few). The preceding definition is useful because, first of all, it achieves some measure of harmony between the principles of self-interest and altruism. It suggests that not only can we explore, develop, and appreciate our own unique potential, but that we can use our emerging abilities for the benefit of ourselves, others, and the environment in which we and others live. Consequently, we can reaffirm our own worth and sense of belonging while also expressing a concern and value for others through positive actions. In a sense, we can contribute to create a better society, as well (Morris and Stiehl 2002).

This definition also has proven useful because, crucial to developing a program that nurtures responsibility, it incorporates the key notion that responsibility is not imposed from the outside. Rather, it is a voluntary act that involves choice. It is internally motivated, a positive consequence to a positive choice. Fundamental to this program is the idea that children are capable, choice-making individuals. We assume that they are capable of accepting responsibility for their own actions and for the consequences of their own behaviors. For example, they can be accountable for making healthy choices about what they will do and not do with their bodies, and about what substances they will allow or not allow into their bodies.

Three stages of responsibility

In order to create an environment that would continually support the development of responsible choices and behavior among our students, we decided to develop content and instruction in the three stages of responsibility: personal, social, and environmental (referred to in the program as surroundings). Irrespective of the stage, a fundamental assumption in our work is that children who learn more about choices and how to make more choices for themselves, learn that not only do they have hope, but they are literally able to create their own opportunities to change. Not only can they cope with the future, they can design it.

Stage one: personal (self-) responsibility

Becoming personally responsible means being able to say: 'I matter, I am valuable and worthwhile; I can be trusted to be accountable for my language and actions. I am willing and am capable of being accountable for my language (personal language/affirmations), I am willing to also be responsible for my thoughts and feelings (recognizing that thoughts and feelings are mine, what I do with them is up to me).' It entails making and keeping agreements; setting goals and creating the support structure necessary for achieving them; accepting the consequences of one's choices; and acknowledging personal accomplishments and actions.

Stage two: others' responsibility

Becoming responsible with others means communicating with people in a manner that enables and ennobles them, rather than demeans them; honoring other students' rights, dignity, and worth; cooperating, or working together toward common goals; negotiating problems and conflicts successfully; and creating opportunities for others.

Table 4.1 Responsibility matrix

	Stage one: *w/self*	*Stage two:* *w/others*	*Stage three:* *w/surroundings*
Feelings			
Thoughts			
Language			
Actions			

Stage three: surroundings responsibility

Having learned how to be accountable for one's actions, how to honor the consequences of one's actions, thus developing a sense of self-control with their lives, students generally choose to expand their sense of caring. Becoming responsible for one's surroundings means becoming conscious of the varied contexts in which we function. It means respecting property and becoming the stewards of equipment, the classroom, the school, and the larger community; recognizing the importance and power of the individual in taking care of one's surroundings; and influencing others also to take care of our surroundings.

Is there a responsibility strategy?

We have found it useful to employ a three-step (i.e. awareness, practice, choice) general strategy when we present the responsibility activities to students. First, we attempt to enhance awareness of language and behaviors that are irresponsible (that is, do not support the well-being of oneself, others, or surroundings). Next, we offer alternative language and behaviors that we encourage children to practice. Finally, we underscore the child's and the teacher's opportunity: a choice is now available. We employ this general strategy with both teachers and students. If students are to become more responsible, then certain behaviors on the part of teachers must occur. At all times the responsibility journey travels along a two-way street. Consequently, in the pages that follow we have suggestions that pertain to teachers' and students' language, and their respective actions.

We begin with a belief that acting in a responsible manner is empowering and offers everyone a freedom to live life to its fullest. We believe that every student is capable of being accountable for his or her feelings, thoughts, language, and actions. The matrix shown in Table 4.1 above provides a comprehensive overview for our set of beliefs.

The matrix suggests the following message to each individual: initially, each one learns about becoming personally responsible for his or her thoughts, feelings, language, and actions. This puts the individual in charge of behavioral decisions he or she makes – this is stage one in becoming a responsible human being. It enables the individual to gain personal control.

Once learned, stage two of responsibility development is available, learning to be responsible for others in the world. Likewise, students understand that the preceding matrix suggests that they are willing on a daily basis to be accountable for the language and behavior they use with other people. They refrain from 'illegal use of the mouth', ridicule, put downs, blame, complaining and find themselves acknowledging others, thanking people, and being someone that others want to be with. Additionally, they become respectful of property, we see them taking care of equipment, using it appropriately and ensuring its safe return.

In stage three, the student applies the responsibility concepts to people, property and groups in the larger context of life – their surroundings. Implicit within the matrix is the concept of choice, the result of conscious decision making. Once an individual engages in the aforementioned responsibility strategy it is possible to make decisions within each of the three stages of responsibility regarding feelings, thoughts, language, and actions. Thus, acquisition of responsibility behavior does appear to follow a developmental sequence. Once stage three is attained, individuals may and do operate freely within the matrix.

None of the preceeding occurs overnight and certainly none of it occurs in the absence of knowing how to speak and act. This program is about assisting students in overcoming the barriers that get in the way of being responsible. It is important to note that these three stages are not absolute. During the course of life, we all seem to participate in one or more of these responsibility stages. For example, there are times when we only want to be accountable to ourselves – so we insist on having some 'alone time'. At times, we find ourselves helping others, and/or we get involved in state or national organizations. We do these things out of personal choice! This program is about each student realizing that he or she has a choice in the matter of being accountable.

After your students begin to practice the skills and concepts found within each stage, you can use the matrix to help your students create daily, weekly, and monthly responsibility goals. For example, today, your students may enter your classroom and indicate that they will be working on their language and associated actions within stage one. On another day they may choose to examine their feeling and thoughts as they dictate their behavior; again stage one. The number of goal choices in the matrix is enormous. By setting simple goals students tend to focus and remain focused on the idea of being responsible. This application of our responsibility matrix applies to all physical education curricula models.

Common elements for teaching social responsibility within different curricula models

I have read the research, performed social responsibility research and worked for many years in the public schools teaching children physical education. During this time I discovered several common elements found in all successful social responsibility programs. These elements are not affected or influenced by one's gender, ethnicity, or socio-economic status. These elements are also common to all physical activity curricula models.

First, the development of trust and a sense of community within the educational setting are the foundation (prerequisites) upon which the remaining program is built. This is accomplished by utilizing messages that empower, supportive language that enhances children's sense of self, and feedback words that enable children to perceive themselves as competent. We know that a teacher's language is crucial to establishing a climate enabling all students to begin to trust one another and adults. Likewise, students' language (self-talk for increasing internal locus of control, language that children can use for making and keeping agreements, words that invite support, language that acknowledges others, aids in cooperation, and language that helps them negotiate conflict) is equally important. If a climate of trust and support is to exist within a class, students must also possess effective language skills. The program follows the aforementioned responsibility strategy. In addition we employ sense of community activities that serve as educational opportunities to teach the language and behaviors of trust and community.

Second, we begin teaching stage one responsibility knowledge and skills. This stage presents the skills and knowledge for a student to learn how to become accountable for his or her feelings, thoughts, language, and actions. Up to this point in the program the teacher has only created an environment that fosters the opportunity for students to gain personal control over their lives. Students are now ready to acquire new knowledge and skills that will enable them to display self-control. Stage one offers:

- a definition of responsibility;
- strategies for becoming responsible;
- learning about commitments;
- learning how to be accountable for all the choices students make during a day.

Third, we then begin teaching stage two responsibility knowledge and skills. This stage relies on students successfully experiencing all of the preceding concepts. The focus of this stage is upon individuals learning how to be accountable with their individual behavior as they relate to other people. We have found a variety of additional skills and knowledge is necessary for students to possess if they are to become responsible contributors to other people. This stage is divided into the following components:

- establishing agreements;
- communicating with others;
- honoring others;
- expectations impact upon actions;
- learning how to give;
- surrender;
- negotiating conflict.

The concepts are presented individually and accompanying activities are offered. We provide no presentation schedule, rather, we suggest you infuse the concepts and the activities within your existing program.

Fourth, we begin teaching stage three responsibility knowledge and skills. The purpose of this final stage is to introduce some additional concepts and skills that will enable your students to become responsible for other people in their local, state, and national areas and beyond. This stage assumes your students have successfully moved through the previous two stages. We build upon the previous lessons and revisit some of the concepts; however, we do add a twist to each. Students first learn to be responsible for themselves, then they learn to express concern for others around them, and finally they are able authentically to assume concerns and considerations for people, things, and the environment beyond their immediate world – we call this surroundings responsibility. Recognizing that the world does not revolve around them, students, by choice, reach out and begin to help others in their community, state, nation, and world.

The majority of the material in this stage enables students to practice what they have previously learned. The topics include the following:

- step by step;
- change;
- creating a project;
- practicing a short term project;
- handling breakdowns;
- practicing strategies for breakdowns;
- classroom projects;
- school projects/community projects.

As your students gain additional skills and knowledge and begin to feel more and more comfortable with the creation of their own destiny, you will observe them demonstrate respect, honor, and consideration towards other people and other things.

Let us review the foregoing. I have proposed that social responsibility can be infused within anyone's physical activity program. It is useful to begin such an emphasis by first developing a sense of trust and community within one's class. There are responsibility skills and knowledge that can then be acquired and practiced. A social responsibility matrix has been presented that suggests both a sequential and interaction representation of these skills and knowledge. Finally, I have suggested that a student may then operate from a position of choice and control with regards to all of the preceding responsibility ideas. Students can establish daily, weekly, monthly responsibility goals enabling a good life to be led.

The remainder of this chapter will present examples for each of these common elements drawn from our program. You will see that this approach can be accommodated by any curriculum model, it only requires the belief that this is important for students, all students!

Development of trust and a sense of community

The following identifies a few of the ideas regarding the language teachers can use in support of designing a class grounded in a social responsibility framework.

We broadcast messages to students through our speaking and our actions. What students hear and the interpretations that students attach to these messages can bolster (or undermine) their sense of self. Our messages may ultimately influence a student's sense of self and the degree to which he or she is capable of becoming responsible. When messages are positive, students can become powerful. Powerful here does not connote force, manipulation or control, but rather, a sense of being able, a sense of empowerment. A child who is powerful possesses a sense of being valuable and capable.

Supportive language, by the teacher, allows students to know, 'You are capable. You are worthwhile. You matter.' When conveyed honestly, these messages can enhance two aspects of becoming responsible: locus of control and perceived competence. Children with an internal locus of control are less susceptible to the opinions of others regarding their own self-worth and potential actions. They believe that what happens to them is largely a result of the choices they make. When they cannot influence what happens, they can still decide how they will let circumstances affect them.

Perceived competence refers to a child's subjective idea about his or her own competence. Frequently, it includes an objective assessment of one's own ability to meet challenges, with success being based on skill demonstration. Perceived competence is influenced by one's own skill assessment as well as by the judgments of others who are viewed as important. Children are remarkably aware of their abilities. They constantly receive feedback from their surroundings about these abilities. Inoculating students with bland admonishments will change nothing about their notions of who they are, and can lead to a distrust of adult communications.

Thus a teacher's words should advance each child's sense of self. For some, this requires speaking in ways that provide a wider range of possibilities in the classroom. We believe strongly that teachers' words and actions should not detract from, but rather should advance each child's sense of self. A teacher's way of speaking and acting should promote an internal locus of control and a positive perception of competence. It is helpful for teachers to become more alert about the messages they send to students.

Trust is the foundation of all successful interaction among people (Glenn and Nelson 1987). We suggest that modeling language and actions that reflect responsible behavior is absolutely necessary for children to become responsible. We now realize that we have control over the words we use with ourselves as well as with others. Words help us express our thoughts, beliefs, and feelings and are a form of action we engage in each time we speak. The importance of language has been previously stated, it is up to *us* to be clear with ourselves regarding the intentional use of words.

Do we intend for children to become powerful? Do we choose to support children in their quest for empowerment? Do we want children to become responsible? If we answer yes to these questions, then we suggest that the words that teachers use are critical to such development. There is a language that supports children becoming responsible and likewise there is a language that promotes dependency, inadequacy, and irresponsible behavior.

For example, have you ever had a youngster approach you with one more question about a new physical education concept? The thought that flashes in your head is 'Geez, I'm tired and this kid is baaack! It would be easy to give her the answer and she'd return to her activity.' Providing the answer ensures dependence, allowing her to work through the question enables and ennobles her. The words used dictate the nature of the outcome. What are you committed to, your comfort or the well-being of the child?

We have found a language that invites, encourages, and enrolls children into your class – in other words it is a language of acceptance. Children are apt to choose to be accountable if they perceive themselves as valued. To that end we suggest a language that creates a climate of respect. We give children feedback and acknowledgement constantly about lots of things. The type we give fosters responsible behavior. Children often attribute success and/or failure to someone or something outside themselves. It is useful for them to begin clarifying what we call performance attributions. For example, the following represents one of our language ideas.

Use effective praise

As teachers we have been taught to reinforce behavior. From college courses to workshops, the value of reinforcement has been presented to us. We have learned a variety of techniques coupled with their purported outcomes. Often, we mix reinforcement with the idea of praise. Part of being a teacher is to offer appropriate praise to our students. We do this to promote certain behaviors, eliminate others and foster a positive sense of self within every student. Have you also discovered any of the following reactions to praise? Sometimes praise produces these reactions:

- students deny the authenticity of your words;
- viewed as manipulation (What does the teacher want from me now?);
- students become anxious (I'll never get another hit, I'm already 2 for 2);
- focus is upon weaknesses (Good shooter, you must be kidding, I can't hit the broad side of a barn door);
- lead to denial (Always kind, should have heard me talk to my brother this morning).

When we first started working with students, we offered lots of kind words, frequently (one of our professors said this was important to do) and discovered rejection on the part of the students. We could not believe what was happening.

The results flew in the face of what we had learned about praise. Then we reflected upon our own childhood and started remembering how we had reacted, then we started an inquiry into the use of language and its impact upon behavior and sense of self. The words we use are critical to the development of students. We discovered that praise often contributed to inappropriate behavior. We soon learned that the nature of the praise used was the issue, not that praise itself was incorrect. We all enjoy a pat on the back; an acknowledgement and/or appreciation sent our way. What and how it is delivered becomes the focus. Generally, value words such as great, good, wonderful, beautiful (words that evaluate) often make students feel uncomfortable. We have discovered that the primary feedback use of value or words of praise, over time, actually decreased our students' sense of self. However, if praise is delivered in a helpful manner the reverse is observed. Therefore, praise should describe with appreciation what the student sees or feels and then the student can learn to praise him or herself. It is useful to provide corrective feedback or neutral feedback to students. This gives the student the necessary information to make changes in performance and/ or behavior. The result is students learn to make personal evaluations, make corrections if necessary and in turn feel part of the school community.

Use effective language

We also encourage students to become more conscious of their speaking. Their language must provide self-validation and an increase in internal locus of control. When they speak with others, their communications must be clear and supportive.

Students are capable of acquiring language that affirms who they are and that empowers them. They may need to learn alternative ways of speaking because they may have become prone to adopting language that frequently assigns responsibility to people and circumstances outside of themselves. By acquiring a different way of speaking, children can create positive, healthy beliefs about themselves and others (Morris and Stiehl 2002).

There is a caveat, however. The language of responsibility seldom occurs naturally; one must work at developing it. First of all, it may be initially uncomfortable. If you speak as though you are not responsible for something, then you do not have to do anything about it. Second, some people prefer that we do not speak in self-supporting ways. For example, advertisers want us to believe that we cannot do without their products and that we cannot look good, do well, or be good without their help. Both children and adults can be very susceptible to advertising claims. Therefore children, and adults, must be taught to be skeptical when encountering those claims.

Nevertheless, there is clear evidence that even young children can begin to speak in ways that allow them to be more responsible for themselves with others and with their surroundings. We may not change every barrier and circumstance that confronts a student, but we can begin to shift how students perceive and deal with those circumstances. Words program us like a computer; that is, they structure or build our thoughts. If we think about the same words often enough, we frequently turn them into beliefs. Our actions become a result of those beliefs. Let us examine a phrase: *makes me*. The *makes me* phrase is used all of the time.

'Melanie makes me nervous.'
'My teacher makes me happy.'
'Smoking makes me cool.'
'The ground made me fumble the ball.'
'Juan made me hit him.'

Makes me is an example of irresponsible language (Morris and Stiehl 2002). It says that you are not responsible. As a matter of fact, it tells you that someone or something else is in control. This can lead you to believe that you are not responsible for your reactions to the people, events, and other things in your life. Therefore it is disabling to you.

We give students a *home fun* assignment. As part of the awareness stage of irresponsible language, they are asked to develop a list of *makes me* messages from their observations of people, TV, music, newspapers, and magazines. In a subsequent stage we initiate discussions about alternatives to such language. For example, 'The teacher makes me upset,' might become 'I'm choosing to be upset.' 'He annoys me,' might be replaced with, 'I let myself be annoyed by him.' Students are reminded that although it may be easier to place responsibility for their feelings or reactions onto someone or something else, e.g. they can blame others, they will lose in the long run because they will convince themselves they are not in control.

There are many lessons designed to assist students in becoming responsible for their language, feelings, thoughts, and actions. For example, the following is an example of a lesson physical educators can use to assist students in learning about commitments and promises (Morris and Stiehl 2002).

Stage one: personal responsibility example

ACTIVITY

Understanding about commitments and promises.

DESCRIPTION

The purpose of this activity is to draw a distinction between commitments and promises, and then to use these two concepts in order to facilitate being reliable. From previous activities, students might have noticed that sometimes they are not especially effective in their attempts to be reliable. Two new concepts, commitments and promises, may offer some help.

With students sitting randomly in a large group, ask them what a commitment is. Give them time to think and share. Next, ask them to get a partner; inform them that each one has one minute to share with the other what he or she thinks a commitment is. Following their sharing, invite them to share their thoughts with the entire group. Record their suggestions on the chalkboard. Then offer the following:

> A commitment is something that you say you'll do – or something that you say will happen – even if you have no evidence you can do it or have no past record of ever being able to do it. It is giving someone your word and it is most powerful when you make it public – tell someone else. Let's try out this new idea. For example, what commitments might be possible for you to make in our physical education class?

Record their responses. Some typical responses might include:

- I will get into better shape.
- I will eat healthily.
- I will learn to juggle.
- I will control myself during class time.

Repeat this using other classroom examples, e.g. use of computers, doing home work, studying for quizzes/exams, keeping desks clean, behavior in and out of class.

Once your students seem to understand this concept move onto the notion of promise. Most people think they are the same as commitments, hence the need to offer the following distinction. Perhaps ask this question:

> What then is a promise?

Again, allow each member of the couples about a minute to discuss the item, and then allow couples to share their ideas with the larger group.

Next, offer the following:

> A promise is the action you agree to take in order to support your commitment. A promise is the ACTION you agree to take so your commitment will become a reality. What promises might be appropriate for some of the commitments you already mentioned?

Record their responses. Typical responses include:

Regarding fitness:
- I promise to exercise 4 times per week.
- I promise to exercise for 20 minutes each time.
- I promise to do 3 sets of sit-ups.
- I promise to exercise, even when I don't want to.

Regarding healthy eating:
- I promise to eat only healthy snacks after school.
- I promise to eat 3 healthy meals daily.
- I promise to eat ice cream once a month only.
- I promise to give to my parents some healthy recipes.

Regarding skills:
- I promise to practice basketball shooting 4 days each week.
- I promise to practice for 10 minutes per day.
- I promise to ask my teacher for help if I'm not performing any better.

Regarding self-control:
- I promise to be aware of when I get angry.
- I promise to walk away when I'm angry with someone.
- I promise not to say the first thing that comes to mind when I'm upset.

Again, repeat this exercise using other classroom examples. End the day's session with these questions:

What commitment(s) will you make in today's class?
Furthermore, what promises may help you to maintain that commitment?

Give students the opportunity to state commitments and promises for today's class only. Indicate that as a subsequent activity, students will be given a chance to create 'personal responsibility' projects.

Stage two: others responsibility example

ACTIVITY

Establishing agreements.

DESCRIPTION

The purpose of this activity is to establish agreements for appropriate behavior in a group. We will consider two types of agreements. First, those that involve interactions between the teacher and students; and second, those involving interactions among the students. The important teacher–student agreement to be addressed here is the student's capability (hence responsibility) to understand and follow directions. The student–student agreements are those that the teacher can generate in collaboration with the students; these commonly accepted 'promises' become a crucial foundation for all subsequent group interactions. Indeed they become the basis for all activities that follow this one.

1 Agreements between teachers and students

There are times when some students may not be fully involved in a lesson because they do not perceive themselves capable of understanding it. Their simple remedy is to avoid full participation. In other words, they elect not to be responsible for their lack of involvement. They say, 'I didn't hear you', or 'I didn't understand', or 'I didn't know what we were supposed to do.'

At the beginning of class, invite students to pay attention in class today. Conduct a conversation in the following vein:

> In our class you must be able to follow directions and know what to do. I'll call that 'staying tuned in' to what I'm saying. In other words, staying 'present', please don't go off to another planet. Do you understand?

Invite questions and explain why this is important. Offer in a non-punitive, yet assertive way:

> It will help if, when I'm talking, your eyes are looking at me and your lips are together. From time to time we will have a 'tuning' check to see if everyone is here and accounted for. The way I'll know if you are present and 'tuned in' is that you will be on task (doing whatever is appropriate at that time) or you will be looking at me when I'm talking.

During this activity you might wish to introduce another idea; i.e. making requests of your students. Offer the following:

> I will be making requests of you from time to time. You have three choices with every request. You can:
>
> 1   accept the request,
> 2   decline the request,
> 3   present a counter-offer. Is that clear?

Answer any questions they may have and then make your first request, for example:

> I request that you . . . (insert here a task from today's physical education lesson, such as: . . . stay involved at your station for the next seven minutes. If you need assistance, I will help you as soon as I can). Seeing no hands, am I to understand that everyone will honor this request?

Begin the lesson. If they go off task (or somehow do not honor your request) approach them privately, ask them if they are clear about the request, and then hold them accountable. Let them know it is OK not to know, and it is not OK to continue not knowing! It is their responsibility to be absolutely clear regarding requests made of them. Will they agree?

This can be quite a breakthrough for some students. It means that they now must become responsible for listening to directions. If they are unclear or do not know, it is their job to mention this to you. The teacher, then, has a responsibility to accept the fact that a student may not know, and must act accordingly. With this agreement in place, students will feel more comfortable in seeking information, clarifying ideas, and accepting coaching. They will leave the class knowing!

Hold students accountable for their agreements. Do not make them wrong when they break an agreement. Rather, provide a renewed opportunity for them to again honor the agreement.

2 Agreements between students

Before beginning, tell the group that if the class is going to work effectively together, everyone must agree on some rules for appropriate behavior. The whole class will engage in some activities that will help the class work together as a team.

If the class is to work together as a team, some basic agreements must be in place (much the same as the commitments and promises that were developed in the previous activities on self). Invite the group to suggest agreements that would help them to work better as a team. It is important that the group generates most, if not all, of the agreements. However, the teacher must ensure that agreements are clear, appropriate, and supportive of a positive class climate.

The following is a list of agreements that we have compiled from various classes:

- I agree that my hand must be raised to be called on.
- I agree that if someone is speaking, I must listen and not interrupt.
- I agree that anyone may say what he or she wishes, and there are no right or wrong answers.
- I agree to respect everyone's contributions.

The following represent some bold, yet extremely powerful, agreements. Most of them were not generated at the beginning of a class, but were added as the students began to appreciate the value of agreements as the bedrock of a successful group.

- I choose to be in school and I agree to be responsible for that choice.
- I choose to make and keep my agreements.
- I agree to support my classmates in keeping their agreements.
- I agree to be responsible for creating value for myself in this class.
- I agree to be on time to all classes.
- I agree only to be absent from school in the event of an emergency (Webster defines 'emergency' as a 'sudden, generally unexpected occurrence or set of circumstances demanding immediate action'), otherwise, I will attend school!
- I agree to respect the confidentiality of anything that anyone says while in this class.
- I agree to handle any complaints I may have by communicating them only to someone who can do something about the situation. I agree not to criticize or

complain to someone who cannot do anything about it. I agree not to receive, from anyone, complaints that I can't do something about, but to redirect the person to someone who can do something about it. (This one ended up posted on the refrigerator in a Teacher's Lounge!)

• I agree to do whatever homework is assigned.
• I agree that if I fail to keep any of my agreements, I am willing to be supported by my classmates and my teacher in looking at and taking responsibility for my actions.

Although not necessary, we have found it useful to post the agreements in a conspicuous place, and to provide each student with a copy (this can be an especially important part of a journal). Sometimes I have each student sign and date it in the form of a personal agreement (or binding contract; or their word).

Stage three: surroundings responsibility

ACTIVITY

School projects.
In our school we could:

1　Check in and out all of our recess and physical education equipment.
2　Make sure the playground area is safe, friendly and inviting.
3　Establish a recycling center for all of our paper, metal and plastic materials – use this as an ongoing school fundraiser.
4　Keep our school grounds attractive and a place we would invite everyone to visit.
5　Adopt a teacher/administrator/support personnel in order to enhance their fitness and well-being.
6　Support another class in becoming a healthy group.
7　Engage in salt-free/sugar-free/fat-free weekends.
8　Begin a walking/jogging club – create after-school study teams.
9　Monitor our own recess behavior.
10　Help a student in another class with an academic problem he or she is having – set up a tutoring club.

These are but some of the many examples of actual lessons found in our Becoming Responsible program (Morris and Stiehl 2002). The common elements of this program have served as the basis for an ongoing comprehensive health study sponsored by the Department of Education in California. For a period of four years, 1997–2000, we examined the effectiveness of using multimedia teleconferencing to deliver a comprehensive substance prevention education and training program to teachers. Our Becoming Responsible program (Morris and Bassin 2000) was used as a primary intervention component for Project TRUST (Teaching Responsibility Undoubtedly Stops Tobacco). Middle school children in the Los Angeles area served as the intervention site. The focus was on the physical fitness, health status, substance use and general well-being of *all* the students in the school. The responsibility program was delivered to physical education and classroom teachers. The mode of program delivery included multimedia presentation, on-site delivery, and Internet programming. All participating teachers used the common elements of the program in physical education classes and in academic classrooms. Students were asked to create supportive classrooms, use appropriate language and be responsible for their thoughts and feelings. They made commitments and promises regarding their school work, their fitness goals, and their health objectives. In other words, they did their best to create an entire social setting, within the school that supported students becoming responsible for what they did with their bodies as well as for what they chose to put into their bodies.

Summary

It is believed that focusing upon one specific aspect of a student's life, behavior in physical education class, produces limited results. Our approach attempts to generalize the responsibility concepts to the entire school community serving students. We attempted, in this project, to also introduce these ideas to the greater community of the parents – we had marginal results. Thus we learned the barriers that need to be addressed in the next project. Our work with elementary and secondary students within school settings clearly demonstrates that social responsibility is useful with all students and perhaps should serve as the basis for a school's behavior and performance plan.

There are many others engaging in this kind of work. The delivery systems come in many forms. Jim Stiehl (2000) has successfully operated for a number of years outdoor and adventure programs grounded in social responsibility concepts. Stiehl clearly outlines the differences that exist between adventure and outdoor activities specifically as social responsibility concepts are applied. For example, adventure programs focus upon communication, cooperation, and trust concepts. These often take place within indoor facilities and we see them take place in outdoor challenge rope courses. Outdoor activities occur in open environments, the mountains, fields, lakes, and in the backcountry. Stiehl utilizes a responsibility model approximating Hellison's model discussed previously. He offers four levels of responsibility: expedition behavior, determination, independence, and leadership. I urge readers to examine Stiehl's program found in 'Youth development and physical activity' (2000).

There are any number of venues in which one can apply the responsibility concepts. Kallusky (2000) offers how they can be incorporated into what he calls 'in-school programs'. Others offer examples of extended day clubs (Hellison and Cutforth 2000), still other possibilities can be found in mentor programs (Martinek and Parker 2000). Suffice it to say that where one employs social responsibility as a basis for one's program the only limit is caused by one's thinking and commitment.

I suggest that becoming responsible is not a new idea or notion. Educators, parents, and many others in our society have stressed the importance of its impact upon human behavior for many, many years. We all have witnessed and experienced the product of irresponsible behavior. Much has been written, much has been presented on video and TV. I began this chapter by sharing some negative outcomes of irresponsible behavior. As a culture we seem to have focused upon a society that seems to shun responsibility. The result has been to develop programs for specific groups of people whose daily life practice is to be irresponsible. Daily there are many more examples available to us that promote living examples of society acting very responsibly. It is important to note that every day tens of millions of adults arrive safely and on time to work. Furthermore, a like number of students arrive at school, homework in hand, and function positively every day. For a society to function well, we must cooperate, trust one another, and willingly hold ourselves accountable for our individual actions. If we collectively accomplish this, our cultures interact well, our lives are enriched, and we can then enjoy our humanity. Becoming responsible is for all of us being able to live together in a world that works.

References

Armstrong, C.F. (1984) 'The lessons of sports: class socialization in British and American boarding schools', *Sociology of Sport Journal*, 1: 314–331.

Beedy, J.P. and Zierk, T. (2000) 'Lessons from the field: taking a proactive approach to developing character through sports', *Community Youth Journal*, 1(3): 1–12.

Burchard, J.D. (1979) 'Competitive youth sports and social competence', in M. Kent (ed.), *Social Competence in Children*, Hanover, NH: University Press of New England, 171–196.

Cutforth, N. (1997) 'What's worth doing: Reflections on an after-school program in a Denver elementary school', *Quest*, 49: 130–139.

DeBusk, M. and Hellison, D. (1989) 'Implementing a physical education self-responsibility model for delinquency-prone youth', *Journal of Teaching In Physical Education*, 8: 104–112.

Dryfoos, J. (1991) 'Adolescents at risk: a summation of work in the field-programs and policies', *Journal of Adolescent Health*, 12: 630–637.

Gatz, M., Messner, M. and Ball-Rokeach, S. (2002) *Paradoxes of Youth and Sport*, Albany, NY: State University of New York Press.

Glenn, H.S. and Nelson, J. (1987) *Raising Self Reliant Children in a Self Indulgent World*, Rocklin, CA: Prima Publishing

Grineski, S.C. (1989a) 'Children, games, and prosocial behavior: insights and connections', *Journal of Physical Education, Recreation, and Dance*, 60: 20–25.

—— (1989b) 'Effects of cooperative games on the pro-social behavior interactions of young children with and without impairments'. Unpublished doctoral dissertation, Grand Forks, ND: University of North Dakota.

Hellison, D. (1978) *Beyond Balls and Bats: Alienated Youth in the Gym*, Washington, DC: AAHPERD.

—— (1983) 'Teaching self-responsibility and more', *Journal of Physical Education, Recreation, and Dance*, 54: 23.

—— (1985) *Goals and Strategies for Teaching Physical Education*, Champaigne, IL: Human Kinetics.

——(1986) 'Cause of death: physical education', *Journal of Physical Education, Recreation and Dance*, 57: 27–28.

——(1993) 'The coaching club: teaching responsibility to inner-city students', *Journal of Physical Education, Recreation and Dance*, 64(5): 66–70.

——(1999) 'Promoting character development through sport: rhetoric or reality?' *New Designs for Youth Development*, 15(1): 23–27.

Hellison, D. and Cutforth, N. (2000) 'Extended day clubs', in D. Hellison, N. Cutforth, J. Kallusky, T. Martinek, M. Parker and J. Stiehl (eds), *Youth Development and Physical Activity*, Champaigne, IL: Human Kinetics, 115–134.

Hellison, D. and Georgiadis, N. (1992) 'Teaching values through basketball', *Strategies*, 1: 5–8.

Hellison, D., Cutforth, N., Kallusky, J., Martinek, T., Parker, M. and Stiehl, J. (1995) *Teaching Responsibility Through Physical Activity*, Champaigne, IL: Human Kinetics.

Jewett, A.E. and Bain L.L. (1985) *The Curriculum Process in Physical Education*, Dubuque, IA: WC Brown.

Kallusky, J. (1996) 'This ain't English', *Teaching Secondary Physical Education*, September: 6–7.

——(2000) 'In-school programs', in D. Hellison, N. Cutforth, J. Kallusky, T. Martinek, M. Parker and J. Stiehl, *Youth Development and Physical Activity*, Champaigne, IL: Human Kinetics, 87–114.

Kirst, J. (1991), as reported in J. Patterson and P. Kim, *The Day America Told The Truth*, NY: Prentice Hall, 115.

Laker, A. (1996) 'Learning to teach through the physical, as well as of the physical', *British Journal of Physical Education*, 27(4): 18–22.

——(2000) *Beyond the Boundaries of Physical Education and Sport: Educating Young People for Citizenship and Social Responsibility*, London: RoutledgeFalmer.

——(2001) *Developing Personal, Social and Moral Education through Physical Education: A Practical Guide for Teachers*, London: RoutledgeFalmer.

Lawson, H. (1997) 'Children in crisis, the helping professions, and the social responsibilities of universities', *Quest*, 49: 8–33.

Lickona, T. (1997) 'The teacher's role in character education', *Journal of Education*, 179(2): 63–80.

Martinek, T. (1997) 'What we should know about under-served youth', *Quest*, 49: 3–7.

Martinek, T. and Hellison, D. (1997) 'Fostering resiliency in under-served youth through physical activity', *Quest*, 49: 34–49.

——(1998) 'Values and goal-setting with under-served youth', *Journal of Physical Education, Recreation and Dance*, 69(7): 47–52.

Martinek, T. and Parker, M. (2000) 'Mentor programs', in D. Hellison, N. Cutforth, J. Kallusky, T. Martinek, M. Parker and J. Stiehl, *Youth Development and Physical Activity*, Champaigne, IL: Human Kinetics, 155–178.

Martinek, T., McLaughlin, D. and Schilling, T. (1999) 'Project effort: teaching responsibility beyond the gym', *Journal of Physical Education, Recreation and Dance*, 79(6): 59–65.

Morris, G.S.D. (1993 'Becoming responsible for our own actions: what's possible in physical education?', Editor, *Journal Physical Education, Recreation and Dance*, 64(5): 36–38.

Morris, G.S.D. and Bassin, S.L. (2000) *Project TRUST – A Final Report*, Research project funded by State of California Education Department, Sacramento, CA.

Morris, G.S.D. and Stiehl, J. (2002) *Becoming Responsible*, Los Angeles: MOST Publisher.

Orlick, T. (1981) 'Cooperative play Socialization among preschool children', *Journal of Individual Psychology*, 37: 54–63.

Parker, M., Kallusky, J. and Hellison, D. (1999) 'High impact, low risk: ten strategies to teach responsibility', *Journal of Physical Education, Recreation and Dance*, 70(2): 26–28.

Patterson, J. and Kim, P. (1991) *The Day America Told The Truth*, NY: Prentice Hall.

Raush, H (1965) 'Interaction sequences', *Journal of Personality and Social Psychology*, 2: 487–499.

Shields, D. and Bredemeier, B.J. (1995) *Character Development and Physical Activity*, Champaigne, IL: Human Kinetics.

Skubic, E. (1956) 'Studies in little league and middle league baseball', *Research Quarterly*, 27: 97–110.

Stiehl, J. (2000) 'The way it is', in D. Hellison, N. Cutforth, J. Kallusky, T. Martinek, M. Parker and J. Stiehl, *Youth Development and Physical Activity*, Champaigne, IL: Human Kinetics, 3–16.

5   Reflective practice goes public

Reflection, governmentality and postmodernity

Doune Macdonald and Richard Tinning

What we know about something will depend on the questions we ask of it (Postman 1989). Accordingly, what we know about reflective practice will depend on the questions we ask of it. When the editor contacted us to engage our work for this chapter he framed what we should do as follows: 'Much has been written about reflective practice. . . . Many programs are aspiring to produce reflective practitioners.' Accordingly we were asked to respond to the following questions regarding reflective practice:

- Has it lived up to expectations?
- Is it realistic to expect teachers to change their practice as a result of self (or aided) reflection?
- How has reflective practice benefited the profession?
- How can we make a good idea work in practice?
- What derivation of reflective practice will emerge?

Of course, such questions beg further questions. For example, whose understanding of reflection are we talking about? Whose expectations are we talking about? Moreover, there is also the consideration of what questions are *not* asked. For example, why reflection now? Whose interests are served by particular notions of reflection? Clearly the plot thickens particularly given a focus upon the postmodern conditions in which we work.

This chapter will explore questions of past and future reflective practice using both postmodernist and poststructuralist referents. Our distinction here is that postmodernism refers in part to a critique of Western civilization's fundamental assumptions of reality, research and knowledge (Scheurich 1997) while poststructuralism provides us with more explicit theoretical frameworks with which to investigate the social construction of selves in and through specific relations of power (Macdonald *et al.* 2002). Lather contends that:

> In essence, the postmodern argument is that the dualisms which continue to dominate Western thought are inadequate for understanding a world of multiple causes and effects interacting in complex and non-linear ways,

all of which are rooted in a limitless array of historical and cultural specificities.

(Lather 1991: 5)

Poststructuralism gives us a way to understand these historical and cultural shifts through attention to mean-making and power.

> For post-structuralists, meaning is not fixed in language or in other cultural symbols and neither is it fixed in consistent power relationships. It shifts according to the way in which a range of linguistic, institutional and cultural factors come together. . . . Such a view of meaning then, calls attention to the particular rather than the general, to discontinuity and instability rather than continuity and stability, to plurality, diversity and difference rather than to similarity and commonality and to the complex and multi-faceted rather than the essential.

(Kenway 1992: 3)

Accordingly, it will be argued that as we move further into the complexities of postmodernity, reflective practice has become less about a personal, moral self/teacher and more about public performance in line with codified practices as demonstrated, for example, by the proliferation of teaching standards that specify 'reflection'. In order to better explain the shifts in, and possible futures for, reflective practice, we will draw upon the poststructuralist concepts of governmentality and performativity.

Governmentality suggests 'a focus on the techniques of the self as well as the institutional technologies that perpetrate the art of government in ways that make it acceptable to the populace' (Popkewitz and Brennan 1998: 21). Within this process, the 'teacher' becomes constructed through accountability regimes and their practices, and, in turn, bodies are codified and routinized in appropriate ways. Foucault (1977) uses the example of the bumble bee that rules the hive but does not need a sting to reinforce particular power relationships. Through the conflation of discourses of professionalism, leadership, and caring, teacher governance has relied upon reflection to structure teacher practices. This form of site-based governmentality has required the self-disciplined, self-surveilling teacher to engage in reflective practice on behalf of their students and education systems.

More recently, the nature of governmentality has shifted and the stipulation for self-surveillance has been codified within a corporatist education regime. Education systems have sought to describe, observe/measure, and report upon teachers' reflective practice through registration requirements, professional standards, appraisal mechanisms, and the like. Self-governance has become supplemented with accountability technologies and the proliferation of performativity criteria (Smart 1992: 174).

Performativity, another poststructuralist concept, helps us to focus upon teachers' practices within a managerialist culture that prizes efficient performance (see Lyotard 1986). Performativity embodies technologies of power (Usher and Edwards 1994). 'Power is not only good performativity, but also effective verification and good verdicts' (Lyotard 1986: 47). Observable action, skilled performance and certification have become highly valued in the demonstration of efficient and competent practice. Within this context, performativity has heralded new ways of seeing reflective practice in line with shifts in governmentality. Thus both governmentality and performativity are concepts that allow us to analyse control of the postmodern teachers' practices.

The first section of this chapter will consider reflective practice as we have known it and the impact that it has had on the physical education profession. The second section, reflection goes public, will address the implications of the shifts of education systems to managerialist priorities for teachers' practice together with other emerging poststructuralist dilemmas surrounding teachers' subjectivities and schooling of the future.

Considering reflection in physical education

The field of physical education has been engaged in the discussions regarding the nature of reflection for some time. Indeed, a decade ago one of the leading professional associations in the field, AIESEP (The International Association for Physical Education in Higher Education), devoted an entire international conference to the theme: 'How can you train teachers to be reflective teachers?' The theme foregrounded technical 'how to do it' issues to be practised by individual teachers and tacitly ignored important questions concerning the ends or purposes of reflection, yet such issues were certainly not ignored by some of the conference presenters (e.g. Crum 1995; Dodds 1995; Tinning 1995).

There have been many attempts by various authors to clarify the numerous interpretations and uses of reflection and reflective teaching. Significantly there is no consensus over the meaning of the term (Tsangaridou and Siedentop 1995; Ovens 2002). As Tsangaridou and Siedentop suggest, 'reflective teaching has different meanings, different approaches towards implementation and little consensus on what ought to be the object of reflection' (1995: 213). We agree completely and hence we recognise it is a difficult task to talk about reflection 'in general'. Accordingly what we offer in the first instance is a little languaging (Kirk 1991).

Languaging reflection

Scholars interested in the notion of reflection have for some time recognised problems with the meaning that is ascribed to the term. For example, Smyth expressed concern that reflection is such a commonsensical notion that '. . . who could possibly be against reflection; it's an indisputable notion like "quality" and "excellence"' (1992: 285). Also, because of its universal appeal, reflection can mean all things to all people and, accordingly, 'it runs the risk of being totally evacuated of all meaning' (Smyth 1992: 285). Smyth suggested that:

. . . we are witnessing . . . a kind of conceptual colonization in which terms like reflection have become such an integral part of the educational jargon that not using them is to run the real risk of being out of educational fashion.

(Smyth 1992: 286)

Hellison and Templin (1991) also expressed a similar concern claiming that reflective teaching had become a buzzword in the educational community and Martinez (1990: 20) was concerned that even by the end of the 1980s critical reflection was becoming 'the patchwork panacea of teacher educators of all theoretical persuasions'.

According to Kirk (1991) there are many terms we use in education (and life in general) for which there is a tacit assumption that there is a shared meaning. As he argues, it is often the seemingly simple terms that create the most problems in terms of language use. For example, the meaning of good, education or even teacher are often more controversial than more sophisticated specialist terms such as aerobic fitness or epidemiology.

As part of the languaging process it is important to recognise something of the history of the term and to draw some distinctions between the possible forms of reflection. It was John Dewey (1933) who led the educational theorizing on the nature of reflective teaching this century (at least in the English-speaking countries). He first distinguished between reflective action and routine action. Routine action is guided by tradition, authority. It takes ends for granted and focuses attention on the means to achieve particular ends. Reflective action, on the other hand, involves the consideration of the assumptions underpinning any belief or form of knowledge and the consequences which might follow from action which incorporates such beliefs or knowledge. Importantly, Dewey identified three attitudes which he claimed are prerequisite to reflective action. First, there must be an attitude of open-mindedness in which there is a desire to see more than one side of an argument, in which full attention is given to alternative possibilities, and in which there is recognition of the possibility that even our dearest beliefs might be wrong. Second, there must be an attitude of responsibility which means that the consequences of our actions are considered. Third, there must be a whole-heartedness in which both open-mindedness and responsibility are central components in one's life.

Forty years after Dewey, Van Manen (1977) considered it necessary to make a distinction between technical, practical and critical forms of reflection. These distinctions are based on Habermas's (1972) notions of knowledge-constitutive interest in which knowledge is construed, guided and shaped differently depending on the human interests being served. According to Van Manen's distinctions, technical reflection is characterised by the application or implementation of existing knowledge to the attainment of given ends. This reflection culminates in instrumental action. Practical reflection is a form of contemplative inquiry that involves clarifying the assumptions underpinning practical actions. It is concerned with moral, ethical and value considerations in that all actions are linked with value commitments. Critical reflection has similar moral and ethical considerations but is also concerned with identifying the ideological forces that might constrain practice.

Grimmett and Erickson (1988) conceived a categorization of reflective teaching that is useful to consider in concert with these forms of reflection. They provide a categorisation that is based on which particular purposes of reflective teaching are foregrounded and which are backgrounded. In their first category reflection essentially represents thoughtfulness applied to action. Research findings are applied to practice. It represents a form of reflection in which reflection would lead to control over or direction of practice. This has sympathies with Van Manen's technical reflection. Their second category sees reflection as the source of knowledge that will inform practice. Reflection is essentially a deliberation among choices of competing versions of good teaching and understanding the context of educational events is seen as fundamental in such deliberations. This has sympathies with practical reflection. Their final category sees reflection reconstructing experience, providing new possibilities for action and/or new understandings of the taken-for-granted assumptions about teaching. This has sympathies with critical reflection.

Tsangaridou and O'Sullivan (1997: 4) argue that it is useful to think of reflection on two 'levels'; micro-reflection 'gives meaning to or informs day-to-day practice whereas macro-reflection 'gives meaning to or informs practice over time'. Although this might be a useful distinction to make, we make our contribution to languaging reflection by conflating the two 'levels' and locating them in the broader term reflective practice.

The term, reflective practice, which titles this chapter is a broader concept than the more common reflective teaching or reflection. The distinction is significant. We consider reflective practice to be an intellectual disposition which functions like a set of lenses through which to view all educational and cultural practices (both micro and macro). We concur with Collins (2002: 4) who claims that, 'The quality of reflection on practice is dependent on the concepts and theories: the ways of seeing; to which teachers have access'. Moreover, these 'ways of seeing' will be taken beyond the classroom and reflective practice will be 'applied to' more than the act of teaching. Reflective practice will also engage issues relating to schooling and education as inherently political and ideological social structures. In this sense it will be critically oriented.

The questions we ask

There are many things upon which a teacher can reflect. Some can be rather trivial, others more significant. We realise that who defines what is significant and what is trivial is a key issue of power/knowledge within teaching and teacher education and we consider that such power/knowledge relationships should be revealed and considered as always inherently problematic.

According to Grossman (1992: 176) reflective teachers are those who 'ask worthwhile questions of the teaching [and] continue to learn from their practice'. Although this is a useful perspective at one level, it leaves the nature of a 'worthwhile' question unasked, and unanswered. For some (for example Siedentop 1991), worthwhile questions relate to the development of teaching skills as defined by the research evidence concerning effective teachers. For others, for example those who advocate a critical enquiry orientation to reflective teaching (see Kirk 1986; Fernández-Balboa 1995; Prain and Hickey 1995), what is considered a worthwhile question (on which to reflect) would be very different indeed. While all forms of reflection might have a place in the repertoire of the reflective teacher, it is technical, individualised, and practical forms of reflection that have tended to be foregrounded in many Physical Education Teacher Education (PETE) programs (Tinning 1991).

Hellison and Templin, in *A Reflective Approach to Teaching Physical Education* (1991), contend that reflective teaching involved asking two questions throughout a teaching career, 'What's worth doing?' and 'Is what I'm doing working?' (Hellison and Templin 1991: 3). They considered that the first of these questions required reflection on beliefs and values, and the second on subject matter and pedagogies. They argue that in the field of physical education there have been a range of conceptualisations of reflective teaching from ethical social, and political issues, through values and goals, assumptions and consequences of the teaching act, to at the opposite end of the continuum an analysis of teaching strategies.

In a collaborative text written for Australian and New Zealand undergraduate PETE students titled *Becoming a Physical Education Teacher: Contemporary and Enduring Issues* (Tinning *et al.* 2001) we were explicit in our aim to encourage student teachers to become reflective practitioners. We encourage them to think about their teaching by means of two orienting questions that provide a point of focus for reflection: 'What are the implications of what I choose to teach?' and 'What are the implications of how I teach?'

But not all questions posed in reflection are as opened ended and generative of enquiry. Kincheloe and Steinberg (1998: 222) is of the opinion that reflection has come to be just another checklist-type competency-oriented question asked in the process of making judgements on a teacher's performance. In this sense:

> reduced to a set of procedures, teacher reflection becomes little more than a skill to be learned as part of a larger battery of competencies. (Did the teacher employ humour in the lesson? Was a personal example used to illustrate the information presented? Did the teacher *reflect* on the success or failure of the lesson?)
>
> (Kincheloe and Steinberg 1998: 222)

Viewed in this way, reflection sits alongside other technical skills such as classroom management, planning and pupil discipline as competencies to be demonstrated. In this manner, reflection for student teachers becomes simply the rational exercise of determining the gap between their current level of competency and the required level needed for certification. In this context questions relating to the value or meaning of the actual competencies themselves are unlikely to be asked.

Most often, reflection will be oriented towards the central problems that are seen to require attention in teaching (or in teacher education). As Hal Lawson (1984) observed, understanding the process of 'problem setting' (defining the problems) involves asking questions about why a particular problem is considered a problem in the first place, by whom is it considered a problem and the interests served by defining a problem in a particular way. For some teacher educators the central problem is: how can we train student teachers to become effective teachers? (e.g. Cruickshank 1987; the AIESEP conference of 1993) and how can we best develop the teaching skills of student teachers?' (e.g. Siedentop 1991). For others it is: how can we educate teachers to be reflective of their work in ways which embody a critical social perspective? (see Kirk 1986; Tinning 1987). Of course it does not have to be an either/or proposition – we are talking here about emphasis.

A question of discourse community

Ovens (2002) argues that part of the reason for confusion over the meaning of reflection is that meaning is often linked to the various contexts within which it is embedded. He claims that there are different 'discourse communities' of reflection and that individuals within each community will share somewhat different meanings of the concept of reflection. From this perspective scholars such as Siedentop and Kirk for example would locate themselves (and be located) in different discourse communities with respect to reflection and therefore their understandings of the concept of reflection will be different. As Ovens (2002) points out, considering reflection as a discursive practice enables us to recognise how different discourses may draw on much the same literature to support quite different conceptualisations of the concept. Tsangaridou and Siedentop (1995) cite Gore's (1993) example of how many contemporary scholars' use Dewey's notions of reflection to advocate very different versions of reflective teaching. According to Gore they:

> . . . draw on Dewey's (1933) distinction between routine and reflective action to make their cases. In this instance the 'will to truth' functions in such a way that the same language is used to make vastly different claims about the 'truth' of reflective teaching.
>
> (Gore 1993: 49)

In *Becoming a Physical Education Teacher* (Tinning *et al.* 2001) we articulated what we called a principled position with respect to the purposes of schooling and reflection as an educational practice. We argued that reflective practice should work towards making the physical education experiences for young people meaningful, purposeful, enjoyable, and just (fair). Such experiences would be underpinned by the assertion that schools should be about reproducing the best of our culture and challenging the worst aspects such that they might be improved. This was an avowedly social reconstructionist vision of schooling and it foregrounded reflection as political action. Importantly, as authors we all shared a common discourse community with respect to teacher education and accordingly we found common ground in the orienting questions for our work in the book. In this sense we were sympathetic to Kemmis's notion of reflection as political action.

Kemmis (1985: 140) makes a number of significant propositions with regard to forms of reflection which are distinct from passive contemplation. He argued that:

1   Reflection is not a purely 'internal', psychological process; it is action-oriented and historically embedded.
2   Reflection is not a purely individual process; like language, it is a social process.
3   Reflection serves human interests; it is a political process.
4   Reflection is shaped by ideology; in turn, it shapes ideology.
5   Reflection is a practice which expresses power to reconstitute social life by the way we participate in communication, decision making and social action.

This set of propositions is, however, a claim for what Kemmis (who was strongly influenced by Habermas) thinks reflection *should* be rather than a claim for what it is. We recognise that there is a difference between what is claimed on behalf of reflection and what it looks like in practice. We share, with others of the critical reflection discourse community, some concerns over what reflection has become in contemporary educational discourse.

Considering the success of attempts to develop reflective teachers

If becoming reflective were simply a rational process, we could indeed train teachers to be reflective (Tinning 1995). The problem, however, is that many of the issues upon which we believe teachers should reflect are not merely a matter of rational argument. Rather, issues of politics and education have a large measure of emotion and subjectivity embedded within them. Opinions about, for example the place of competition in physical education classes, are influenced by our emotional/subjective experiences and commitments as much as by rational arguments. We must remember that any pedagogical moment occurs against a backdrop (or better still within a cultural context) of one's discursive histories and the power of the moment can only be understood in the context of that background. A student teacher's discursive history is a complex mosaic of ideas, experiences and emotions. The predictability of any pedagogical encounter which attempts to develop reflective practice of the sort that we desired in our principled position is limited to say the least.

Gore (1990), for example, wrote of her struggle to implement a critical pedagogy with physical education teacher education students through a reflective teaching approach. She wrote of how she shifted '. . . from a discourse of teacher effectiveness, to a discourse of ideology-critique' (Gore 1990: 130) and later (in a reanalysis of an earlier study) to a discourse of critical cultural studies. For Gore, the discourses of reflective teaching (as a form of critical pedagogy) were inconsistent with her lived experience of teaching the PETE students.

Almost a decade after Gore's attempt, Macdonald and Brooker (1999) reported on an action research project that they conducted with their PETE students in the late 1990s. Reflective teaching underpinned the action research and was central to their notion of critical pedagogy. Their intent was to implement a critical pedagogy in which socially critical subject matter, negotiation, reflection and praxis worked together in developing 'socially responsible professionals'. Over a two-year period they monitored student reactions to the critical pedagogy and their own feelings, frustrations and joys throughout the process. At the conclusion of the project they claimed that: 'For those students who could make sense of the critical subject matter, the outcomes seemed to be worthwhile in that they had grasped fresh perspectives on taken-for-granted practices' (Macdonald and Brooker: 57).

Recently, Cassidy (2000) completed her PhD thesis investigating the enactment of critical pedagogy within a teacher education course. Again the notion of critical reflection was central to the critical pedagogy process. Some student teachers come to their course with an emotional commitment that might be said to be coherent with the agenda of critical pedagogy. For such students there is a real possibility of developing their reflective practice further. For others (the majority), the intellectual rationale for a socially critical curriculum and a reconceptualist vision of schooling is insufficient to change their practice. For a small minority it may even be that engaging a socially critical perspective precipitates a serious life crisis (see for example Devis-Devis and Sparkes 1999). Not surprisingly Cassidy (2000: 241) concluded that: 'Implementing a socially critical pedagogy in this period of late modernity is not an easy task nor is it possible to provide a "how to guide"'. The reference to late modernity (postmodernity) is important here for it is through the lenses provided by postmodernism that we can begin to recognise the problematic nature of the modernist search for progress in the form of a perfect solution.

In essence, other than for forms of brainwashing, we do not have ways of making a student teacher think (reflect) as we might like them to think (Tinning 1993). We cannot make them think that the issues which we (in our shared discourse community) believe to be central to the mission of education should be central to them also. Certainly, we can assess written, oral or other products in an attempt to measure what they have learned in our programs, but the success of such endeavours is problematic. Students can speak or write responses which fit our particular regime(s) of truth, but how do we know if it is merely strategic rhetoric (see Sparkes 1991) or a real shift or change in thinking.

Teaching the skills of technical reflection on teaching seems well within our grasp in teacher education but pedagogies for the development of reflective practice as political action remain illusive. Perhaps, given the power of mass culture in postmodern times, the development of reflective practice in children of the information age is more difficult than ever. But probably that is only a concern if you share the discourse community in which a social reconstructivist view of education is favoured.

We are confident that the emphasis that many contemporary teacher education programs give to the development of the skills of technical reflection (e.g. the ability to analyse ALT-PE or the nature of teacher feedback in lessons) has produced teachers who have the ability to think more critically about their teaching. We are also confident that attention to critical reflection on possible learnings from the hidden curriculum (such as sexism, equity or stereotyping) within teacher education and professional development workshops has certainly raised the consciousness of physical education teachers to such issues. The extent to which such consciousness translates into an ongoing self-reflection by physical education teachers is not known. Our guess would be that it does for some teachers and not for others.

As we know from considerable research over the past 30 years, there is a great deal about school physical education that is less than satisfactory. While some physical education teachers are inspiring, caring and competent, there are also those who give less than adequate attention to their teaching and for whom the cliché of 'rolling out the ball' was coined. Larry Locke (1977) once said that physical education was not so much plagued by poor teaching as it was by mindless teaching. In his view, just going through the motions, metaphorically and literally 'rolling out the ball', in the absence of purposeful teaching has become too common. We suggest that mindless teaching is another name for unreflective teaching. Reflective practice, however, is a necessary but not sufficient condition for improving physical education.

A decade ago O'Sullivan, Siedentop and Locke (1992) argued that teachers of physical education were 'pragmatists to the core' and the same year Smyth (1992) expressed concern that the kind of reflection most appealing to many teachers is one grounded in pragmatism – a technical form of reflection. The tendency in such pragmatism is for reflection to be an individualistic process that can very easily lack any understanding of the wider social and structural influences on schooling and teaching. Smyth claims that reflection as a notion evolved from an individualistic and psychologistic origin and has been appropriated as an individualist solution to the problems of education and schooling. Further, according to Smyth (1992: 286) '. . . processes like reflection, which give the outward appearance of modernity and teacher autonomy, can in fact be used as rhetorical flourishes and a very effective cover with which to acquire even greater control over teachers.'

In what follows we argue that reflection, from technical to critical, has operated through governmental technologies that rely on the individual 'teacher as professional'. In our view the notion of reflection that has become most popular within education (and physical education) is as an individual rather than a social process. In this sense reflection has been seen less as political action and more as a technique for improving an individual teacher's educational practice. Ironically, however, this individualistic perspective has been 'made public' through various systemic appropriations of the idea of reflection. We examine how the idea of reflection while remaining essentially an individualist *process*, has shifted from an individual's professional *responsibility* to a more public, codifed and accountable activity. In order to understand this apparent paradox we need to consider the contemporary postmodern context in which reflection has become institutionalised within educational discourse.

Reflection goes public

Governmentality and the performance of reflection

Smyth *et al.* (2000) have identified a number of control regimes or forms of governmentality that shape the new labour process of teaching and, in turn, the place of reflection within this process. These regimes provide a way of understanding how teachers can be positioned within, and make sense of, educational reform as they occupy contradictory positions within discourses of marketisation, deprofessionalisation, increased accountability and intensification on one hand and collaboration, community and civility on the other. 'Some control regimes have served to partially deskill teachers' work, while at other times control has operated more subtly and allowed teachers a greater measure of control over their work' (Smyth *et al.* 2000: 39).

The control regimes may be used more specifically to explain current manifestations of reflective practice. Smyth (2001) describes the regulated market, technical, bureaucratic, corporate, ideological and disciplinary control regimes. In practice, these control regimes do not operate in isolation but come to be through complex systems and strategies enacted in different contexts and historical moments. While all six help to explain trends in reflective practice, it is the last three that are most useful in this context. Corporate control can be closely linked with postmodern shifts to globalised, competitive economies that require highly efficient management systems in both private and public sectors. Corporate control, they argue, is maintained through an ideological control in the form of hegemonic beliefs, ideas and language, emphasising responsibility and self-regulation. Further, corporate and ideological control underpin the regime of disciplinary power that gives 'permission for certain subjects to be talked and written about in certain ways, and established who has permission to speak and with what authority' (Smyth 2001: 45). Disciplinary power shapes not only the systematic bodies of school knowledge, but also the appropriate behaviours of teachers through external and self-surveillance.

Thus, in many Westernized education systems, postmodernity has required organisational transformation of educational management and delivery due to the effects of globalisation and increased international competitiveness, the need to enhance school outcomes particularly in government schools that seek to maintain their market share, and organisational flexiblility to match discontinuous and rapid change (Lingard *et al.* 2002). Management has become 'a theoretical and practical technology of rationality geared to efficiency, practicality and control. . . . It represents the bureaucratization of the structure of control via job descriptions, line management relations and the establishment of fixed flows of communication, and committee-style decision-making' (Ball 1990: 157). In practice, what has occurred are shifts to school-based decision making and leadership alongside more centralised accountability and control mechanisms in the form of codified teaching 'standards', core curricula and centralised testing.

Reflective practice is one dimension of teachers' work that has been codified into performance standards. The General Teaching Council in England (GTCE) has the goal of raising the status of the teaching profession with a view to guaranteeing high standards of teaching and learning. To this end it has a code of professional values and practice for teachers that includes 'Teachers continually reflect on their own practice, improve their skills and deepen their knowledge' (GTCE 2000). The requirement of teachers to reflect sits alongside other behaviours such as 'taking responsibility', 'adapting', 'respond sensitively', 'have insight' and 'support' (ACDE 1998). The Australian Council of Deans of Education (ACDE 1998), in their graduate standards and guidelines, employ the concept of 'critical' and 'reflection' frequently. Graduates should have a 'critical awareness of how their own background (social, cultural, financial, educational, geographic, religious) shapes their approach to teaching and the assumptions they will make as teachers' (ACDE 1998: 9), the ability to critically assess relevant curriculum documents, 'their rationales and perspectives' (ACDE 1998: 12–13), and should be able 'to make explicit, critically reflect on, and modify as appropriate their theories of teaching' (ACDE 1998: 14).

In the United States the National Board for Professional Teaching Standards (NBPTS) for middle childhood/generalist standards lists as one of the eleven standards 'Reflection' explained as follows: 'Accomplished teachers regularly analyze, evaluate and strengthen the effectiveness and quality of their practice' (NBPTS 2000: 25). Reflection and/or reflective practice appear regularly throughout the articulation of standards across subject specialisations and teaching levels. The NBPTS for Physical Education (1999: 31) has as Standard Ten, 'Reflective practice and professional growth' specifying that 'Accomplished physical education teachers participate in a wide range of reflective practices that foster their creativity, stimulate personal growth, contribute to content knowledge and classroom skills, and enhance professionalism'. Interestingly, Standard Ten talks further about 'introspective self-assessment', teachers 'tak(ing) responsibility for their own professional growth and development', and re-invigorating themselves professionally (NBPTS 1999: 31). The thrust of the NBPTS in Physical Education is clearly upon self-assessment and self-renewal positing the responsibility for governmentality with the individual teacher while at the same time using performative mechanisms of public submissions and appraisal as evidence of reflective practice. The language of these behaviours is indicative of the shift to performativity and the statements are worded as performance imperatives.

More generally, Ball (1990: 159) talks about the appraisal process as 'a formal ritual of power and ceremony of visibility. . . . The appraisee is there to be known, and recorded, by the appraiser.' The physical educator wishing to be appraised as a highly competent teacher prepares a portfolio of their work (written and videotaped), seeks peer references and undertakes a discipline-based knowledge test (Macdonald and Beckett 2002). These processes reflect a performative subjectivity where 'the subject presents itself' (active voice), rather than earlier forms of governmentality where 'the subject is visible' (passive voice) (Fendler 1990: 181).

Now we turn again to the question asked earlier: What does reflective practice mean? We then reconsider it with respect to the context of new managerialism and control regimes. What questions should teachers now be asking? What practices should they be interrogating? What outcomes should they be seeking? In response to these silences, and with a view to enhancing the learning of all students, the Queensland School Reform Longitudinal Study (QSRLS) in Australia, modelled on the work of Newmann and associates (1996) in Canada, has sought to identify and measure 'productive pedagogies' across a range of schools as a 'way to reflect upon which pedagogies might make a difference for different groups of students' (Lingard *et al.* 2000: 96). It is important to emphasise that the project leaders came to this large-scale measurement task with socially critical lenses, a somewhat hybrid position increasingly common in postmodern enquiry. Cross-cutting their enquiry were both structuralist (e.g. class, gender, location) and poststructuralist (e.g. difference, diversity) points of reference (see Macdonald 2003, in press).

Which pedagogies will contribute to the enhancement of the academic and social performance of all students? The QSRLS response was to hypothesise that there are at least four dimensions of classroom practice which are potentially necessary conditions for improved and more equitable student outcomes: intellectual quality, relevance, supportive classroom environments, and the recognition of difference (School of Education 2001: 4). More specifically, the QSRLS team monitored classroom practices looking at, for example, where critical analysis was occurring. Is there an attempt to connect with students' background knowledges? Do students have any say in the pace, direction or outcomes of the lesson? Is the classroom a socially supportive and positive environment? Does the teaching build a sense of community and identity? (Lingard *et al.* 2000: 101–102).

After scoring twenty dimensions of productive pedagogies, the project has been able to recommend to teachers, schools, communities, and the state education system where individual, structural and systemic reforms might be best directed. What the process has given Australia, much like that provided by the authentic pedagogy work in Canada, is a more specific, practice-referenced, and publicly shared language with which to reflect upon practice. Also, by emphasising both the teacher and his or her systemic support and resources, the responsibility *for* reflection, while still located within the individual in terms of performativity, now also includes a more public dimension in the form of a shared responsibility within teacher professional learning communities. Following the authentic/productive pedagogy projects has been the encouragement of teacher professional learning communities (Lingard *et al.* 2000) as a way of enhancing student outcomes across a school community. These professional learning communities function as communities of practice or discursive communities (Ovens 2002) that serve to open up the possibility for reflection as political action (Kemmis 1985).

Louis, Kruse and Marks (1996) describe learning communities as emphasising *reflective collaboration* focusing upon the links between pedagogies and student learning outcomes, thereby further deprivatising practice and exemplifying performativity. Such collaborative pedagogical work can also be enhanced by changed school structures in terms of the management of teachers, time and space to allow for team teaching, collaborative preparation and moderation, mentoring and the like. The QSRLS found, in addition to these features, that schools with more productive pedagogies had more extensive individual and collective professional development, a philosophy that created a coherence across the schools' curriculums, and an alignment of curriculum, pedagogy and assessment, leadership that supports a robust emotional economy that encourages innovation and risk, and substantial connections to other schools, universities or education systems (Lingard *et al.* 2000).

Thus, we have reflective practice being recast in some important ways. In a sense reflective practice is increasingly becoming deprivatised. Here reflective practice is not posited in self-assessment on the one hand or systemic imperatives on the other, but at the interface between the individual teachers, their colleagues, the schools structures, policies, resources and leadership, and community and systemic support. While still functioning as a governmental technology, the subject/teacher presents himself or herself to colleagues and the community as competent and responsible practitioners.

Reflective futures

Having suggested that discourses of reflection are becoming more codified, public and, indeed, collaborative we want to now argue that there are still some important silences. Initiatives such as teaching standards have given flesh and direction to reflective practices. However, postmodern times and poststructuralist lenses have highlighted new questions that extend the reflective gaze. Here we present two possibilities for reflective practice beyond teachers' school work. They are derivations of reflective futures, futures that also might entail reflective practices addressing other contemporary issues for physical educators such as citizenship and multiculturalism.

Performativity and embodiment

While reflection is embodied through the public monitoring of teachers' practices, little has been asked of physical educators with respect to their embodied identities. Identity (McLaren 1998) and embodiment (Giddens 1991) are central to the postmodern context yet until recently physical educators' work has been particularly disembodied. Identity is not something constructed, polished and finished but is now an ongoing process of reflection, adjustment and becoming (Giddens 1991). Significantly for physical education teachers the '[b]ody and self are inextricably folded within each other. Rather than a unity of body and self there is a doubling: an embodied self' (Kenworth Teather 1999: 9).

As 'the politics of identity is increasingly wrapped around configurations of the body' (Elliott 2001: 99), physical educators' reflective practices will be influenced by their embodied identities shaped by the central place that physical activity and sport plays in their daily lives. Work by Macdonald (1995) and Webb (2001) on teachers' concerns with their ageing bodies and Sparkes and Silvennoinen (1999) writing on the injured body highlights how teachers understand their competent performance as embodied (able, muscular, fit, energetic). With the increasing commodification of the body and physical activity (Tinning 1995), we argue that physical educators need to understand the relationship between embodiment and performativity; how their bodies are central to their private and public selves, how the management of their bodies is integral to contemporary governmentalities, and how their embodied selves can shape their relationships with parents, students and other teachers.

Further, we argue that curriculum shifts raise new questions and challenges for teachers of physical education as syllabuses increasingly focus upon the concept of healthy lifestyles. As a technology of government (Rose 1996), the physical education curriculum is buying into a 'politics of lifestyle' (Giddens 1991: 214). Through participation in physical education students are expected to learn to make choices that promote health and personal development in their lives beyond the school gate. They are encouraged to take care of the self through self-regulation of diet, exercise, and prudent risk management (Tinning and Glasby 2002). This focus also behoves physical educators to ask new questions about their practices; how they sit with respect to politics of the body, corporeal management, and lifestyle management. However, lifestyle-oriented reflection may be(come) more like self-surveillance which is predominantly individualistic (perhaps even narcissistic) and not necessarily embrace a critical perspective that might stimulate political action.

Reflection beyond physical education

Alongside the increasing emphasis on lifestyle in the physical education curriculum, there are also substantial shifts in how and where students learn, again raising new challenges and broader questions for the reflective practitioner. 'A postmodern curriculum will accept the student's ability to organize, construct and structure, and will emphasize this ability as a focal point in the curriculum' (Doll 1989: 250). It may be a more open system of learning with constant flux and complex interactions requiring interactive and holistic frameworks for learning that bypass bureaucratic control. Thus, curriculum documents that embrace a postmodern perspective will no longer be stories of 'the translation of an academic discipline, devised by "dominant" groups of scholars in universities, into a pedagogic version to be used as a school subject' (Goodson 1988: 177). The institutionalisation of knowledge via disciplines and subjects limits the possibilities for freedom or autonomy for teachers and students and for making meaningful connections across schooling. In Australia, for example, the clustering of subject matter into learning areas that extend beyond subjects is being accompanied by students learning through new technologies, and in learning partnerships with those who lie outside educational bureaucracies and the teaching profession.

If the school curriculum is to become an emancipatory experience for a much larger section of each cohort of students, this is going to require much greater involvement of many people who currently have no direct links with school, including parents and employers, and many activities by teachers and pupils which are not confined to the school nor, in conventional terms, are usually defined as 'educational' at all (Young 1998: 32).

Consequently, as we noted earlier, reflective practice undertaken by physical educators needs a broader gaze beyond physical education, beyond the learning resources of the classroom, and beyond the school gates. Young people's inter-action with the curriculum is becoming similar to that of a consumer and a product and for many young people their preferred engagement with physical activity lies outside the school. As they become increasingly disillusioned with curricula that are irrelevant (Tinning and Fitzclarence 1992) and aware of multiple pathways and places for learning, as critical consumers they can bypass pre-selected, given and inert curriculums and seek alternative products. Global media and technologies give many young people access to ideas and opportunities for the engagement in forms of physical activity that lie outside their local culture. We suggest that physical educators need to reposition themselves, not as those concerned with the delivery of physical education knowledge and skills, but as facilitators for young people to access and learn about the place, meaning and potential of physical activity in their lives. Accordingly, reflective practice will require physical educators to ask questions of their curriculum in relation to the totality of young people's learning and the extent to which they are helping young people to be critical consumers and 'manage' their own access to physically active lifestyles.

Conclusion

Returning to our opening reference to Postman's (1989) claim that what we know about a subject depends on the questions we ask about it, it is important that some of the questions we consider important in reflective practice are those that have the tendency to make the familiar strange (see Kirk 1994). Questions related to: What counts for truth in physical education? Whose truth is it anyway? and Why do they hold it as true? have the capacity to challenge the taken-for-granted of physical educators' practices and the taken-for-granted in how teachers work is implicitly and explicitly governed. Teachers who develops a reflective orientation to their work that is underpinned by the notion of reflection as political action and collaboration (as distinct from acquiring a few technical skills for personal reflection) will learn to be careful about how things appear and the assumptions that they make. They will understand the need to ask open-ended type questions and to look beneath the surface of their own and others' pedagogies and subject matter and beyond the school to their own and others' subjectivities.

However, making the familiar strange can be an unsettling process. It can upset one's ontological security. Ontological security refers to 'the confidence that most human beings have in the continuity of their self-identity and in the constancy of the surrounding social and materials environments of action' (Giddens 1991: 92). Importantly it is an emotional rather than a cognitive phenomenon. It is anchored in practical consciousness which enables individuals to accept certain routine actions as part of their normal functioning in the world (Giddens 1991). Yet, the new landscape for reflective practice is a postmodern one with managerialist systems of order, procedure, and accountability as well as old professional discourses of responsibility and trust. Together these increase teachers' sense of insecurity as they engage in both self-surveillance and systemic critique. While it may be particularly challenging for teachers to embrace reflective practice as political action concurrently with satisfying publicly monitored standards, it is perhaps more important now than ever that physical educators individually and collectively have both the disposition and the capacity to ask questions of schooling, society and themselves.

References

ACDE (1998) *Preparing a Profession: National Standards and Guidelines for Initial Teacher Education*, Canberra: Australian Council of Deans of Education.

Ball, S. (ed.) (1990) *Foucault and Education: Disciplines and Knowledge*, London: Routledge.

Cassidy, T. (2000) 'Investigating the Pedagogical Process in Physical Education Teacher Education', unpublished doctoral thesis, Deakin University.

Collins, C. (2002) *Envisaging a New Education Studies Major: What are the Core Educational Knowledges to be Addressed in Preservice Teacher Education?* Available: http://scs.une.edu.au/CF/Papers/Collins.htm

Cruickshank, D. (1987) *Reflective Teaching: The Preparation of Student Teachers*, Reston, VA: Association of Teacher Educators.

Crum, B. (1995) 'The urgent need for reflective teaching in physical education', in C. Pare (ed.), *Training of Teachers in Reflective Practice of Physical Education*, Trois-Rivières, Quebec: Université du Quebec à Trois-Rivières.

Devis-Devis, J. and Sparkes, A. (1999) 'Burning the book: A biographical study of a pedagogically inspired identity crisis in physical education', *European Physical Education Review*, 5(2): 135–152.

Dewey, J. (1933) *How We Think: A Restatement of the Relation of Reflective Thinking to the Educative Process*, Chicago, IL: Henry Regnery Co.

Dodds, P. (1995) 'Reflective teacher education (RTS): Paradigm for professional growth or only smoke and mirrors?', in C. Pare (ed.), *Training of Teachers in Reflective Practice of Physical Education*, Trois-Rivières, Quebec: Université du Quebec à Trois-Rivières.

Doll, W. (1989) 'Foundations for a post-modern curriculum', *Journal of Curriculum Studies*, 21(3): 243–253.

Elliott, A. (2001) *Concepts of the Self*, Oxford: Polity Press.

Fendler, L. (1990) 'Making trouble: Prediction, agency and critical intellectuals', in T. Popkewitz and L. Fendler (eds), *Critical Theories in Education*, London: Routledge.

Fernández-Balboa, J.-M. (1995) 'Reclaiming physical education in higher education through critical pedagogy', *Quest*, 47: 91–114.

Foucault, M. (1977) *Discipline and Punish: The Birth of the Prison* (trans. A. Sheridan), Harmondsworth: Penguin.

General Teaching Council for England (2002) http://www.gtce.org.org.uk (28 April 2002).

Giddens, A. (1991) *Modernity and Self-identity*, Stanford, CA: Stanford University Press.

Goodson, I. (1988) *The Making of Curriculum*, London: Falmer Press.

Gore, J.M. (1990) 'Pedagogy as text in physical education teacher education: Beyond the preferred reading', in D. Kirk and R. Tinning (eds), *Physical Education, Curriculum and Culture: Critical Issues in the Contemporary Crisis*, Basingstoke: Falmer Press.

—— (1993) *The Struggle for Pedagogies: Critical and Feminist Discourses as Regimes of Truth*, New York: Routledge.

Grimmett, P. and Erickson, G. (1988) *Reflection in Teacher Education*, New York: Teachers College Press.

Grossman, P. (1992) 'Why models matter: an alternate view on professional growth in teaching', *Review of Educational Research*, 62(2): 171–179.

Habermas, J. (1972) *Knowledge and Human Interest*, London: Heinemann.

Hellison, D. and Templin, T. (1991) *A Reflective Approach to Teaching Physical Education*, Champaigne, IL: Human Kinetics.

Kemmis, S. (1985) 'Action research and the politics of reflection', in D. Boud, R. Keogh and D. Walker (eds), *Reflection: Turning Experience into Learning*, London: Kogan Page.

Kenway, J. (1992) 'Making "hope practical" rather than "despair convincing": some thoughts on the value of post-structuralism as a theory of and for feminist change in schools', paper presented to the Annual Women's Studies Conference: Sydney.

Kenworth Teather, E. (1999) *Embodied Geographies: Spaces, Bodies and Rites of Passage*, London: Routledge.

Kincheloe, J. and Steinberg, S. (1998) *Unauthorized Methods: Strategies for Critical Teaching*, New York: Routledge.

Kirk, D. (1986) 'A critical pedagogy for teacher education: Toward an inquiry-oriented approach', *Journal of Teaching in Physical Education*, 5(4): 230–246.

—— (1991) 'Languaging physical education teaching', paper presented to the AIESEP/ NAPEHE Convention, Atlanta, GA.

—— (1994) 'Making the present strange: sources of the current crisis in physical education', *Discourse*, 15(1): 46–63.

Lather, P. (1991) *Feminist Research in Education; Within/Against*, Geelong: Deakin University Press.

Lawson, H.A. (1984) 'Problem-setting for physical education and sport', *Quest*, 36: 48–60.

Lingard, R., Mills, M. and Hayes, D. (2000) 'Teachers, school reform and social justice: challenging research and practice', *Australian Educational Researcher*, 27(3): 93–109.

—— (2002) 'Developments in school-based management: the specific case of Queensland, Australia', *Journal of Educational Administration*, 40(1): 6–30.

Locke, L. (1977) 'Research on teaching in physical education: new hope for a dismal science', *Quest*, 28: 2–16.

Louis, K., Kruse, D. and Marks, H. (1996) 'Schoolwide professional community', in F. Newmann and Associates (eds), *Authentic Achievement Restructuring Schools for Intellectual Quality*, San Francisco: Jossey-Bass.

Lyotard, J. (1986) *The Postmodern Condition: A Report on Knowledge*, Manchester: Manchester University Press.

Macdonald, D. (1995) 'The role of proletarianization in physical education teacher attrition', *Research Quarterly for Exercise and Sport*, 66: 129–141.

—— (2003, in press) 'Curriculum change and the postmodern world: Is the school reform project an anachronism?' *Journal of Curriculum Studies*, 35(2).

Macdonald, D. and Beckett, L. (2002) 'A case for HPE professional teaching standards: A review of the arguments', *ACHPER Healthy Lifestyles Journal*, 3–4(173): 7–13.

Macdonald, D. and Brooker, R. (1999) 'Articulating a critical pedagogy in physical education teacher education', *Journal of Sport Pedagogy*, 5(1): 51–63.

Macdonald, D., Kirk, D., Metzler, M., Nilges, L., Schempp, P. and Wright, J. (2002) 'It's all very well, in theory: a review of theoretical perspectives and their applications in contemporary pedagogical research', *Quest*, 54(2): 133–156.

McLaren, P. (1998) 'Revolutionary pedagogy in post-revolutionary times: rethinking the political economy of critical education', *Educational Theory*, 48(4): 431–462.

Martinez, K. (1990) 'Critical reflections on critical reflection in teacher education', *Journal of Teaching Practice*, 10(2): 20–28.

NBPTS (1999) *Physical Education Standards*, Arlington, VA: National Board for Professional Teaching Standards.

—— (2000) *2000–2001 Guide to National Board Certification*, Southfield, MI: National Board for Professional Teaching Standards.

Newmann, F. and Associates (1996) *Authentic Achievement: Restructuring Schools for Intellectual Quality*, San Francisco: Jossey Bass.

O'Sullivan, M., Siedentop, D. and Locke, L. (1992) 'Toward collegiality: competing viewpoints among teacher educators', *Quest*, 22: 266–280.

Ovens, A. (2002) 'Discourse communities and the social construction of reflection in teacher education', paper presented to the HERDSA Annual Conference, Perth.

Popkewitz, T. and Brennan, M. (1998) *Foucault's Challenge: Discourse, Knowledge and Power in Education*, New York: Teachers College Press.

Postman, N. (1989) *Conscientious Objections: Stirring Up Trouble About Language, Technology and Education*, London: Heinemann.

Prain, V. and Hickey, C. (1995) 'Using discourse analysis to change physical education', *Quest*, 47(1): 76–90.

Rose, N. (1996) *Inventing Our Selves: Psychology, Power, and Personhood*, Cambridge: Cambridge University Press.

Scheurich, J. (1997) *Research Method in the Postmodern*, London: Falmer Press.

School of Education (eds) (2001) 'School reform longitudinal study: final report', Brisbane: The University of Queensland.

Siedentop, D. (1991) *Developing Teaching Skills in Physical Education*, Mountain View, CA: Mayfield Publishing.

Smart, B. (1992) *Modern Conditions, Postmodern Controversies*, London: Routledge.

Smyth, J. (1992) 'Teachers' work and the politics of reflection', *American Educational Research Journal*, 29(2): 267–300.

Smyth, J. (2001) 'What's happening to teachers' work', Landsdowne Lecture, 18 July, University of Victoria, British Columbia.

Smyth, J., Dow, A., Hattam, R., Reid, A. and Shacklock, G. (2000) *Teachers' Work in a Globalizing Economy*, London: Falmer.

Sparkes, A.C. (1991) *Curriculum Change and Physical Education – Towards a Micropolitical Understanding*, Geelong: Deakin University Press.

Sparkes, A. and M. Silvennoinen (eds) (1999) *Talking Bodies: Men's Narratives of the Body and Sport*, Jyvaskyla: SoPhi.

Tinning, R. (1987) *Improving Teaching in Physical Education*, Geelong: Deakin University Press.

—— (1991) 'Teacher education pedagogy: Dominant discourses and the process of problem solving', *Journal of Teaching in Physical Education*, 11: 1–20.

—— (1993) 'We have ways of making you think, or do we? Reflections on "training" in reflective teaching. Training of teachers in reflective practice of physical education', Trois-Rivières, Quebec: Université du Quebec à Trois-Rivières.

—— (1995) 'We have ways of making you think, or do we? Reflections on 'training' in reflective teaching', in C. Pare (ed.), *Training of Teachers in Reflective Practice of Physical Education*, Trois-Rivières, Quebec: Université du Quebec à Trois-Rivières.

Tinning, R. and Fitzclarence, L. (1992) 'Postmodern youth culture and the crisis in Australian secondary school physical education', *Quest*, 44: 287–304.

Tinning, R. and Glasby, P. (2002) 'Pedagogical work and the "cult of the body": Considering the role of HPE in the context of the "new public health" ', *Sport, Education and Society*, 7(2): 109–119.

Tinning, R., Macdonald, D., Wright, J. and Hickey, C. (2001) *Becoming a Physical Education Teacher: Contemporary and Enduring Issues*, Melbourne: Prentice Hall.

Tsangaridou, N. and O'Sullivan, M. (1997) 'The role of reflection in shaping physical education teachers' educational values and practices', *Journal of Teaching in Physical Education*, 17: 2–25.

Tsangaridou, N. and Siedentop, D. (1995) 'Reflective teaching: A literature review', *Quest*, 47: 212–237.

Usher, R. and Edwards, R. (1994) *Postmodernism and Education*, London: Routledge.

Van Manen, M. (1977) 'Linking ways of knowing with ways of being practical', *Curriculum Inquiry*, 6: 205–228.

Webb, L. (2001) 'Leadership in health and physical education: A case study of a female head of department', *ACHPER Healthy Lifestyles Journal*, 48(1): 14–18.

Young, M. (1998) *The Curriculum of the Future*, London: Falmer Press.

6 The pedagogy of motor skill learning

Teachers and students

Stephen Silverman

When I was asked to write this chapter I was not sure I was the best person to analyze the research that has been my professional focus for over two decades. I am invested in the concept that empirical research can answer questions about what helps students learn motor skills in physical education. I believe that having data that can serve as a basis for making informed decisions about teaching and learning in physical education is necessary if we are to grow as a profession. In addition, I believe that many issues in physical education should be discussed with more than just a gut feeling or with the view that something is correct because we have always done it that way or because the way we have always done it has not worked so this way must be better. I definitely believe that research has the potential to influence practice and help practitioners make decisions (Locke *et al.* 1998).

As I reflected further I realized that there are other things I believe about the research I do. First, I think we should be very cautious about making prescriptions for practice based on a single study. Second, I think that we must consider context when thinking about the application of results to professional practice. Third, I believe we should acknowledge that different questions demand different research methods to answer them and that there is not just one way to do research (Locke *et al.* 2000). And, further, I think that as a profession we have, at times, been somewhat intolerant about how others answer their questions and do their work (e.g. see Schempp 1987; Siedentop 1987). We have taken pot shots at each other based on the paradigms we use for our research when, in fact, we as a community of practice (Pallas 2001) should celebrate the successes of others based on our mutual desires to better understand physical education.

So I accepted the task of writing this chapter. My purpose is to examine the research on teaching in physical education (RT-PE) and to celebrate the successes and discuss the aspects that were less successful. As the editor of this volume directed, I will use a critical lens to discuss both the research and those who have critiqued it. In order to accomplish this I will: (a) provide a little background on the evolution of RT-PE; (b) discuss the misconceptions about the methodology of RT-PE; (c) discuss the problems with some of the RT-PE research; (d) review what we have learned and what is less clear about RT-PE; (e) discuss how my own program of research has evolved in response to what we have learned;

and (f) provide some ideas for where I think we should be heading in the future. Throughout these sections I will provide my own perspective of each of these issues, while, I hope, at the same time acknowledging that others may disagree with that perspective.

Background on RT-PE

For this chapter, as I have in similar ways in other places (Silverman 1987; Silverman and Skonie 1997; Silverman and Ennis in press; Silverman and Manson 2003), I am defining RT-PE as research on the processes, social dynamics, and outcomes (motor skill, attitude, social responsibility, and physical activity and fitness) of physical education. This would include, among other things, research that examines how teachers teach physical education, what students do in class, what teacher and student processes are related to student achievement, the effect of different teaching methods on student processes or achievement, and research on student attitudes and perceptions about physical education. Since most of my research has utilized quantitative research methods and that was the editor's intended focus for this chapter, most of what follows focuses on quantitative RT-PE.

For decades people have been doing RT-PE – or at least thinking that is what they were doing. As Locke (1977; Nixon and Locke 1973) has noted RT-PE is rooted in motor learning research. Much of the motor learning research asks similar questions as RT-PE research, but the context is so different that it is not logical to apply it directly to a teaching situation. For example, feedback has been found to influence learning in motor learning studies (Magill 1993), but RT-PE has not found that feedback influences learning in any appreciable or direct way (Lee *et al.* 1993; Silverman *et al.* 1992). There has been a good deal of discussion of why motor learning research and RT-PE research may produce different results (e.g. see Magill 1994; Silverman *et al.* 1994). In attempting to extend motor learning research to the gymnasium, Magill (1994) has suggested that the skill being taught and the type of feedback provided may influence whether feedback helps learning. I believe, however, that it is hard to make prescriptions to practice from research that occurs in laboratories with one college-aged subject who is delivered a treatment and monitored by computer to teachers teaching younger students of varying skill – and 30 or more at a time – in a less controlled environment (Silverman *et al.* 1994). Motor learning research certainly has informed my research and has great value, but it is not RT-PE. The differences are too profound to suggest immediate application.

In the 1970s (Lee 2003), research in physical education moved from motor learning laboratories to research in gymnasiums, natatoriums, and on fields. Those doing this research examined students and teachers and primarily focused on motor skill. This research has evolved from descriptions of physical education to studies looking at complex relationships between teacher and student processes and achievement. It is this research upon which I will focus in the remainder of this chapter. As I will note later some of the research has provided information for teachers to consider when planning instruction and other research, because of design issues or the questions that were asked, has been less helpful and may, in fact, provide erroneous conclusions. For example, Behets (1997) found that teachers who were more effective provided more feedback. They also provided more time for practice and a conclusion about feedback without controlling for time may mislead those who might use the results in their instructional decision making.

In the next two sections I will deal with general issues related to RT-PE. The first section, misconceptions about quantitative RT-PE, focuses on misconceptions I believe some accept about quantitative RT-PE – and perhaps quantitative research in general. My focus is on a perspective of RT-PE research that I perceive as negative and which I believe is a caricature of RT-PE research and researchers. The second section, concerns about quantitative RT-PE, focuses on legitimate problems with RT-PE that complicates what faith we can place in the results and whether the research is of any value at all.

Misconceptions about quantitative RT-PE

As the area of sport pedagogy has evolved we have expanded the areas and the foci of research. Where once virtually all sport pedagogy research focused on teaching and used quantitative methods (Lee 2003), there is now research that focuses on teacher education and curriculum and a variety of methods are used (Silverman and Ennis in press). As this evolution has occurred some have seen fit to denigrate quantitative research on teaching (see Gage 1989 for a discussion in education), perhaps in an attempt to raise what they do to a higher status. While some of this discussion has been very public (e.g. Schempp 1987; Siedentop 1987; McKay *et al.* 1990; O'Sullivan *et al.* 1992), most has not and has occurred during presentations at conferences or around the table over a drink afterwards.

I will focus here on three misconceptions that I believe influence how some perceive RT-PE. These issues are (a) restrictions in quantitative research, (b) the role of the researcher in quantitative methods, and (c) what we can learn from quantitative research. Since these represent my perceptions of discussions that have occurred where citations are not possible, this selection will reflect my views.

Restrictions in quantitative research

In my view many perceive quantitative research as consisting of a rigid, inflexible set of rules that all researchers must follow in designing and analyzing their research. While I acknowledge that, as in other forms of research, there clearly are accepted guidelines and preferred ways of doing things (Locke *et al.* 1998, 2000), and that some presentations of quantitative research in our field reinforce this notion (Chen and Zhu 2001), it really is not that simple.

Good quantitative researchers do not design their research using a step-by-step formula. There is much creativity in this research. Instead of thinking of it as a formula, a better way might be to consider it to be similar to what happens when an experienced cook uses a recipe. The experienced cook has a goal, creates a dish making adjustments to his or her taste and that of the others who will share the meal, and then presents the product to others. In quantitative research there are many adjustments that are made and instances where creativity and the good sense of the researcher are more important than some simplistic formula. The researcher must decide how to ask questions: how to change and modify methods during pilot studies, the trade-offs in recruiting participants in school settings, how to best analyze the data in a way that is parsimonious and that the results are meaningful and do not violate statistical assumptions, and how to present and discuss the results so that readers understand what was found and what it means without going beyond the data. While, like me, I suspect many quantitative RT-PE researchers have guidelines, a great deal of creativity occurs during the process of designing, conducting, and reporting research (Locke *et al.* 1998).

The role of the researcher in quantitative research

At meetings when discussions occur, I believe people impute upon quantitative RT-PE researchers qualities that are stereotypes at best and simplistic thinking at worst. At one reception during an American Educational Research Association meeting a member of the sport pedagogy community said to me: 'You're not at all what I expected you to be. I figured someone who does the research you do would see the world in a way that I didn't.' As we talked further the person told me that because I do quantitative research it was assumed that I saw the world in black and white with no shades of gray. Some discussions of method in our field may imply that – by making quantitative research and quantitative researchers appear to be unidimensional. As the person and I were talking I thought of the nerdy researcher proposing hypotheses and chasing facts. Like Kerlinger (1973) I do not believe this is true and in fact have gone on record in a public forum (Silverman and Solmon 2001) suggesting quantitative researchers can be nice people! For many of us who have sustained a long-term program of research, and I will discuss my own research later, our focus changes and grows and the research can be put in perspective. It is not reasonable, in my opinion, to believe that quantitative researchers test hypotheses and believe there are direct and clear implications for our understanding or practice in physical education.

What we can learn from quantitative research

Related to the topic above is the issue of what can we learn from quantitative RT-PE. It is unreasonable for quantitative researchers and others to expect that any individual study will provide results that tell us everything we need to know about how learning occurs in physical education. In fact, it is not appropriate to make the assumption that quantitative researchers expect that non-replicated, individual studies tell us more than what occurred in this setting. As Cronbach (1976) noted some years ago, and it is true today, an individual study tells us what occurred in this setting, at this time, with these children. Much replication in a variety of contexts is needed before anyone should be certain what impacts learning. In fact, the physical education setting, the teacher, the students, and how the study was conducted demands that context be a part of interpreting results and those who do not, or who assume it does not matter to quantitative researchers, are making a large mistake about what we can learn from any study. The concepts of quantitative research we learned about (e.g. true experiments and generalizability) in science classes and in research methods classes rarely if ever happen in RT-PE research. Each study is just a sample of what occurs and we should not believe that there is more there than there really is.

Concerns about quantitative RT-PE

While in the previous section I suggested that there are misconceptions in the way many perceive quantitative RT-PE, I also believe there are concerns or problems that must be addressed. These concerns clearly impact the quality of RT-PE. I believe there is great creativity in RT-PE research. I also think there are some aspects of research design, analysis, and reporting that are troubling because researchers are not considering the literature that discusses these issues and notes where we have problems. Some of the decisions researchers make are based on expediency and cause good ideas to result in poor research from which we should be very cautious in designing other studies or making prescriptions for practice. I will discuss three of the issues here that I think are especially problematic in RT-PE. These issues revolve around (a) the use of experiments and the investigation of teaching methods, (b) how we analyze data, and (c) overextending what we learned from a study.

Experiments and teaching methods research

The literature (e.g. see Silverman 1983, 1985a; Silverman and Solmon 1998 for discussions) suggests that doing research that compares the efficacy of one teaching method against another for student motor learning is fraught with problems. In the minds of many, these studies, because they are experiments or quasi-experiments, are likely to yield the most valid conclusions. The problem, however, is that it is difficult to do good experimental studies. Unless we acknowledge that, we will continue to waste time doing this research and without adding to what we know about teaching physical education. I do not mean to imply that good experimental research is impossible, just that it is very difficult. The research of Thom McKenzie and his colleagues (see McKenzie 2003, for a review) on physical activity and physical education clearly indicates quality research is possible and can add a tremendous amount to the knowledge of our field.

Most experimental research in physical education does not have the resources, time, or sustained track record of McKenzie. Typical of many experimental studies in physical education is one where the researcher has participants in two classes and has one teacher teach using a new method and the second teacher teach using a 'traditional method.' At the end of the intervention learning by each group is compared. These are not good experiments since the teachers are probably providing a weak treatment (the teaching method) and it is at least as likely that the individual teacher is the reason for any differences as it is the treatment. Despite the problems with a small number of teachers and classes, limited training to implement the method, and verifying that the method actually was implemented as intended, there are still many studies that compare teaching methods (Silverman 1987; Silverman and Manson 2003; Silverman and Skonie 1997). Although there are many of these studies, their volume should not overwhelm the inherent problems with the research.

Analyzing data

Similarly, many researchers conduct RT-PE studies where the analysis is not appropriate. Some of this occurs because while designing the study the researcher did not consider what the appropriate unit of analysis should be (e.g. class or student, see Silverman and Solmon 1998 for an in-depth discussion) and therefore had insufficient classes or participants to do any meaningful analysis. Or, in other cases, the researcher uses analyses that others suggest or that they believe are more rigorous. Often in these cases the analysis is not suited to answer the question and an attempt at statistical rigor produces results that may or may not be correct. While I believe that Chen and Zhu (2001) provide us with guidelines that are far too restrictive, I also believe that many RT-PE results are clouded by the analysis.

Overextending the conclusions

Before looking at RT-PE results, one other issue needs to be addressed. That issue is when researchers overextend the conclusions that can be made from their study. As was discussed above, context is an important issue. Taking one study and providing teachers or teacher educators with 'should' statements about practice, without any qualification, does not consider the context and may send others to try methods that have no possibility of success.

I was reminded of the implications of this at a recent professional meeting. A newly minted doctoral graduate had just concluded a presentation where part of her dissertation was presented. When she was finished someone in the audience asked whether the result suggested that teachers should consistently do something in a certain way. The presenter responded affirmatively. It would have been much better if the response had been something like: 'It depends on how much your situation – grade level, setting, resources, and what has occurred previously in physical education – is like the one I described. Also, remember that this is one study and just provides some inkling as to what may help students learn.' Without considering the context, researchers extend the conclusion too far (Locke *et al.* 1998). As my doctoral students who teach in New York City remind those who teach in areas with larger gyms and smaller classes: 'This is great, but there is no way it applies to my school and my students. We'll never have the gym space or resources to try these things!' We should be very careful in saying what works in physical education because situations are so different.

Wanting to over generalize results may be a natural reaction. Researchers in pedagogy often come to their research with strong backgrounds as practitioners. As teachers, we want to try to provide solutions that can help others improve their practice. As researchers, we want our research to be meaningful to more than a few other researchers. While wanting to generalize and help improve the field is a noble pursuit, it is unlikely that broad generalizations will be appropriate from a single study.

What we have learned from quantitative RT-PE

Although I acknowledge the difficulties in doing RT-PE research and that there is a body of research of which we should be suspicious, I also believe we have learned a great deal. The results of RT-PE provide a basis for understanding student learning and for teaching motor skill in physical education classes. In this section I will not duplicate extensive reviews of the literature (e.g. Rink 2003). I will present three examples of conclusions from the RT-PE literature in which I believe we can have faith. While there may be other results that are important, space permits only a few and I have included those I think are most important and permit me to emphasize particular aspects of research. These results are: (a) time is important, but practice is more important; (b) content development is the key to good practice; and (c) teacher feedback may not play the role in student motor skill learning that we once thought.

Time is important, but practice is more important

Like the field of education, RT-PE began looking at those teacher-controlled factors that influence learning (Lee 2003). Based on the process–product model of classroom learning posited by Dunkin and Biddle (1974), the assumption was that teachers do things that impact student learning. This model often made the assumption that teachers design lessons and implement them, students do as they are told, and then learning occurs. Many believed that this downplayed the role of the student. Doyle (1983) suggested that students mediate what teachers tell and expect them to do and that studying educational processes without studying the student will only tell us so much.

In RT-PE the role of time and practice emphasize why students are important. There was a tremendous amount of research on time usage and its effects in physical education (for reviews see Lee and Poto 1988; Metzler 1989). We learned that generally the more time devoted to motor skill learning the more students learned, but that some components of time that were presumed to facilitate learning had the opposite effect (Silverman *et al.* 1988). For example in that 1988 study, skill practice enhanced learning but time spent in scrimmage was negatively correlated with learning. Time is important, but all time devoted to learning is not the same.

The research on time led to a focus on research on individual student practice. Appropriate student practice (Piéron 1983; Dugas 1984; Silverman 1985b, 1990; Ashy *et al.* 1988; Buck *et al.* 1991) is correlated with student learning – and this is perhaps the strongest finding from the RT-PE literature. By changing our focus to students we learned that class level variables (time and organization) are mediated by what individual students do and that there may be wide variations in what they do. In addition, we learned that some practice, that which is too hard or too easy for the individual student, is counterproductive to learning (Silverman 1990). Changing the focus from time to practice permitted a far greater understanding of how children learn in physical education.

Content development is the key to good practice

Judy Rink and her colleagues (French *et al.* 1991; French *et al.* 1990; Rink 1994, 2003; Rink *et al.* 1992) have done extensive research examining how teachers communicate with children and how they structure learning tasks, i.e. what students do to learn motor skill. Rink (2002) has proposed a variety of teaching tasks (i.e. informing, extension, refinement, application, and repeat) that provide a framework for moving students from simple tasks to those that are more complex and more like actual games. Her research supports the notion that teachers who consider student performance and design the next task based on that performance, can enhance the appropriate practice students engage in and the learning that occurs. This research is powerful in supporting the notion that there is not just one way to do things, but teachers who select tasks based on a lot of information can help students learn. Rink (2001) suggested that the selection of the learning task may be one of the most important things a teacher does. I believe that is not an overstatement.

Teacher feedback may not play the role in student motor skill learning that we once thought

In the section of this chapter that provided definitions and discussed the evolution of RT-PE, I pointed out that research on teacher feedback in physical education did not turn out as might be expected. It differs from results in motor learning laboratories and what teacher educators once believed, that teacher feedback is important for learning. It appears from many studies (see Lee *et al.* 1993 for a review) that the evidence does not suggest a relationship between feedback and motor skill learning in physical education.

The analysis of the feedback literature is complex. For example, my colleagues and I (Silverman *et al.* 1992) found that certain types of feedback contributed to the variance in learning, but only about 2% of that variance. While comparisons of more and less effective teachers suggest more effective teachers provide more feedback (e.g. Behets 1997) they also provide more practice time and other research has demonstrated a relationship between time devoted to practice and the amount of feedback teachers provide (Silverman *et al.* 1998). While Graber (2001) has suggested that these results do not provide any clarity about feedback and achievement, I believe the opposite is true. She is correct that the overwhelming volume of research has not shown meaningful relationships between feedback and achievement. These results only lack clarity if we assume there is a strong relationship. It is likely that long-held beliefs of the role of feedback in skill learning in physical education are probably wrong. If we consider that research has taken place in many studies and that there are relatively consistent results, that the studies have been conducted with different students, teachers, and settings, and that those studies suggesting a strong relationship may not have controlled for other important variables, such as practice time, then perhaps it is clear. What we thought was occurring is not. That is as important to understand as is getting a verification of what we thought should happen.

The evolution of a research program

Part of taking on the assignment of writing this chapter was to examine my own research program. I will do this by presenting the several phases of my research and those things that I have learned about doing research from having completed various studies. In many ways, my research mirrors the evolution of RT-PE, and in some ways my main body of research has been more tightly focused than others might think prudent. I cite studies below from my RT-PE that focused on processes and achievement in physical education. It is important to understand that additional research was conducted to determine the validity of research methods (e.g. Silverman and Zotos 1987). Without this type of research, other studies would not have been possible.

Like many of our colleagues in sport pedagogy I went to graduate schools with an idea of what I wanted to study. As a physical educator, I wanted to know what made teachers effective in teaching motor skill. At the time I thought that was the question. Now, as I have learned more and have worked as a researcher in the field for over two decades, I realize that my original questions were much too simplistic and that had I focused solely on the teacher, while still assuming teachers had a direct effect on learning, I would not have learned much.

I was very fortunate to begin my doctoral studies by being able to participate in research with strong faculty members and other graduate students (Placek *et al.* 1982; Shute *et al.* 1982; Silverman *et al.* 1984). These and other descriptive RT-PE studies told us a lot about what was happening in physical education. However, they made assumptions about good teaching based on the classroom literature and on what was commonly believed to be effective teaching. Many of the conclusions about effective teaching in the reports of descriptive research in physical education were not influenced by research evidence – there was little in physical education – and the context and students participating in the research often were not considered. My colleagues and I were among the first to look at student characteristics in descriptive research (e.g. special needs status and sex) but we were missing other, perhaps more important, characteristics that needed to be considered in order to more fully understand what was occurring in these classes.

As we were conducting these descriptive studies, I began to think about my dissertation research. I wanted to study what occurred in a physical education class and how that impacted motor skill learning. I had been influenced by our descriptive work and by process–product research in physical education and in education. In addition, I had been thinking about the work of Cronbach and Snow (1981) that supported the notion that stable student characteristics such as aptitude might mediate the teaching treatments to which they were exposed. My initial explorations in the early 1980s have led to at least three research phases. These phases are presented diagrammatically in Figure 6.1. The solid arrows indicate studying a direct relationship between or among variables. For example, in the first phase at the top of the figure, the direct relationship between practice and skill learning was investigated. You will note that all of the arrows go both ways, suggesting that it is not a one-way effect but a two-way relationship. For example, in all three phases student characteristics, in most cases student skill level, are affected by instruction and the student characteristics, in turn, mediate the instruction. Finally, the broken arrows in the last phase denote studying an indirect effect and making an assumption based on previous research. In this case, for example, we have strong evidence that appropriate practice influences learning so practice can serve as a proxy for learning.

The first major phase of my research involved looking at the relationships between what teachers plan and do in class, how students spent their time, and student skill learning. As indicated on the right side of Figure 6.1, the mediating effect of student characteristics on the relationships being studied was a part of this work and, in a somewhat restricted form, all of my research. Initially I focused on how students spent time in practice (Silverman 1985b). We learned there was a relationship between practice time and achievement in these college swimming classes and that the relationship was different based on skill level. The time–achievement relationships were moderate and this suggested that the way in which we had been measuring student engagement (i.e. time) might have lacked precision. In the same report (Silverman 1985b) a follow-up study demonstrated that appropriate individual student practice was positively correlated with achievement and that skill level mediated these relationships. It was clear that how we conceived student practice and who the students were (Silverman 1985c) affected the results and conclusions.

As a part of this research phase it became quite clear that, while I was learning both about teaching effectiveness and how to do research in field settings that considering individual variables only provided one level of information. We were learning about practice and achievement, but what about teachers' time use, accountability, teacher communication and feedback, and a whole array of other variables. Many things occur in physical education classes and they do not occur in isolation. Doyle's work (1983; Doyle and Carter 1984) suggested teachers and students react to each other during instruction and that it goes both ways. Doing research that considered the interactions among student and teacher variables and achievement clearly would provide a more sophisticated – and accurate – understanding of what influenced learning.

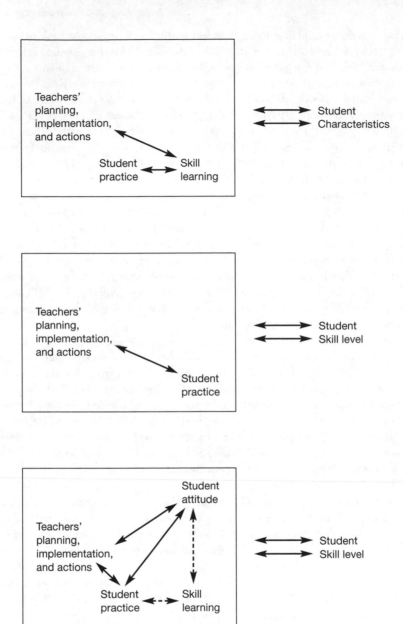

Figure 6.1 The various phases of Silverman's research program

To address these issues I created a large databank of physical education classes on videotape. This research occurred with middle school teachers and students as participants and focused on skill learning in volleyball. The databank included videotapes of all instruction and pre-test and post-test scores for the two skills that were taught. This large-scale effort was designed so that each study could be informed by the previous study and that data could be combined across studies to examine the interactions that might occur.

A number of research reports came out of this databank. Among the variables my colleagues and I studied were teachers' time use (Silverman *et al.* 1988), practice (Silverman 1990), accountability (Silverman *et al.* 1995), feedback and its interaction with practice (Silverman *et al.* 1992) and how student skill level interacted with process variables in predicting achievement (Silverman 1993; Silverman *et al.* 1993). We learned a lot about teaching physical education and those variables that influence student learning.

I believe I learned additional things too. For example, it became clear that RT-PE benefits from replication. These studies indicated that the relationship of practice with achievement was robust and occurred across age groups and types of skill. It also was clear that studies that ignored student skill level would provide only a limited view of what was occurring. In addition, we learned that sometimes what we think is happening during class cannot be supported by data (i.e. a simple relationship between teacher feedback and student achievement, or that more practice is good, no matter what type of practice). Finally, we learned the importance of considering that the interactions of many variables is necessary to understand just some of the nuances that take place during instruction. We do not get even a remotely complete picture of teaching and learning without aiming our lens in a number of different directions.

I would like to be able to say that each of the things presented in the previous paragraph was clear from the start. They were not. For example, I was convinced that the reason previous studies had not found a relationship between teacher feedback and achievement was because they were not strong studies. In my opinion we were designing a study that would be rigorous by collecting very specific information on teacher feedback with a large sample size across a number of classes. As you may have guessed from the previous discussion, we did not find the relationship despite the strength of our study. No matter how often we lamented that our statistical power was very strong, the relationships we initially hypothesized did not emerge. Sometimes we do not find what has become traditional wisdom because the traditional wisdom is wrong.

These studies presented a pretty good indication of what teacher and student process variables influence student achievement. From a number of the analyses, other variables influenced achievement indirectly through appropriate student practice. The question in the next phase of the research was what do teachers do that has an effect on the quantity and quality of student practice (represented in the middle panel of Figure 6.1). What we had learned in previous studies and from the work of Rink and her colleagues suggested that teachers made decisions before and during class that influenced practice and that the way teachers did this may depend on a number of factors.

To address these questions another videotape databank was created. This databank differed from the previous one, in that a number of activities were represented and that pre-test and post-test data were not collected. We were concerned with the relationships of teacher variables and practice. Process data were collected with an instrument that permitted us to tie each aspect of practice and feedback to the task and teaching strategy used by the teacher. Because the research was based on the premise that students and teachers influence each other, tying together all aspects of our study was necessary. The reports from this research phase (Silverman *et al.* 1988; Silverman *et al.* 1998; Silverman *et al.* 1999) suggest, among others, that the way teachers structure and modify instruction influences student practice and, that again, student skill level is important in interpreting results. The role of the teacher in designing instruction was important in these classes. For example, when teachers structured practice so that students practiced individually (e.g. each student had his or her own piece of equipment) instead of having students in groups waiting in lines, students received more practice. In addition, students' practice was appropriate practice because the teacher could extend or refine the task on an individual basis.

Reflections on my research up to this point lead to the next phase, the one in which I am currently pursuing, and which is presented in the bottom panel of Figure 6.1. I was fortunate to have a graduate student, Raj Subramaniam, with similar interests in teaching processes. What became evident, based on the literature on motivation (see Chen 2001, and Solmon 2003, for reviews) and student attitude (see Silverman and Subramaniam 1999 for a review) and our discussions, was that the focus on motor skill only addressed one aspect of learning in physical education. This caused us to be concerned that if students develop skill, but do not develop good attitudes they may never care to use the skill. There, again, looking at physical education from one direction probably is not providing a detailed understanding of what happens in gymnasia.

We have validated an instrument that measures attitude in complex ways that is based on attitude theory (Subramaniam and Silverman 2000a), collected interview data that provides student perspectives on their attitudes (Subramaniam and Silverman 2002), and learned more about how student variables influence attitude (Subramaniam and Silverman 2000b). Our next step is to create another multi-faceted databank to examine the interaction of student and teacher process variables, student skill level, and student attitude.

As in my other research the unexpected findings of our initial attitude research is as important as those we expected to find. For example, in validating the attitude instrument we found that the students provided strong guidance in designing items and that no matter how much we wanted to think like them a PhD student and his professor thought differently than middle school students. When the data were collected, the teacher and curriculum, two of the hypothesized factors, were found to be aspects of both the affect and knowledge components of attitude and these are consistent with discussions of student attitude in physical education. We also found that although peers were a factor in most discussions, the psychometric data did not bear this out, no matter how many times the instrument was revised and tested (Subramaniam and Silverman 2000a). Again, sometimes we have to change and adjust our perceptions and research direction to be consistent with what actually is occurring in physical education

My intent in the discussion of my own research was to demonstrate that RT-PE moves forward when researchers adjust their perceptions, think about physical education from a number of perspectives, and do not ignore the many variables that may complicate things. It would be great for me to be able to provide simple black and white prescriptions to teachers about motor skill acquisition in physical education. The simple black and white picture would not be accurate and provide far less detail than a finely focused color picture. The details matter, and simple explanations may work for some students in some settings, but probably do not work for many students in other settings.

The future of RT-PE

By conducting RT-PE research over the last 30 years we have learned a great deal about student and teacher processes in physical education and what promotes student learning. We have results that we can safely say permit us to make general statements about effective teaching and learning in physical education. For example, I believe it is quite safe to say that a student who gets more appropriate practice will learn more than if he or she got less appropriate practice. The problem, however, in statements such as these is that how appropriate practice is increased requires the teacher to make many decisions and to tailor these decisions to the setting and students. We have some guidelines, but there still is much to learn.

In order to move forward, I believe there are a number of research areas that will bear fruit. It will come as no surprise if you have read the rest of the chapter, that I believe we must look at multiple process variables and how they interact with each. While single studies can provide some information, studies that acknowledge the multidimensional nature of teaching and learning are likely to be more productive. To do this, researchers need to have a program of research and to focus on the long-term benefits from doing this.

If we want students to learn skill and move toward a physically active lifestyle, the focus of our research needs to go beyond motor skill. RT-PE research has addressed physical activity and fitness, but there is still much to learn about that outcome. Although we know a little about attitude (Silverman and Subramaniam 1999; Subramaniam and Silverman 2000a, 2000b) and motivation (Chen 2001; Solmon 2003) in physical education, investigating these topics will give us greater insight into how students feel and perceive physical education, how physical education influences their desire to participate in physical education and other physical activity, and how student motivation affects participation. Combining attitude and motivation research with research on motor skill and physical activity will permit us to investigate the interaction of these factors, which is what happens in physical education classes.

Teacher and student cognition is an area in which further research is merited and is needed. There is an emerging body of research on student thinking in physical education (for reviews see Lee 1997; Lee and Solmon 1992). Since students mediate teachers' instruction and intents, understanding student thought processes is essential in order for us to get a full picture of what is occurring. While I believe we will need to contextualize this research and consider many variables (e.g. the physical education program the student has gone through, the age of the student, student skill level, attitude and motivation, and the school and neighborhood environment) insight into what students are thinking will help us understand what is needed for teachers to prepare and adjust lessons that are receptive to students' needs.

While there is less research on teacher cognition in physical education, there are some examples (e.g. Housner and Griffey 1985). This research gives insight into what teachers do while planning and delivering instruction. If we can get a better understanding of what successful teachers do, that may provide a basis from which to help others make decisions. I suspect based on the literature that is available, that good teachers think through changes they will need to make based on student responses before entering the gymnasium to start the lesson. They likely have a repertoire of responses to change tasks and motivate students and learn which works in which situations with which students. Having more information on how teachers and students respond to each other in various situations will tell us much about the teaching–learning process.

In order to conduct research on motivation, attitude and cognition, I believe physical educators need to work together by combining research methods. For example, in attitude research both quantitative and qualitative studies provide a wealth of knowledge (Silverman and Subramaniam 1999). In the work I have done with Raj Subramaniam on student attitude it is apparent that quantitative (Subramaniam and Silverman 2000a) and qualitative (Subramaniam and Silverman in press) data complement each other and the richness of what we learn is greatly enhanced by combining methodologies. Each type of research allows us to explore different questions and, as a result, we learn a great deal more by working together and learning to do research from more that one approach.

Finally, I need to return to what I stated earlier and what has been a central theme throughout this chapter. In any research – and on the applications to practice – context is extremely important. If we want to learn more about teaching and learning in physical education, we must consider who the students are and the instructional setting. Attempting to put all students and physical education environments into a single pile obscures the diversity and uniqueness of teachers and students. Only when we consider the context and build our knowledge by progressive research programs, which consider more than single aspects of instruction, will we have a chance to better understand instruction in physical education.

References

Ashy, M.H., Lee, A.M. and Landin, D.K. (1988) 'Relationships of practice using correct technique to achievement in a motor skill', *Journal of Teaching in Physical Education*, 7: 115–120.

Behets, D. (1997) 'Comparison of more and less effective teaching behaviors in secondary physical education', *Teaching and Teacher Education*, 13: 215–224.

Buck, M., Harrison, J.M. and Bryce, G.R. (1991) 'An analysis of learning trials and their relationship to achievement in volleyball', *Journal of Teaching in Physical Education*, 10: 134–152.

Chen, A. (2001) 'A theoretical conceptualization for motivation research in physical education: an integrated perspective', *Quest*, 53: 35–58.

Chen, A. and Zhu, W.M. (2001) 'Revisiting the assumptions for inferential statistical analyses: A conceptual guide', *Quest*, 53: 418–439.

Cronbach, L.J. (1976) 'Research on classrooms and schools: formulation of questions, design, and analysis', Stanford, CA: Stanford Evaluation Consortium, School of Education, Stanford University.

Cronbach, L.J. and Snow, R.E. (1981) *Aptitudes and Instructional Methods*, New York: Irvington.

Doyle, W. (1983) 'Academic work', *Review of Educational Research*, 53: 159–199.

Doyle, W. and Carter, K. (1984) 'Academic tasks in classrooms', *Curriculum Inquiry*, 14: 129–149.

Dugas, D.M. (1984) 'Relationships among process and product variables in an experimental teaching unit', *Dissertation Abstracts International*, 44: 2709A (University Microfilms No. 84-00, 193).

Dunkin, M.J. and Biddle, B.J. (1974) *The Study of Teaching*, New York: Holt, Rinehart and Winston.

French, K., Rink, J., Rikard, L., Mays, A., Lynn, S. and Werner, P. (1991) 'The effects of practice progressions on learning two volleyball skills', *Journal of Teaching in Physical Education*, 10: 261–275.

French, K.E., Rink, J.E. and Werner, P.H. (1990) 'Effects of contextual interference on retention of three volleyball skills', *Perceptual and Motor Skills*, 71: 179–186.

Gage, N. (1989) 'The paradigm wars and their aftermath: a "historical" sketch of research on teaching since 1989', *Educational Researcher*, 18(7): 4–10.

Graber, K.C. (2001) 'Research on teaching in physical education', in V. Richardson (ed.), *Handbook of Research on Teaching*, Washington, DC: American Educational Research Association, 4th edn, 491–519.

Housner, L. and Griffey, D. (1985) 'Teacher cognition: differences in planning and interactive decision making between experienced and inexperienced teachers', *Research Quarterly for Exercise and Sport*, 56: 45–55.

Kerlinger, F.N. (1973) *Foundations of Behavioral Research*, New York: Holt, Rinehart and Winston, 2nd edn.

Lee, A.M. (1997) 'Contributions of research on student thinking in physical education', *Journal of Teaching in Physical Education*, 16: 262–277.

—— (2003) 'How the field evolved', in S.J. Silverman and C.D. Ennis (eds), *Student Learning in Physical Education: Applying Research to Enhance Instruction*, Champaigne, IL: Human Kinetics, 2nd edn.

Lee, A.M., Keh, N.C. and Magill, R.A. (1993) 'Instructional effects of teacher feedback in physical education', *Journal of Teaching in Physical Education*, 12: 228–243.

Lee, A.M. and Poto, C. (1988) 'Instructional time research in physical education: contributions and current issues', *Quest*, 40: 63–73.

Lee, A.M. and Solmon, M.A. (1992) 'Cognitive conceptions of teaching and learning motor skills', *Quest*, 44: 57–71.

Locke, L.F. (1977) 'Research on teaching physical education: new hope for a dismal science', *Quest*, 28, 2–16.

Locke, L.F., Silverman, S.J. and Spirduso, W.W. (1998) *Reading and Understanding Research*, Thousand Oaks, CA: Sage.

Locke, L.F., Spirduso, W.W. and Silverman, S.J. (2000) *Proposals That Work: A Guide for Planning Dissertations and Grant Proposals*, Thousand Oaks, CA: Sage, 4th edn.

Magill, R. (1993) 'Augmented feedback in skill acquisition.', in R.N. Singer, M. Murphey and L.K. Temant (eds), *Handbook of Research on Sport Psychology*, New York: Macmillian, 193–212.

Magill, R.A. (1994) 'The influence of augmented feedback on skill learning depends on characteristics of the skill and the learner', *Quest*, 46: 314–327.

McKay, J., Gore, J. and Kirk, D. (1990) 'Beyond the limits of technocratic physical education', *Quest*, 42: 52–76.

McKenzie, T. (2003) 'Health-related physical education: physical activity, fitness, and wellness', in S.J. Silverman and C.D. Ennis (eds), *Student Learning in Physical Education: Applying Research to Enhance Instruction*, Champaigne, IL: Human Kinetics, 2nd edn.

Metzler, M. (1989) 'A review of research on time in sport pedagogy', *Journal of Teaching in Physical Education*, 8: 87–103.

Nixon, J.E. and Locke, L.F. (1973) 'Research on teaching in physical education', in M.W. Travers (ed.), *Second Handbook of Research on Teaching*, Chicago: Rand McNally, 1210–1242.

O'Sullivan, M., Siedentop, D. and Locke, L.F. (1992) 'Toward collegiality: competing viewpoints among teacher educators', *Quest*, 44: 266–280.

Pallas, A. (2001) 'Preparing education doctoral students for epistemological diversity', *Educational Researcher*, 30(5): 6–11.

Piéron, M. (1983) 'Teacher and pupil behavior and the interaction process in p.e. classes', in R. Telama, V. Varstala, J. Tiainen, L. Laakso and T. Haajanen (eds), *Research in School Physical Education*, Jyväskylä, Finland: Foundation for the Promotion of Physical Culture and Health, 193–202.

Placek, J., Silverman, S., Dodds, P., Shute, S. and Rife, R. (1982) 'Active learning time in a traditional elementary physical education setting: a descriptive analysis', *Journal of Classroom Interaction*, 17(2): 41–47.

Rink, J.E. (1994) 'Task presentation in pedagogy', *Quest*, 46: 270–280.

—— (2001) 'Investigating the assumptions of pedagogy', *Journal of Teaching in Physical Education*, 20: 112–128.

—— (2002) *Teaching Physical Education for Learning*, New York: McGraw-Hill, 4th edn.

—— (2003) 'Effective instruction in physical education', in S.J. Silverman and C.D. Ennis (eds), *Student Learning in Physical Education: Applying Research to Enhance Instruction*, Champaigne, IL: Human Kinetics, 2nd edn.

Rink, J., French, K., Werner, P., Lynn, S. and Mays, A. (1992) 'The influence of content development on the effectiveness of instruction', *Journal of Teaching in Physical Education*, 11: 139–149.

Schempp, P.G. (1987) 'Research on teaching in physical education: beyond the limits of natural science', *Journal of Teaching in Physical Education*, 6: 109–110.

Shute, S., Dodds, P., Placek, J., Rife, F. and Silverman, S. (1982) 'Academic learning time in elementary school movement education: a descriptive-analytic study', *Journal of Teaching in Physical Education*, 1(2): 3–14.

Siedentop, D. (1987) 'Dialogue or exorcism? A rejoinder to Schempp', *Journal of Teaching in Physical Education*, 6: 373–376.

Silverman, S. (1983) 'The student as the unit of analysis: effect on descriptive data and process-outcome relationships in physical education', in T. Templin and J. Olson (eds), *Teaching in Physical Education* (Big Ten Body of Knowledge Symposium Series, Volume 14), Champaigne, IL: Human Kinetics 277–285.

——(1985a) 'Critical considerations in the design and analysis of teacher effectiveness research in physical education', *International Journal of Physical Education*, 22(4): 17–24.

——(1985b) 'Relationship of engagement and practice trials to student achievement', *Journal of Teaching in Physical Education*, 5: 13–21.

——(1985c) 'Student characteristics mediating engagement-outcome relationships in physical education', *Research Quarterly for Exercise and Sport*, 56: 66–72.

——(1987) 'Trends and analysis of research on teaching in doctoral programs', *Journal of Teaching in Physical Education*, 7: 61–70.

——(1990) 'Linear and curvilinear relationships between student practice and achievement in physical education', *Teaching and Teacher Education*, 6: 305–314.

——(1993) 'Student characteristics, practice and achievement in physical education', *Journal of Educational Research*, 87: 54–61.

——(1994) 'Communication and motor skill learning: what we learn from research in the gymnasium', *Quest*, 46: 345–355.

Silverman, S., Dodds, P., Placek, J., Shute, S. and Rife, F. (1984) 'Academic learning time in elementary physical education (ALT-PE) for student subgroups and instructional activity units', *Research Quarterly for Exercise and Sport*, 55: 365–370.

Silverman, S. and Ennis, C. (in press) 'Enhancing learning: an introduction', in S.J. Silverman and C.D. Ennis (eds), *Student Learning in Physical Education: Applying Research to Enhance Instruction*, Champaigne, IL: Human Kinetics, 2nd edn.

Silverman, S., Kulinna, P. and Crull, G. (1995) 'Skill-related task structures, explicitness, and accountability: Relationships with student achievement', *Research Quarterly for Exercise and Sport*, 66: 32–40.

Silverman, S. and Manson, M. (2003) 'Research on teaching in physical education doctoral dissertations: a detailed investigation of focus, method, and analysis', *Journal of Teaching in Physical Education*, 22: 280–297

Silverman, S. and Skonie, R. (1997) 'Research on teaching in physical education: an analysis of published research', *Journal of Teaching in Physical Education*, 16: 300–311.

Silverman, S. and Solmon, M. (1998) 'The unit of analysis in field research: issues and approaches to design and data analysis', *Journal of Teaching in Physical Education*, 17: 270–284.

——(2001) 'Quantitative research: more than a unidimensional construct', paper presented at the preconference meeting of the American Educational Research Association Special Interest Group: Research on Learning and Instruction in Physical Education, Seattle, WA, April.

Silverman, S. and Subramaniam, P.R. (1999) 'Student attitude toward physical education and physical activity: a review of measurement issues and outcomes', *Journal of Teaching in Physical Education*, 19: 97–125.

Silverman, S., Subramaniam, P.R. and Woods, A.M. (1998a) 'Task structures, student practice, and student skill level in physical education', *Journal of Educational Research*, 91: 298–306.

——(1998b) 'Task structures, student practice, and student skill level in physical education', *Journal of Educational Research*, 91: 298–306.

Silverman, S., Tyson, L.A. and Krampitz, J. (1992) 'Teacher feedback and achievement in physical education: interaction with student practice', *Teaching and Teacher Education*, 8: 333–344.

——(1993) 'Teacher feedback and achievement: mediating effects of initial skill and sex', *Journal of Human Movement Studies*, 24: 97–118.

Silverman, S., Tyson, L.A. and Morford, L.M. (1988) 'Relationships of organization, time, and student achievement in physical education', *Teaching and Teacher Education*, 4: 247–257.

Silverman, S., Woods, A.M. and Subramaniam, P.R. (1998) 'Task structures, individual student feedback, and student skill level in physical education', *Research Quarterly for Exercise and Sport*, 69: 420–424.

——(1999) 'Feedback and practice in physical education: interrelationships with task structures and student skill level', *Journal of Human Movement Studies*, 36, 203–224.

Silverman, S. and Zotos, C. (1987) 'Validity of interval and time sampling methods for measuring student engaged time in physical education', *Educational and Psychological Measurement*, 47: 1005–1012.

Solmon, M. (2003) 'Student issues in physical education classes: attitude, cognition, and motivation', in S.J. Silverman and C.D. Ennis (eds), *Student Learning in Physical Education: Applying Research to Enhance Instruction*, Champaigne, IL: Human Kinetics, 2nd edn.

Subramaniam, P.R. and Silverman, S. (2000a) 'The development and validation of an instrument to assess student attitude toward physical education', *Measurement in Physical Education and Exercise Science*, 4: 29–43.

——(2000b) 'Student attitude toward physical education: grade level and gender influences', paper presented at the annual meeting of the American Educational Research Association, New Orleans, April.

——(2002) 'Using complementary data: an investigation of student attitude in physical education', *Journal of Sport Pedagogy*, 8: 79–91.

7 Sport education

Peter Hastie

Few people would argue with the position that games and sport have a quintessential place within the physical education curriculum. If we were to survey a number of men and women on the street, they would certainly believe the place for learning about how to play to games and sports belonged within this particular subject. Indeed, Taggart (1988) has gone as far as to say that sport is one of the historic cornerstones of physical education, and physical education cannot exist without it. From students' perspectives, sport and games are seen as an important part of the physical education program. In a study of middle and high school students' attitudes towards physical education, Tannehill and Zakrajsek (1993) reported that game play was regarded as the most important component of physical education.

The foregrounding of sport within physical education has not always been the case. In the United States, for example, the earliest physical education saw no mention of sports. More likely, students were engaged in formalized gymnastics training based upon systems that had German and Swedish origins. The focus of these programs was organic development accompanied by activities that promoted graceful movement. For the few girls who participated in physical activity in schools, the curriculum included horse riding, archery and swimming. Indeed the 'battle of the systems' conference of 1889 in Boston saw deliberate efforts by all to keep sport out of the physical education discussion.

While the playing of sports made inroads into 20th century physical education, the focus on physical education as a primary site for developing physical fitness continued to have peaks of interest. Cries from community, government and medical authorities were particularly persuasive in physical education taking a strong focus on the development of cardiovascular and muscular system health. The catalyst for these cries for a refining of physical education from its 'soft' games focus to a specific fitness goal was the poor performance of soldiers in wartime tasks or the release of specific data showing lower than desirable levels of youth fitness (see Siedentop 2001).

The inclusion of sport within physical education has also tended to have a political dimension. That is, in a number of countries, particularly those who at the time were experiencing poor international competitive performances, certain government officials have called for a strengthening of the place of the traditional national team sports within physical education. In Britain, one particular physical education order (DES 1991) reflected the dominant central government view of physical education as virtually synonymous with sport with priority given to traditional team games. Indeed, one English prime minister called for every school 'to put sport back at the heart of weekly life' (Major 1996: 3).

In Australia, the national sporting federations who at the time were witnessing decreases in participation rates in out-of-school sporting clubs heavily supported the introduction of Aussie Sport (and likewise Kiwi Sport in New Zealand). Though promoted on grounds of providing 'sport for all' through modified games suitable to the developmental appropriateness of younger children, Aussie and Kiwi Sport were seen as ways of improving the base of the sport, with the pyramidal theory suggesting that when more youngsters participate at the ground level, the performance of the national teams can only be promoted.

The question remains as to whether sport within physical education should replicate the processes and systems by which it is conducted in the community (and hence follow a socializing function), or whether sport within physical education should operate within the context of schools as change agents and educate students to be critical consumers of negative sport practice? For example, Kirk (1983) presented the idea that sport within physical education should teach students to become intelligent performers. That is, Kirk commented that there is more to games than simply knowing facts or being able to reproduce skills. Students should not only become skillful at the mechanics and techniques of games, but should be able to select which skill to use at the appropriate time and also be able to read a game. As a result, Kirk distinguished between competent performance and intelligent performance. An intelligent performer is one who can accommodate both the familiar and the unfamiliar.

Accompanying this call for the development of intelligent performers was the creation of a new model for teaching sport within physical education. Called Teaching Games for Understanding, the model was based upon the premise that the main emphasis on teaching games should be an understanding of the game, as it exists (see Bunker and Thorpe 1983). This idea developed from the beliefs that there was a deficiency of players, spectators and administrators who think or know much about anything but skills. Bunker and Thorpe (1983) were particularly critical of the traditional approach to teaching games in which the game itself was subservient to technique.

Irrespective of one's belief about the place of sport within physical education, many authors have been particularly damning concerning its practice. While sport is suggested to be an avenue where students can learn a number of positive social skills, we also know that sport has the potential to marginalize and otherwise alienate students. Many authors provided significant evidence of negative student outcomes from their participation in sport in physical education when it is replicated directly from the community setting (see Ennis, 1996). In addition, criticism has also been directed towards the lack of content mastery developed by traditional teaching, as well as the presentation of irrelevant content.

Concerns with traditional physical education

Lack of content mastery

One particular criticism of the teaching of sport within physical education is that the units of instruction are too short for the development of substantive learning outcomes. As Taylor and Chiogioji note:

> The proliferation of and emphasis on teaching too many activities in too short a time – has made these goals (fitness, self-esteem, and cognitive/social development) more difficult to attain. The smorgasbord approach of requiring team sports, individual sports, dance, physical fitness activities, all within the space of one year lessens those student's opportunities to master any one activity through which they can meet the stated goals .
>
> (Taylor and Chiogioji 1987: 22)

Discriminatory and abusive practices

Criticisms of sport within physical education include the permitting of dominant aggressive male players to control the game, marginalizing and alienating low-skilled girls and boys (Ennis 1999). As large-sided games take place within physical education, frequently in numbers that exceed the regulation for play (e.g. 10-a-side volleyball, or 14-a-side softball) the intimidation by higher skilled students leads to participation patterns of avoidance of those of a lower skill. This can often lead to the development of 'competent bystanders' (Tousignant and Siedentop 1983), those students who migrate to areas of lesser involvement and fake involvement when being monitored by the teacher. Griffin (1984) has noted that many girls also chose to take roles that served to reduce their playing involvement and hence become generally nonassertive.

We are all also familiar with the potentially humiliating scenarios of students who are less skillful having to endure the very public selection process as they wait to be selected among the last students, and even have to suffer the ignominy of verbal displays of disappointment when they are finally allocated to a team.

Boring and irrelevant content

Even in cases where the playing of sport is accompanied by sensitive teachers who do not allow for harassment or other inappropriate student interactions, sport in physical education that replicates the community or interscholastic participation model, often neglects to embrace the components of institutionalized sport that indeed make those experiences authentic. Criticisms of sport units have also come from students who claim that most of their experiences are with boring and repetitive content (Carlson 1995a). Students also make claims of content irrelevance where activities are alien to their homes and communities.

The genesis of sport education

Sport education is a curriculum and instruction model developed by Siedentop (1994) to counter the criticisms of academics and students about the way sport is presented in physical education. Focusing essentially on the notion of authenticity, it is Siedentop's belief that the essential features of sport that lead to its attractive-ness are rarely reproduced in physical education. As Siedentop comments, this happens in several ways:

> Skills are taught in isolation rather than as part of the natural context of executing strategy in game-like situations. The rituals, values, and traditions of a sport that give it meaning are seldom even mentioned, let alone taught in ways that students can experience them. The affiliation with a team or group that provides the context for personal growth and responsibility in sport is notably absent. [In summary] physical education teaches only isolated sport skills and less-than-meaningful games. Students are not educated in sport.
>
> (Siedentop 1994: 7)

Siedentop lists six key features of the sport experience that make it authentic (and hence attractive). These include: (a) that sport is done by seasons, (b) players are members of teams and remain in that team for the entire season, (c) seasons are defined by formal competition, which is interspersed with teacher and student directed practice sessions, (d) there is a culminating event to each season, (e) there is extensive record keeping, and (f) there is a festive atmosphere in which the season (and particularly the culminating event) takes place. Siedentop contrasts these features with the typical sports unit within physical education where units rarely last longer than three weeks, team selection is changed daily and is usually ad hoc, and that very little (if any) of that sport's culture and ritual is transmitted through the experience.

The aim of sport education is to create competent, literate and enthusiastic sports players. A system of tasks and class activities are planned that will result in students not only becoming more skillful, but understanding the histories, traditions and nuances of the sport, as well as becoming willing participants within the wider sport culture. Sport education places students in small-sided teams and takes them through a series of skill practices (planned and carried out by teachers and peer coaches), through developmentally appropriate games conducted as authentic competition. That is, in contrast to the more common ad hoc game context of physical education where students play in nonconsequented matches, students in sport education become members of teams that stay together for the entire length of a season, and they play in games that are modified in the number of players per team (4-a-side volleyball). Let us look at one vignette of a typical sport education lesson.

> A class of 45 students is divided into 9 teams. Each of these teams selects its own captain, coach and manager. They also choose a name, and may have

team pictures taken or adopt a uniform color. The first part of the season involves skill training, where the teacher provides a number of technique-focused drills in which the group participates as a whole. A small segment of time at the end of each lesson is allocated for team coaches to run practices with their teams. Each team is assigned a 'home space'.

After a series of lessons in which the basic skills are learned and practiced, a pre-season competition is held. During this phase of the season, students practice becoming referees, learn how to keep score and take statistics, and are involved in many of the managerial tasks such as setting up the field, running the time clock, and having all the equipment ready for play.

As the season progresses, refining and practicing skills takes less of the class time, and formal competition becomes the focus. It is a team competition, so the major goal is to win the competition by compiling points for winning matches, but also for good sportsmanship, being organized, and completing any set managerial duties. At the completion of the finals series, a variety of awards are presented; final ranking, referee awards, fair play awards and participation awards.

Sport education is not, however, a direct simulation of institutionalized sport. It differs in three distinct ways: participation requirements, developmentally appropriate competition, and diverse roles. First, all students play all the time. There are no substitute players in sport education. Large-sided teams are seen as inappropriate, because these typically provide lower numbers of opportunities to play for those with lesser skill. Basketball games in sport education are more likely to be between teams of 3 rather than 5, and 5-a-side softball is the norm as opposed to 9-a-side. The second fundamental difference is the notion of developmentally appropriate competition. Equipment and rules are modified to make the game more accessible and attractive for students. Games are also played over a shorter period of time, requiring a high level of intensive play. Third, students will take roles other than player during the season. That is, students will referee, keep scores and statistics, may become a team manager responsible for the upkeep and allocation of equipment, or a first aid officer. In addition, many students will become members of a class committee – a group of students charged with the organization of the league itself or some component (e.g. setting parameters for the appropriateness of student conduct or the development of specific local rules). This handing over of the responsibilities for many of the decisions of the practice of sport by teachers to students is potentially empowering. It also helps students understand the development of a good and sane sport culture in ways in which they will hopefully protect and nurture appropriate sport practices for youth in the future.

As sport education has developed, more and more teachers are designing ways to create novel competition formats. For example, in one particular soccer league (see Bell and Darnell 1994), students begin by playing 1-v-1 games, progressing as the season develops to 2-a-side and finally 4-a-side contests. The results from all matches contribute towards a season league score. These additions in the number of players come about when students are able to handle the skill and tactically related components of the game.

Research on sport education

Research on sport education since the middle 1990s has provided us with more and more answers as to whether the model has been able to achieve its objectives. As a general summary, research with regard to enthusiastic participation is solid and replicated, while evidence of literacy and competence is best described as emerging and consistent.

Enthusiasm

Numerous studies have reported substantive enthusiastic participation by students during seasons of sport education. Grant (1992) in New Zealand, as well as Taggart and Alexander (1993) and Carlson and Hastie (1997) in Australia, provide specific examples of student eagerness and increased engagement. The general commentary from students is that they seem to work harder in sport education seasons and take this work more seriously than in their previous physical education units. In North America, many students have reported a strong preference for the persisting team concept. They enjoy playing with the same players over a long period of time (Hastie 1998a). Students also report a preference for peer coaching to instruction from teachers and other adults. They also perceive they have increased responsibility for leadership, teamwork, and administrative roles (Hastie 1996). Carlson (1995b) has reported that lower-skilled students have a great level of enthusiasm in sport education over other sport contexts in that they are seen as important team contributors, most particularly when in a positive and supporting team environment. Hastie (1998b) notes that those who perceive themselves as alienated in large teams report being particularly empowered when on a small team of four or five, especially where they have some responsibility and their team mates help them improve.

Literacy

By definition, a literate sportsperson is one who understands and values the rules, traditions, and values of a sport, and one who can also distinguish between good and bad sport practices. Research on sport education shows robust evidence that students do indeed develop sports literacy. Hastie (1996) has reported that students do take their nonplaying (e.g. referee, scorer, statistician) roles seriously, while the students in that study commented that they became more knowledgeable about the sport they were studying. Moreover, while students took their roles seriously, they also demonstrated competence in those roles. Students were rarely off-task, and were accurate in their decision making for significant percentages of time.

Carlson and Hastie (1997) identified learning as one key theme of students' perceptions of their experiences in sport education. This learning included the learning of isolated physical skills, applying learned skills in game situations and increased understanding of team strategies and tactics, increased knowledge of the rules, and learning various personal/social techniques that maximized team functioning.

With regard to this learning, however, there seem to be differences in learning dependent upon skill level. For example, more highly skilled students are less likely to believe they improve in physical skills or conditioning, but make strong reference to gaining affective or coaching skills. Lower skilled players, on the other hand, did develop strong beliefs that they learned more about how to play the game and how to apply the skills in game settings (Hastie and Carlson 1998).

Competence

With reference to competence, Siedentop (1994) suggests that a competent sportsperson has sufficient skills to participate in games satisfactorily and can understand and execute strategies that are appropriate to the complexity of the game being played. Studies by Carlson and Hastie (1997), as well as Grant (1992) have anecdotal accounts from teachers and students reporting skill and game play improvements. In particular, lower skilled students hold this as their strongest perception. We are also beginning to see empirical evidence showing that students do indeed improve in skills. Hastie (1998a) showed that these students made significant improvements in selection and execution dimensions of the game during an extensive season of frisbee, while Ormond *et al.* (1995) reported that a class of students playing basketball following sport education principles 'play a better game' than those engaged in a traditional unit of skill practice followed by game play (Ormond *et al.* 1995: 12). By 'play a better game,' these authors suggest that students in the sport education setting show more attempts to share the ball, utilize offensive and defensive strategies, and that higher skilled students demonstrate a willingness to pass the ball to lower skilled students.

Perceptions of teachers about sport education

One of the major attractions for teachers of sport education is the freedom that it offers them. That is, as the teacher is released from much of the formal instructional demands of lessons (Alexander and Luckman 2001), they can then attend to more pressing needs which often do not receive attention. Teachers report these needs as focusing more on student assessment, helping individual students develop specific skills, and attending to the affective domain. Alexander *et al.* (1996) describe these features as serving to revitalize teachers' enthusiasm towards teaching physical education, giving them a 'spring in their steps.'

Nonetheless, there are some challenges for teachers as they begin to develop their first sport education seasons. In particular, the handing over of responsibility to students is often considered problematic. As noted, the fate of an entire season will depend upon how well students can perform their nonplaying roles (Hastie 2000). Additionally, some teachers struggle with what they see as ineffective student coaches. Research has shown that peer coaches characteristically spend more time playing games with their teams than teaching skills. While teachers spend more time in refining and extending tasks, peer coaches spend more time in organization, demonstration, and application tasks (Hastie 2000).

Reasons for the attractiveness of sport education

So why do so many students find sport education attractive? Carlson and Hastie (1997) suggest the answer lies in the students' social system. In traditional games unit, the students' social agendas (minimizing work and socializing) often interfere with the teacher's instructional agenda. In contrast, because there is a change in the way they are able to socialize during class and because of their leadership roles, students in sport education feel as though they have some ownership of the season. In addition, because the competition counts for something meaningful, working hard together as a team to be successful is a way of having fun. This camaraderie and task commitment has been shown in the collegiate setting in addition to schools (see Bennett and Hastie 1997; Kinchin 2001).

The students' social system is nonetheless one part of a multidimensional program of action operating in sport education. I previously suggested (Hastie 2000) that the high level of enthusiastic student engagement was due to the presence of three vectors, all of which make positive contributions to sustaining the program of action. These vectors include, in addition to the student social system, the teacher's managerial task system and the content-embedded accountability inherent in the curriculum model.

The development and progress of sport education

Since its introduction, the way in which the sport education model has been employed has been greatly diversified. These are not illegitimate iterations of the model, but rather extensions of the key principles to suit local conditions. Essentially, provided that the three key rules are not violated, sport education programs can take many forms. The principles referred to are (a) an extended period of time engaged with the content, (b) that students remain in constant teams and engage in progressive competition, and (c) that students take roles other than player. As a result, sport education seasons have been completed in activities such as hip-hop dance, aerobics, and in gymnastics. Further, teachers have given students considerable choice and options in the development of their seasons. In one particular study, students were members of committees that met daily to discuss issues of game rules, competition format, as well as fair play. In these units, the students gradually developed not only how the game was to be played, but also how the entire season would develop (see Hastie and Carlson 2002).

In another case in New Zealand, students were placed into teams and charged with creating new countries. They spent time in the classroom developing governments and parliaments, and, indeed, invented the games that would ultimately be played. During physical education, the students from each country taught the remaining students the rules of their new game, a process that culminated in an Olympic Games complete with opening ceremony, anthems, and competition.

Teachers have also used sport education as a vehicle through which they have promoted cross-curricular learning. Students in Australia have played in soccer seasons where each team adopted a team from the Italian League. As part of their social studies curriculum, the students were required to discover information about those cities, even to the extent to writing to the respective chambers of commerce or the soccer team's home office. Students then made presentations in class.

Teachers have also become very creative in the ways in which they have promoted their seasons and in particular, the culminating events. One American teacher has students videotape contests during the week, and then edits these tapes into a 'plays of the weeks' highlights video. The video is shown on repeated cycle in the school's lunchroom. In this way, all the students and teachers in the school can see the progress of sport education seasons in a manner that acts as a strong advocate for physical education. Another teacher replicated the entire United States collegiate football tailgating concept on the day of the fourth and fifth grade football championships. Classroom teachers, parents and school administrators and students collectively engaged in a barbecue-like cookout before the championship game. Students made banners which they ran onto the field, there was live commentary by students, and there was even half-time entertainment.

The creation of hybrid models

Perhaps the most radical metamorphosis of sport education has been the creation of almost entirely new models. In both the cases described below, the attractiveness of sport education as a model that can legitimately address multiple objectives led to the use of the template of sport education to create situation specific responses to local issues. Ennis and her colleagues (1999) were primarily interested in enhancing girls' satisfaction in physical education, as well as addressing the difficulty that many urban students experience with regard to engaging in learning and affiliating with others. In due course, Ennis *et al.* (1999) developed a model which they named Sport for Peace.

Sport for Peace is a model that integrates all the crucial curricular structures of sport education (i.e. player roles and responsibilities, as well as developmentally appropriate, authentic competition). In addition, Ennis and her colleagues added the teaching of strategies for conflict negotiation, the requirement that all students play during every class, and rules requiring students to rotate through every position and responsibility (except that of coach). The intent of the model was to create deliberate levels of authentic conflict, and then help students to negotiate and compromise.

During its implementation in urban schools, Sport for Peace was found to cultivate shared responsibility for learning, trust, respect, and a sense of family

(Ennis *et al.* 1999). The authors reported that both high and low skilled girls and boys felt successful and responded positively, creating a class community more conducive to engagement and participation.

Similar to Ennis *et al.* (1999), Hastie and Buchanan (2000) were interested in improving the performance of middle school boys with regard to the fair play requirements of sport education. Those authors used a strong infusion of Hellison's 'Teaching for Personal and Social Responsibility' model (see Hellison 1995) to create a model named Empowering Sport.

A basic model of Empowering Sport would look like this:

> Units begin with a series of work-related problems, the major ones being the creation of even teams as well as a game. This game is born from either a skeleton of primary rules (as was the case in this experience) or may even be totally student centered. The teacher may then provide some leadership in the form of direct skill instruction or may further facilitate team captains (or practice leaders), with the primary agenda being to assist lower skilled students to become more competent and with an increased sense of self-efficacy. The competition format is one in which teams negotiate to play or scrimmage, again within certain parameters put in place by the teacher. . . . Decisions concerning more formal competition within this hybrid model would be a function of the teacher's primary Sport Education agenda in combination with the students' goals for their sport experience. However, the global objective of this model is personal empowerment, particularly through making appropriate personal and social responses.
>
> (Hastie and Buchanan 2000: 34)

Can sport education address current problem issues in institutionalized sport?

As can be seen from the results of sport education research to date, it is clearly providing a viable attractive alternative for the teaching of sport within physical education. The model is specifically addressed to compensate for many of the issues that are the negative components of institutionalized sport. The playing requirements of sport education (everyone plays all the time) means that students become significant players on their teams, and numerous reports have suggested the more skillful players will spend time with those of lesser skill in endeavors to improve those of lower skill. Indeed, when asked what they learned during sport education, more skillful students suggest that they do not in fact learn to become more skillful players, but were more likely to talk about gaining affective or coaching skills than improvement in physical skills or conditioning. To quote one student, 'I didn't get better at netball because I was playing you know below standard that we have to play all weekend [but I learned] more patience' (Hastie and Carlson 1998). As noted, lower skilled players have been most enthusiastic about how they enjoy being a valued part of a team.

The other structural component of sport education that specifically attempts to counter the negative sport culture of institutionalized sport is the foregrounding of fair play. Indeed, winning matches in sport education is only part of becoming a season champion. Siedentop suggests that a complete sport education season will have a ranking for teams' match performance, but also will include data from a team's ability to complete its administrative tasks and measures of adherence to the values of fair play. Indeed, many leagues throughout the world incorporate a fair play award that accompanies the win/loss record of teams. Sport education frequently uses sportsmanship as the tiebreaker between teams with equal records.

However, few of the fair play components of sport education will automatically appear in practice unless teachers make deliberate efforts to help students learn what appropriate sport practices are. These practices need to be modeled, they need to be demonstrated and reinforced. Indeed, there is evidence that students need specific training in sportsmanship for the desired results to accrue. In a study by Hastie and Sharpe (1999) involving high school boys (many of whom were at-risk of school dropout), when competition first began during a sport education season, negative behaviors not only far outstripped positive ones, but also actually increased with increasing competition. It was only after deliberate efforts to help students evaluate their own behaviors and holding them accountable to specific fair play requirements that the shift towards positive interactions took place. The fair play intervention witnessed an increase in the number of positive interaction and leadership statements, as well as a reduction in disputes during the game.

Sport education does then have the potential to reduce the promotion of aggression and competitive play among students, but only if the teacher takes up the opportunity within the season. To go further, in another study in which students were responsible for the development of rules as well as the behavioral accountability system, there was almost total absence of dispute. Many of the students in this seventh grade hockey class acknowledged that there were so few incidences of arguing and negative behavior because they were indeed the ones who developed the acceptable levels of play. Further, all had a voice with regard to personal and social responsibility (see Hastie and Carlson 2002). However, it is fair to note that irrespective of sportsmanship requirements, students treat their games during sport education more seriously and have a greater desire to win in sport education than they do in regular physical education sport contexts (Carlson and Hastie 1996).

This notion of competitiveness leads to the question as to whether sport education presents a setting that is indeed too competitive. Siedentop (1994) would suggest that sport education aims to present good competition. By this he means that first, it is competition in which the consequences of winning or losing are not important outside the competition. That is, there is a particular avoidance of a zero-sum mentality, i.e. I win, therefore you must lose. Cooperation and competition are not seen as mutually exclusive but exist together as participants are bound up in a cooperative effort to create a good game.

The future for sport education

What do we still need to know about sport education?

One of the key attributes of sport education is that it gives students a considerable degree of responsibility and voice. From our research, we suggest that lower skilled players appreciate being on small-sided teams because of the legitimate attention they receive and because they are valued. However, we know little to nothing about the internal dynamics of how teams operate. In any teams there will be positions with more inherent power (e.g. captain or coach) and other roles will be more attractive (e.g. referee versus statistician). It would be worthwhile for us to investigate and understand the ways in which students make decisions about who takes these roles in order to fully understand whether all students have an opportunity to take these roles, or whether certain students in the peer group always seem to dominate.

We still need to know considerably more about skill development during seasons of sport education. What small amounts of data we have show that students do improve during an extended season, but this is from one study only (Hastie 1998a). In particular, we need more understanding about how student coaches operate within their teams. Peer coaches typically spend more time playing games with their teams than teaching skills, while teachers spend more time in refining and extending tasks, peer coaches spend more time in organization, demonstration, and application tasks (Hastie 2000). In summary, student coaches are not the expert instructors that most teachers are. We do, however, need to understand if there are ways we can assist peer coaches develop more systematic skills for improving the performances of their team mates.

We also know nothing about the teaching of strategy by peer coaches. Again, we have data that suggest students will develop some strategic knowledge through an extended period of time playing the game, but we have not yet investigated ways in which we can help students learn tactics. A study that might incorporate an instructional model such as 'Teaching Games for Understanding' into a season of sport education would be a most attractive research endeavor.

We also do not know the effects of long-term participation in sport education. We have no longitudinal data about those students who have played in multiple seasons or years in sport education. First, we might ask whether the novelty of the system of taking roles and being on consistent teams wears off after a certain period. More important, however, would be to gauge the extent to which students are beginning to realize those long-term goals of sport education. Are they indeed participating and behaving in ways that preserve, protect, and enhance sport cultures, whether it is a local youth sport culture or a national sport culture? Perhaps the best yardstick would be to measure how many students decide voluntarily to become involved in sport after-school and outside of school.

Alternately, we know little of the responses by teachers to continued presentation of sport education seasons. Are they conducting programs in which students are invested in more and more responsibility to the extent to where they eventually make significant curricular decisions?

Finally, we need to examine potential of the integration of sport education into classroom learning. Siedentop has proposed, for example, an Olympic curriculum, but we know nothing of its efficacy. We have examples from South Pacific sites of seasons where teachers have integrated social studies into sport education season, but as of yet, we have no empirical data that gives us the perspectives of the classroom teachers concerning student enthusiasm and learning, or information that may help us improve these integrative practices.

Where to from here?

Following its early successes, Tinning (1995) commented on sport education as becoming a remarkable success story. However, in his praise he also provided some concerns. The main tenet of Tinning's argument was that while sport education represents a form of pedagogy that is highly laudable for physical education, its very success has created the possible danger of sport further dominating the physical education offerings in schools. While Siedentop is clear in noting that sport education is but a part of the entire physical education program, Tinning's concern is realized where sports become privileged to the detriment of a well-rounded activity curriculum. By well-rounded, Tinning refers to a curriculum involving more than just games, but inclusive of dance, gymnastics and other individual endeavors.

However, this is not the intent of those who developed the model. One of the areas in which we *do* need to be vigilant is that it is relatively easy to do sport education badly. That is, teachers can simply place students into teams, provide one or two days of skill practice and then present an extended period of competition.

In conclusion, sport education is a flexible model that aims to develop competent, literate and enthusiastic sportspersons. Its particular attraction for teachers is that the model allows for the reinforcement of a number of instructional objectives within an authentic experience. Playing or competition formats are not unchangeable. That is, there is no one best way to do sport education. In addition to the recording of match results, the scoring systems of sport education seasons can reward fair play, personal and team responsibility, or cognitive learning. Sport education also aims to give students considerable power in determining their learning priorities.

Because of its flexibility, the future of sport education is particularly bright. As teachers become more experienced with the model, we should continue to see more and more creative applications in sports that have, to date, not been trialed. This is particularly the case where teachers are using student advisory boards in the design of their programs. Sport education then can fit comfortably as part of a well-rounded physical education curriculum.

It has been eight years since Tinning questioned whether sport education would become a phoenix, bandwagon or a hearse for physical education. Clearly, eight years of continued reports of teacher and student enthusiasm has taken it beyond the category of 'bandwagon,' and given the reports by so many of renewed enthusiasm in their teaching and overall programs, one would have to give credibility to the notion that sport education has indeed saved at least some programs from vanishing.

References

Alexander, K. and Luckman, J. (2001) 'Australian teachers' perceptions and uses of the sport education curriculum model', *European Physical Education Review*, 7: 243–267.

Alexander, K., Taggart, A. and Thorpe, S. (1996) 'A spring in their steps? Possibilities for professional renewal through sport education in Australian schools', *Sport, Education and Society*, 1(1): 23–46.

Bell, C. and Darnell, J. (1994) 'Elementary soccer', in D. Siedentop (ed.), *Sport Education: Quality PE through Positive Sport Experiences*, Champaigne, IL: Human Kinetics.

Bennett, R.G. and Hastie, P.A. (1997) 'A sport education curriculum model for a collegiate physical activity course', *Journal of Physical Education, Recreation and Dance*, 68(1): 39–44.

Bunker, D. and Thorpe, R. (1983) 'A model for the teaching of games in secondary schools', *Bulletin of Physical Education*, 19(1): 32–35.

Carlson, T.B. (1995a) 'We hate gym: student alienation from physical education', *Journal of Teaching in Physical Education*, 14: 467–477.

——(1995b) ' "Now I think I can." The reaction of eight low-skilled students to sport education', *ACHPER Healthy Lifestyles Journal*, 42(4): 6–8.

Carlson, T.B. and Hastie, P.A. (1997) 'The student social system within sport education', *Journal of Teaching in Physical Education*, 16: 176–195.

Department of Education and Science (1991) *Physical Education in the National Curriculum*, London: Her Majesty's Stationery Office.

Ennis, C.D. (1996) 'Students' experiences in sport-based physical education: (more than) apologies are necessary', *Quest*, 48: 453–456.

——(1999) 'Creating a culturally relevant curriculum for disengaged girls', *Sport, Education and Society*, 4: 31–49.

Ennis, C.D., Solmon, M.A., Satina, B., Loftus, S., Mensch, J. and McCauley, M.T. (1999) 'Creating a sense of family in urban schools using the sport for peace curriculum', *Research Quarterly for Exercise and Sport*, 70: 273–285.

Grant, B.C. (1992) 'Integrating sport into the physical education curriculum in New Zealand secondary schools', *Quest*, 44: 304–316.

Griffin, P.S. (1984) 'Girls' participation patterns in a middle school team sports unit', *Journal of Teaching in Physical Education*, 4: 30–38.

Hastie, P.A. (1996) 'Student role involvement during a unit of sport education', *Journal of Teaching in Physical Education*, 16: 88–103.

——(1998a) 'Skill and tactical development during a sport education season', *Research Quarterly for Exercise and Sport*, 69: 368–379.

——(1998b) 'The participation and perceptions of girls within a unit of sport education', *Journal of Teaching in Physical Education*, 17: 157–171.

——(2000) 'An ecological analysis of a sport education season', *Journal of Teaching in Physical Education*, 19: 355–373.

Hastie, P.A. and Buchanan, A.M. (2000) 'Teaching responsibility through sport education: prospects of a coalition', *Research Quarterly for Exercise and Sport*, 71: 25–35.

Hastie, P.A. and Carlson, T.B. (1998) 'Sport education: a cross cultural comparison', *Journal of Comparative Physical Education and Sport*, 20(2): 36–43.

—— (2002) 'The inclusion of participatory democracy in a season of sport education', AERA National Convention, New Orleans, LA, April.

Hastie, P.A. and Sharpe, T. (1999) 'Effects of a sport education curriculum on the positive social behavior of at-risk rural adolescent boys', *Journal of Education for Students Placed at Risk*, 4: 417–430.

Hellison, D. (1995) *Teaching Responsibility through Physical Activity*, Champaigne, IL: Human Kinetics.

Kinchin, G.D. (2001) 'Using team portfolios in a sport education season', *Journal of Physical Education, Recreation and Dance*, 72(2): 41–44.

Kirk, D. (1983) 'Theoretical guidelines for "teaching for understanding" ', *Bulletin of Physical Education*, 19(1): 41–45.

Major, J. (1996) 'Sport – raising the game: Response from the Prime Minister', *The British Journal of Physical Education*, Autumn: 5.

Ormond, T.C., DeMarco, G.M., Smith, R.M. and Fischer, K.A. (1995) 'Comparison of the sport education and traditional approaches to teaching secondary school basketball', paper presented to the Annual meeting of the American Alliance for Health, Physical Education, Recreation and Dance, Portland, OR.

Siedentop, D. (1994) *Sport Education: Quality PE through Positive Sport Experiences*, Champaigne, IL: Human Kinetics.

—— (2001) *Introduction to Physical Education, Fitness and Sport*, Mountain View, CA: Mayfield, 4th edn.

Taggart, A. (1988) 'The endangered species revisited', *ACHPER National Journal*, 121: 34–35.

Taggart, A. and Alexander, K. (1993) 'Sport education in physical education', *Aussie Sport Action*, 5(1): 5–6, 8.

Tannehill, D. and Zakrajsek, D. (1993) 'Students' attitudes towards physical education: a multicultural study', *Journal of Teaching in Physical Education*, 13: 78–84.

Taylor, J. and Chiogioji, E. (1987) 'Implications of physical education report on high school programs', *Journal of Physical Education, Recreation and Dance*, 54(8): 22–23.

Tinning, R. (1995) 'The sport education movement: a phoenix, bandwagon or hearse for physical education', *ACHPER Healthy Lifestyles Journal*, 42(4): 19–21.

Tousignant, M. and Siedentop, D. (1983) 'A qualitative analysis of task structure in required secondary physical education classes', *Journal of Teaching in Physical Education*, 3: 47–57.

Editor's note

The final two chapters of this book make an interesting comparison. Rather like one of those books where readers can make up their own ending; here readers are encouraged to consider both the chapters and make their own decisions as to which they see as being most appropriate to their current situation. Juan-Miguel Fernández-Balboa takes a postmodern stance in describing a brave new world of physical education/activity provision. He clearly takes Kirk's (in Jewett *et al.* 1995) arguments further than many have taken them before. Is this a step too far? We will not know until we get there, but Fernández-Balboa's predictions should have a chilling effect on any teachers of physical education who read them. At the very least, they will cause reflection and pause for thought, and doubt, within the profession.

On the other hand, Anthony Laker takes a more traditional view of the future. Although critical of the current situation, Laker's proposals originate from the body of knowledge and research findings to date. In an attempt to promote a relevant, culturally sensitive, yet socially critical, curriculum he advocates evolution as opposed to revolution. By reforming the legacy of our scientific research past into both a theoretical and practical model, Laker begins an attempt to build the new pedagogy.

Some readers may find this gradual approach more acceptable. The sporting and educational establishments are notoriously slow, and even resistant, to change. Nevertheless, Laker's suggestions might not be radical enough to remedy the ills that face school physical education. Whichever version of the future the reader prefers, they both provide ideas on which to base future discussions.

Reference

Kirk, D. (1995) 'Physical education and cultural relevance: a personal statement', in A.E. Jewett, L.L. Bain and C.D. Ennis, *The Curriculum Process in Physical Education*, Boston, MA: McGraw-Hill, 2nd edn, 369–373.

8 Physical education in the digital (postmodern) era

Juan-Miguel Fernández-Balboa

Education, be it perceived as an activity, an ideology, or a profession, should not be understood outside of its social, political, and historical contexts. Physical education ought to be seen in the same light (Laker 2000). In fact, each of the constituent knowledges of physical education derives from its own grand narrative. For example, performance pedagogy grows out of positivist science and social responsibility grows out of critical theory. Each has its own, self-promoting agenda and theoretical baggage. Historically, physical education has served three main functions; fostering health through the practice of certain physical activities, training bodies for strength and leadership in the battlefield, and preparing workers for more efficient and productive labor. These purposes, no doubt, have been framed by a dominant ideology whose validity must now be questioned (Penney and Chandler 2000). To project the future for physical education requires new conceptual frameworks and more holistic views. Examples of this are the connections among physical education, sport, and sociology (Sage 1997) or the intersections between traditional forms of physical activity, say in outdoor education, with those developing as a result of growing globalization (Jarvie and Maguire 1994; Sicilia 1999).

With this in mind, in this chapter I set out to disrupt the taken-for-granted and to present alternative ways of thinking about physical education from a postmodern perspective, that is, by critically contesting conventional canon (see also Fernández-Balboa 1997a, 1997b). My arguments will be based on present social and political circumstances. I want to take the concepts of postmodernism and physical education a step further. My analysis will be somewhat eclectic in that I will use a mixture of futuristic, scholarly, speculative and critical perspectives. My intention is to provoke a dialogue among readers about the problems and possibilities of physical education in a new world order. In this sense, my 'postmodern' approach reflects more a view of cultural *evolution* (in diverse directions) than that of a radical cultural *revolution*.

Toffler's three waves of civilization

The world is changing at an unprecedented pace. To be able to explain what is happening, Toffler's theory of the three waves of civilization may be useful

(Toffler 1980, 1990). He suggests that the evolution of humans through the millennia has gone through three main stages or waves. These waves, despite having emerged chronologically, are not mutually exclusive, and depending on the context, one is predominant over the others. It is also important to point out that each new wave does not represent a break for its precedent one – it is not the case that one day we are living in one wave and the next day we are living in a totally different one. On the contrary, one wave emerges as a result of the evolution of that which preceded it and, therefore, the new one contains certain elements of the old (Giddens 1993; Harris 1992). By the same token, in societies where the new wave is still too new, it is difficult to know that it really exists since there are so many elements of the old still in place. Yet, as the new wave advances, its characteristics become more obvious, and the patterns of the previous wave become increasingly displaced and problematic (Castells 1998; Seidman 1999). What is worth mentioning is that the third wave, with its new patterns of behaviour, values, technologies, relationships, spaces, and aspirations is establishing itself with tremendous speed and force, to such an extent that ignoring it would be foolish. But before entering into more detail about this latter point, I will briefly describe these three waves.

According to Toffler (1980), the first civilization wave began about 10,000 years ago, as a result of the discovery of agriculture and animal husbandry. Working the fields enabled humans to establish themselves in permanent communities and villages. This, in turn, gave way to a multitude of new social, political, and economic relations that were practically unthinkable up to that time because, previously, people were forced to be nomadic in order to find food. The industrial revolution symbolized the second civilization wave, which emerged between 1650 and 1750. During that period, many of the present modern institutions in Western societies emerged, and therefore a new way of life was established in these societies. As such, in the last 300 years, factories, banks, planes, and trains have affected the way millions of human beings live. The success of large-scale industrialization was based on several principles which, in turn, have come to serve as the basis of both a widely shared social ideology as well as an internalized form of personal psychology. These principles are: (a) standardization (e.g. of measurements, systems of accountability, law, schedules, products, behavior, production, processes, evaluation); (b) specialization in relation to certain professional types of knowledge and functions; (c) synchronization of schedules and labor to add predictability to certain acts and increase the level of efficiency of production and supply; (d) centralization of information and decision-making power in the hands of a powerful few who, through central banks and central governments, join forces to control both money and policy; (e) maximization of performance and production coupled with an obsession with growth; (f) concentration of people in big urban centers, of economic resources in huge banks and corporations, of information in big databanks, of production in huge industrial sectors; and (h) bureaucratization where what matters is the stratification and hierarchy of the processes that seek to maintain the *status quo* as much as possible. The third wave (i.e. the digital era) began roughly around 1955 due to a variety of technological, economic, political, and environmental factors that contributed to a decrease of industrialization in certain countries. During the 1980s and 1990s, in order to reduce the costs of production and taxes (Castells 2000), many factories closed or moved to less developed countries (i.e. countries that were still basically agrarian). In this regard, the United States, for instance, has reached levels of deindustrialization where only 4% of the work force is employed in factories (Toffler 1980). In turn, a paradigm based on digital technologies and an economy based on services is growing exponentially (Tapscott 1998). This paradigm is based on principles practically opposite to those that dominated the industrial era.

Schooling trends in the digital society

In the last hundred years or so, schools (in particular public schools) have reflected and helped legitimize the industrial model of production (Apple 1990). Notice, for instance, that the operative processes, the educational patterns, and the types of knowledge presented in these settings have been based on the aforementioned second-wave principles (i.e. standardization, specialization, synchronization, concentration, centralization, massification, and bureaucratization). As such, the parallels between the school and the factory have also been reinforced by a common discourse. Students are seen as hard or lazy workers, teachers are viewed as managers, homework is assigned as overtime learning, learning is divided into tasks, curriculum seeks outcomes and products, and verbal rewards to students take the form of 'good job' for focusing on their work. If one looks at it from a critical perspective, one can easily see that the whole process of schooling is set up like a huge assembly line where even its schedules mirror those of the factory.

All this is likely to change very quickly in the digital era (i.e. the third wave) because of the emerging technologies, principles, and ideologies. After all, new times demand new forms of teaching and learning. The question, however, remains: What forms of schooling and what forms of knowledge will be necessary in this new era? What seems to be certain is that, for several reasons, digital technologies will play an important role in the development of new thinking about schooling. Digital cameras make face-to-face communication possible among people who live at a distance. Chat-rooms and list-serves via e-mail allow for dialog among, and the distribution of information to, many people at once. Intelligent systems can convert voice into text and translate it into various languages. With all this readily available, people and companies will be able to offer educational services in different countries simultaneously, without worrying about language or bureaucratic barriers. Without a doubt, the explosion and democratization of information (Ratnesar and Stein 2000) and the easy access to a multitude of sources and databases are opening new doors and producing new problems and dilemmas. As such, new alternatives of teaching and learning are already emerging, and parents and educators will have to deal with them. Let us see what some of these alternatives are.

Private sector schools

An option more and more prevalent to public schooling is that provided by private companies, which, despite not having been traditionally associated with educational contexts, see education as a valuable economic investment in light of the new market tendencies (Greenwald 2000; Saymonds 2000; Fernández-Balboa 2001). These private companies or education management organizations (EMOs) have at their disposal a substantial amount of capital, strong connections with the powers-that-be, and a much greater degree of flexibility when compared with their public counterparts. In fact, they have and are developing very advanced and powerful technologies in order to provide specialized and individualized curricula that match the needs of many clients (Pini 2001). To illustrate, Michael Milken, the famous North American financier, has created 'Knowledge Universe', a conglomerate of companies that offers online curricula, testing, test preparations, tutoring, and even management of schools. Milken's companies also share databases and resources and contract among themselves value-added services. While providing educational services for its companies, Knowledge Universe is also amassing a huge databank on childhood learning, skill levels, and online learning behavior through a 'Turbo Twist' toy that feeds information upstream to the company database, where the child's skill level and progress are assessed and tracked. Then the server downloads to the toy a new batch of educational games customized to that particular child's skill level, dovetailing, if needed, with the child's own school curriculum (Pizzo 2001).

In this vein, several critical issues must be raised, however. Perhaps the most concerning one is the lowering of democratic opportunities for the public, since these corporations make autocratic decisions that affect curriculum and schooling, with little or no input from the public (Pini 2001). Second, is the deskilling and proletariatization of teachers, given that those who work for these EMOs are not subject to union privileges and contracts and in many cases their job is relegated to technical tasks. Third, we must acknowledge that the education provided by EMOs tends to benefit those children who can afford the technology through which the curricula are presented. In this vein, the members of the lower socio-economic classes will not have access to the types of knowledge the former students will acquire. This, in turn, will contribute to a wider gap between the haves and the have-nots. Fourth, as we have seen in Knowledge Universe's case, the child's privacy can be jeopardized since his or her behaviour and performance will be recorded somewhere in cyberspace without guarantee that such information will not be used by unauthorized persons.

Home schooling

Home schooling has emerged as a strong alternative to the crowded and standardized conditions of compulsory public schooling. In fact, the public school in the United States was established not only to provide a progressive perspective and enable the masses to have a better quality of life, but was also instituted to furnish factories with efficient and obedient workers, able to speak English and understand and follow commands (Callahan 1962; Apple 1985, 1990). This is one of the reasons why students are stratified, tracked, classified, and arranged by age, socio-economic status, and knowledge level in a meritocratic system. As a result, relatively few public school students have been able to greatly transcend their backgrounds or acquire entrepreneurial values. Moreover, the secular values promoted by schools have been contested by members of certain religious groups who argue that their children must be brought up according to their own religion. From these standpoints, home schooling is seen as a liberating alternative.

The Internet, among other means, has made it possible to access a multitude of educational resources and information settings both locally and abroad. To this one can add that roughly 30 million teenagers log-on to the Internet daily (Tapscott 1998). Tapscott calls them the *Net Generation* or *N-Gen* (see also Bigum and Green 1998; Green 1998; Okrent 1999). In this regard, it is worth mentioning the keen understanding these teenagers possess about the Internet and other digital technologies (Pesce 2000). Adding all these factors together, one can easily see why home schooling is a very viable option, which, by the way, EMOs are beginning to capitalize on.

The detractors of this type of schooling indicate that students thus educated are not as well socialized as their school counterparts, for they have little contact with either other students or adults. Yet, reasonable arguments point to the contrary. First, by and large, students in schools have very little time to relate to one another in informal ways aside from short periods of recess or at meal times. The fact is that in the majority of cases, students in classrooms are forced to work independently and silently. Second, contact with adults is also minimal given that despite having as many as seven teachers a day (which is the case in high school), the teacher has to attend an average of 25 students in a 50 minute period, and assuming that he or she were able to devote the whole period to personally relate to the students (no group lesson here), the total time he or she would be able to dedicate to each student would be scarcely 2 minutes. Let us do the math here: 2 minutes of teacher attention times 7 teachers would amount to a maximum of 14 minutes of contact with adults a day, that being the best case scenario. On the other hand, home schooling, when well organized, can provide a much higher rate of personalized attention with adults. A group of four children tutored by one adult would receive 15 minutes of undivided attention every hour. Besides, in that amount of time, and with such level of personalized attention, they are likely to learn much more than if they were in school all day. Three hours of tutoring would, hence, be worth three days of being taught in school, while leaving plenty of extra time to go out, play, visit museums and libraries, do independent study, and socialize with other children and adults in these alternative settings.

Home schooling does not have to be carried out in isolation, nor should the burden of the teaching fall on one parent only. Several parents may combine time and resources to provide the tutoring and travel, they may even hire certified, specialist teachers or trusted volunteers (e.g. retired professionals with deep knowledge of carpentry, medicine, gardening, libraries) a few hours a week to provide the children with content and skills that parents may not have. Also, there exist many types of curricula from which parents and guardians can choose. These are provided via the Internet and through alternative educational groups. This creates a type of mobile and dynamic classroom where small groups of children can learn a great deal from many people, about a lot of things that suit their own interests and the values of the parents (Mercogliano 1998).

A new type of public school

In third-wave societies, given their needs and the circumstances, the role of schools and teachers alike will have to change in radical ways. Schools will have to have a much better political and financial backing by both the state and the private sector if they are to become better social equalizers than those existing today. This in turn will necessitate a clear vision, a series of strong agreements among interested parties, and a rethinking of priorities in terms of budget and goals. If this happens, it may be an important step toward breaking the link between a poor education and poverty (Kozol 1991, 1995; Forcier 1996). Without political and financial resources, it will be practically impossible to provide the services, technology, tutoring, and facilities the public schools require to properly address the social and economic needs of future societies (Morgan 1999).

The new public school will have to be much smaller so as to create a sense of community and belonging among students and teachers. The huge physical plants built in the last 70 or so years have contributed to the disenfranchising of people within them. The concentration, standardization, and centralization of the present public school system have brought about many problems that, in turn, have justified the culture of control so prevalent in these settings. Needless to say, the more control, the more resistance and rebellion on the part of those being controlled; and the more rebellion, the more need to control by the powers-that-be. The vicious cycle is clear and the fact is that with that approach, it is practically impossible to truly educate.

Tinning and Fitzclarence (1998) point to the necessity to create curricula that balance the present social and economic circumstances with personal development (e.g. teaching students to be informed and critical consumers). From this perspective, it would be absurd to conceive curriculum as something that must be learned in order to justify the achievement of standards as measured by standardized testing and assessment; a reason too often given in the present educational system. Smaller schools, on the other hand, offering a more personalized approach, with smaller groups of students per class, with teachers that belong to the community in which schools are placed, with curricular alternatives also intimately connected to the community, make much more sense in this day and age.

Up until now, concentration, standardization, and centralization have been defended in the name of efficiency in instruction. Yet, with the technological means at our disposal, reducing school size does not necessarily mean a decrease in learning. On the contrary, with the help of digital technology, students and teachers can access all kinds of pedagogical resources (e.g. the Library of Congress) and explore all types of curricular alternatives. Moreover, not all teaching and learning has to be mediated through technology. Students can do supervised internships in local settings thus learning business operations and trades first hand. The possibilities are endless; what is needed is imagination and common sense.

The new type of public school ought not to be compulsory. Instead it should be enticing and inviting enough to attract students. In this regard, if the school ambiance and its spaces are safe, warm, and welcoming; if the staff are caring and capable; if there exists a flexibility of schedules; and if the curriculum is perceived by students as varied and valuable; then, it is reasonable to assume that most youngsters would want to go to school (Leonard 1968).

Still another important factor would be to consider the needs and characteristics of students of many different socio-cultural and economic backgrounds (Kozol 1995; Kirn 2000). Tapscott (1998) has found that the members of the Net Generation distinguish themselves by a deep knowledge of the digital technologies and by a strong sense of independence. By and large, they possess a willingness to be more inclusive of alternative ideas and peoples, have a marked desire to investigate social, moral, and political issues, value freedom of expression, and aspire to be leaders. On the other hand, it goes without saying that there are the hundreds of thousands of children born into poverty, whose life is marked by dangerous and precarious conditions (e.g. delinquency, fear, abuse, violence, and hunger). Very often, these children lack caring and are deprived of happiness and hope. In a sense, it is precisely these children who most need a public school of the future in which they can feel safe and valued, in which, while being fed both food and knowledge they can find alternatives to their presently not-so-bright future. This is not merely an educational matter, but, more importantly, an ethical and political one.

A new type of teacher

Another factor to be considered in the new public school is a new kind of teacher, a person able to cover many needs. For one, given the change in world demographics, and in order to alleviate the crowded conditions of classrooms, many more teachers will be needed. In the United States, as in other countries, the teacher shortage is being felt already. The viable solutions to this problem are many, including actively recruiting students into teaching, offering incentives to attract qualified persons from other professions via alternative routes, rehiring retired teachers and professionals, inviting parent volunteers into the classroom. But only increasing the numbers of teachers, although necessary, will not suffice. The teachers in the new public school will have to be much more than mere transmitters of information or facilitators of learning. Present technologies can do this much better and much more efficiently. Teachers will have to be extremely well prepared, with a great range of knowledge regarding people, society, history, language, science, geography, to name but a few. They will have to be generalists with deep understanding of specific subjects and the connections among them. For that, they will have to engage in on-going independent and communal learning. Furthermore, we must take into account that with the increasing complexity of societies, and consequently their inherent dangers, people will have to make extremely difficult choices. As such, teachers will have to possess an acute sense of pedagogy so as to guide their students toward wise moral, ethical, and political decisions.

In order to do all that, educators will need to have at least two fundamental capacities. First, they will have to have a deep sense of humanity, which in turn will enable them to relate to their students in positive and empowering ways (Armour and Fernández-Balboa 2000); second, they will have to have a strong commitment to the larger world (be it peace, the community, the environment, and so on). The Spanish philosopher Fernando Savater argued: 'To make oneself responsible for the world, does not mean to accept it as is; but instead to be conscientiously aware that it is, because only then one can transform it' (Savater 1997: 150). In this vein, the teacher in the new public school will have to know how to foster human dignity, peace, acceptance of diversity, reason, and empathy (Woldkowsky and Ginsberg 1993; Marina and Válgoma 2000; Villegas and Lucas 2002). In sum, in addition to having a broad and deep background on subject matter content, and on top of also possessing knowledge of psychology, sociology, technology, politics, and pedagogy, teachers will have to show a high degree of personal character, self-esteem, and wisdom. Otherwise, it will be very difficult for them to be the role models needed to truly educate the citizens of the future.

Knowledge alternatives in physical education in the digital era

In the digital era, physical education could be deliverable at home. Imagine that physical education teachers design individualized programs and distribute to students via the Internet, including illustrative text, sound, and image. Imagine that adults of all ages and both genders download exercise programs to do at home or at the office. Nowadays, it is expected that the longevity of the population, at least in the so-called developed countries, will increase. It follows that the need for leisure, recreation and physical activity will also increase. Physical education professionals could create consulting firms through digital media offering all kinds of tips and advice regarding conditioning, diet, coaching, and sociological and psychological commentary. Why not, then, take advantage of the emerging 'learning ecologies' and 'communities of intersection' (Brown 2000) to learn and upgrade our own professional and personal knowledge? What if one could take university courses, say, in football coaching or CPR or classroom management from one's living room? Online universities are already beginning to establish themselves as serious contenders to traditional institutions, offering online courses and all types of degrees. What if, instead of having to travel across the country, professionals could attend physical education meetings and present papers through teleconferencing from one's own school or home? All this is already possible and, given the increasing availability and use of digital technologies, if physical education professionals do not do it, someone else will.

The social and technological transformation will have important implications when it comes to thinking about, and implementing, physical education (Sicilia 1998). For instance, in the previous section I pointed out the possibility (more so, the increasing tendency) toward the privatization of schooling. This is not new in the field of physical activity, given that private health clubs, for instance, have proliferated in the last few decades. Despite this fact, however, physical education has managed to maintain its relative status as a subject in schools. This could radically change in a few years because of the present economic crisis (as of this writing, CNN reports the highest unemployment rates and the lowest consumer confidence rates in the United States in decades). Under these circumstances, it is reasonable to forecast budgetary cuts in many areas in schools. Besides, there will be new pressures to adapt, condition, and equip old buildings to the new techno-logical necessities. Hence, priorities will inevitably shift, and physical education, a subject not too important in the public mind, will be in jeopardy. Hoffman (1987) already warned us of physical education's precarious conditions. I want to put a spin on his warning. Consider this scenario:

Before they had time to react, the four physical education teachers at PS 88 were laid off. The letter attached to the pink slip stated that both the PTA and the Board deemed it necessary to eliminate physical education in order to give way to a new school subject, 'Computers and the Internet.' As an alternative, these teachers applied for a job at Multisport Inc., a subsidiary of Intelcom, a powerful international telecommunications conglomerate that recently established one of its headquarters in town. Multisport Inc. would provide physical activities and services to the employees of Intelcom and their families. It is worth mentioning that despite being in existence for just three years, Multisport Inc. had already 1,700 franchises, one of them located precisely next to PS 88. Also worth pointing out is that the facilities of Multisport Inc. were state-of-the-art, and that it had engaged in an aggressive commercial campaign based on slogans such as 'We give personalized instruction' and 'Satisfaction guaranteed or your money back!' to recruit as many clients as possible. Part of this recruiting campaign was to offer extremely low membership rates (including some scholarships) to the students of PS 88. So successful had been the campaign that of the two local health clubs (quite popular until the arrival of their corporate competitor) one had already gone bankrupt and the other was losing members by the minute.

The members of the community were so pleased with Multisport Inc.'s services and facilities that they began sending their kids there as well. The kids, in turn, not only loved going there because they could openly socialize with their friends; but, also, reported getting physically fit. That, too, influenced the decision of the educational authorities regarding physical education.

Of the four teachers, only Mary Martin was hired by Multisport Inc. After all, she was young, pretty, and fit; had a recent master's degree in exercise physiology; several teaching awards to her credit; and strong letters of recommendation from both the PTA and the PS's Principal. Furthermore, the company needed talented and charismatic instructors, and Mary, with her extreme popularity and strong preparation, would certainly be an asset in many ways – one being to attract many of her students to the club. Still, before fully joining the staff, Mary had to agree to take several company workshops, the aim of which was to teach the company's philosophy and policies to all new employees. As for the remaining three teachers, they were not as lucky. Two of them looked for jobs in other sectors and old coach Kowalsky simply retired.

Tensions between traditional and critical traditions of physical education

The trend toward globalization and the incredible advances in technology in the digital era are having an undeniable effect on the ethical, socio-cultural and political spheres, creating many tensions and conflicts. Needless to say, these tensions and conflicts will also be felt in physical education as the traditional and critical camps struggle for hegemonic power. On the one hand, it is reasonable to affirm that the competitive patterns and the economic tendencies already established in the terrains of sport, recreation and fitness will likely be strengthened by the demands and ideologies of both neo-liberalism and the market, finding new forms of expression and organization (Sage 1987). Also the tendency towards high performance will continue its inexorable path (Tinning 1997). On the other hand, in the last few years the professional literature has reflected a growing effort on the part of several critical commentators in raising awareness about the potential and actual detriments of the *status quo* (Sage 1987; Scraton 1990; Sparkes 1990; Tinning 1990; Evans 1993). I for one, while proposing viable alternatives that promote social justice, have warned about the effects of the prevalent 'poisonous pedagogies' and hidden curricula in physical education and sport whose characteristics foster sexism, racism, elitism, political ignorance, and social stratification (Fernández-Balboa 1993a, 1993b; 1995, 1997b, 1999a, 1999b).

One key component that either perpetuates or problematizes the current values and practices of physical education will be Physical Education Teacher Education (PETE). Up until now, as a general norm, PETE has been considered to be a process mainly technocratic and positivistic (McKay *et al.* 1990; Whitson and Macintosh 1990). New pedagogies in this regard are urgently needed. In Australia, for example, Fitzclarence and Hickey (1997) have highlighted the need to neutralize violence in sport through alternative pedagogies and therapies based on a critical analysis of the social forces that promote violence (see also Fitzclarence 1994; Fitzclarence and Hickey 1997) while promoting personal and social responsibility and respect toward others. These pedagogies and therapies are designed to help athletes and coaches alike to counteract violent practices on and off the sport field. Likewise, in the United States, Hellison (1995) has been promoting and practicing pedagogies of responsibility in the gym. We must take into account that these practices are not only social; they are political as well. In this regard, there exist intimate strong connections between the social structure and the person-as-a-change-agent (Shilling 1999). PETE must become aware, and raise awareness, that the predominant competitive, scientific, and technological approaches carry hidden values that must be subject to careful scrutiny (Postman 1992; Aronowitz *et al.* 1996). PETE must make important choices about whether to promote technocracy or social justice, and develop a new pedagogy that encompasses the benefits of the past with the needs of the future.

In the digital era, thanks to the power of global telecommunications, and despite censure, it will become even more evident that the vast majority of the peoples in the world are suffering. In order to foster social justice, education in general and physical education in particular, pedagogies that are critical, democratizing, and humanizing will have to be foregrounded (Freire 1993, 1999). Pascual (1996) offers us this insight:

> A teacher educator . . . must be a mature person, psychologically balanced, preoccupied with valuable purposes – those that can be justified from an ethical standpoint – and committed to their achievement. In this regard, teacher educators everywhere must begin to radically change, not only in our ways of thinking, but also in our ways of educating.
>
> (Pascual 1996: 77, 88)

As such, a deliberate and constant effort must be made based not only on a deep understanding of society and politics; but, also, on a considerable capacity to reflect and act critically (Pascual 1996,1999; Fernández-Balboa 1999b).

From this perspective, PETE must transcend tradition. One place to start is by acknowledging the fact that the human body is not merely physical, but also it is the result of a series of social, cultural, historical constructions whose interests are in constant tension, fighting for hegemony (Giroux 1988; Fitzclarence 1990; Scraton 1990; Kissling 1991; Kirk 1992; Sage 1998). After all, the body is also considered a commodity – something one can sell, buy, paint, tattoo, pierce, wash, dress (or undress), train, fatten, starve, operate on, caress, drug, incarcerate, bury, classify, fire, hire, educate, beat, kill, etc., depending on what groups are in power, what ideologies are foregrounded, what traditions are in place, and what geographical zone one lives in. Through our bodies, we reject and accept others while being accepted and rejected by others. Also, we do gain or lose status though our looks. With our bodies we establish relationships of power and take actions with moral, ethical, and political consequences. What role does human movement (e.g. physical education, sport, dance) play in all this? In what ways do we oppress, repress, liberate ourselves and others? (Fernández-Balboa 1999a). In addition, it is important to mention the changes in the perceptions of the cultural body as a result of the new digital technologies. Virtual bodies, virtual realities, and video games are already more fact than fiction (Quittner 1999; Fernández-Balboa 2002).

PETE must also avoid propagating 'poisonous pedagogies' (Miller 1990; Fernández-Balboa 1999b), vicious cycles in which certain pedagogical principles are automatically applied as if they were beneficial to students while, in reality, their effects are socially and psychologically pernicious. Examples of these principles can be found in the discourses and practices of violent sport (Hickey *et al.* 2000), the automatic belief that exercise (no matter what type) equals health (Falhberg and Falhberg 1997), and of machismo (Fitzclarence 1994; Dewar 1991). The origins and unjust conditions and contradictions inherent in these ideologies ought to be critically uncovered and contested. Today, as valuable as these critical alternatives are, they are still considered the exception to the norm. PETE will have to take a leading role in mainstreaming them if it wants to stand for social justice in the digital era.

The traditional pedagogies espoused in PETE have largely ignored the needs and circumstances of many students at both ends of the socio-economic spectrum. For instance, at present PETE is doing little to include discourses and deeds of disenfranchised youth. PETE will also have to reinvent methods and purposes so as to educate teachers who in turn will be able to understand and educate the students of the Net Generation who have a tremendous sense of immediacy and independence, students who are used not only to breaking with tradition but also inventing new rules (Tapscott 1998). Even more poignant is the fact that some of these students will be entering PETE programs in the very near future. How will the mainly conservative physical education teacher educators cope with them? Critical physical education could offer multiple educational possibilities appropriate to all these kids through movement forms that foster mutual understanding and personal development. PETE educators and students may want to seriously consider these alternatives (Fernández-Balboa 2002).

Closing remarks

Regardless of whether one agrees with the premises and points I have presented in this chapter, what seems undeniable is that the digital era, with all its complexity, instability, and confusion, will force us to redefine our principles, purposes, and policies. In fact, new economic, ethical, and political forms are already with us, and the lifestyle of millions of people is beginning to experience significant changes, both good and bad. Among this upheaval, it is important to remember that digital technologies, despite their important role in all this, are not the panacea. On the contrary, they constitute a double-edged sword with incredible benefits and terrifying consequences. In this vein, it is reasonable to say that much like the industrial revolution, the digital era will bring advantages to some and misery to others. Some will improve their chances at life while others will inexorably suffer and perish as a result of the new developments. In fact, war, hunger, pandemics, and environmental destruction, for instance, will not go away merely by bringing in more sophisticated computers. Likewise, the inequalities of schooling will not disappear by digitizing didactics (Kozol 1991). Thus, the modern concept of progress must be, at least, problematized in the new times.

After all, most of the problems we presently experience in the world have been created by humans, and, as such, it is humans who have the responsibility to solve them.

Needless to say, educators must play a crucial role, for adopting the attitude of disinterest is irresponsible and dangerous (Tinning 2000). To be sure, educators will have to engage in a tough, balancing act reconciling the pragmatic realities of the new times with the ethics and politics of democratic empowerment. This kind of future will need more and more people with integrity and determination to promote justice, dignity, happiness, and peace (Marina and Válgoma 2000).

As for physical education, the same principles and problems of the digital era also apply. It is fair to suggest that these principles and problems will transform our field and take it in different directions, and that traditional value systems and practices taken for granted until now will be affected and even threatened and suppressed. In view of this, physical education professionals at all levels (PETE included) will have to begin to imagine how best to contribute to the quality of life of the present and future generations (Smith *et al.* 1996). That requires a rare ability to envision what seems impossible. Yet, despite the confusion and the uncertainty, we must commit to begin building the foundations of a good legacy, a legacy full of hope and possibilities for the generations to come.

References

Apple, M.W. (1985) *Education and Power*, Boston: Ark Paperbacks.

——(1990) *Ideology and Curriculum*, New York: Routledge.

Armour, K. and Fernández-Balboa, J.M. (2000) 'Connections, pedagogy and professional learning', paper presented to the CEDAR Conference, University of Warwick, March.

Aronowitz, S., Martinsons, B. and Menser, M. (1996) *Technoscience and Cyberculture*, New York: Routledge.

Bigum, C. and Green, B. (1998) 'New kids on the chopping block? Media culture and educational practice in new times', in L. Fitzclarence, B. Green and J. Kenway (eds), *Changing Education: New Times, New Kids*, Geelong, Victoria: Deakin University Press, 81–86.

Brown, J.S. (2000) 'Growing up digital: the web and a new learning ecology', *Change*, 32(2): 11–20.

Callahan, R.E. (1962) *Education and the Cult of Efficiency*, Chicago, IL: University of Chicago Press.

Castells, M. (1998) *La Era de la Información: Economía, Sociedad y Cultura*, Madrid: Alianza.

——(2000) 'Materials for an exploratory theory of the network society', *British Journal of Sociology*, 51(1): 5–25.

Dewar, A. (1991) 'Feminist pedagogy in physical education: promises, possibilities, pitfalls, *Journal of Teaching in Physical Education*, 62(6): 68–77.

Evans, J. (ed.) (1993) *Equality, Education and Physical Education*, London: Falmer Press.

Falhberg, L. and Falhberg, L. (1997) 'Health, freedom and human movement in the postmodern era', in J.M. Fernández-Balboa (ed.), *Critical Postmodernism in Human Movement, Physical Education, and Sport*, Albany, NY: Suny Press, 65–86.

Fernández-Balboa, J.M. (1993a) 'Los aspectos crítico y cívico de los profesionales de la educación física', *Apunts*, 34: 74–82.

—— (1993b) 'Socio-cultural characteristics of the hidden curriculum in physical education', *Quest*, 45: 230–254.

—— (1995) 'Reclaiming physical education in higher education through critical pedagogy', *Quest*, 47: 91–114.

—— (1997a) *Critical Postmodernism in Human Movement, Physical Education, and Sport*, Albany, NY: Suny Press.

—— (1997b) 'Physical education teacher preparation in the postmodern era: toward a critical pedagogy', in J.M. Fernández-Balboa (ed.), *Critical Postmodernism in Human Movement, Physical Education, and Sport*, Albany, NY: Suny Press, 121–138.

—— (1999a) 'Pedagogía crítica y educación física en la escuela secundaria', *Conceptos de Educación*, 6(2): 9–14.

—— (1999b) 'Poisonous pedagogy in physical education', paper presented to the AIESEP World Congress, Long Island, New York, July.

—— (2001) 'Digital telecommunications technologies, critical pedagogy, and teacher education in the 21st century', in T. Ariav, A. Keinan and R. Zuzovsky (eds), *The Ongoing Development of Teacher Education: Exchange of Ideas*, Tel Aviv: The Mofet Institute, 366–381.

—— (2002) 'El cuerpo y la educación física en la era digital', keynote address, XX Congreso Nacional de Educación Física y Universidad. Guadalajara, Spain, July 3–7.

Fitzclarence, L. (1990) 'The body as a commodity', in D. Rowe and G. Lawrence (eds), *Sport and Leisure: Trends in Australian Popular Culture*, Sydney: HBJ, 96–108.

—— (1994) 'Gender, power, violence: implications for teachers', in *Schooling What Future? Balancing the Education Agenda*, Deakin, Victoria: Deakin Centre for Educational Change, 113–122.

Fitzclarence, L. and Hickey, C. (1997) 'Confronting yourself in narrative: the search for new pedagogy', paper presented to the Invitational Conference on Gender, Sport and Education, Deakin University, Geelong, September.

Forcier, R.C. (1996) *The Computer as a Productivity Tool in Education*, Englewood Cliffs, NJ: Prentice Hall Inc.

Freire, P. (1973) *Education for Critical Consciousness*, New York: Seabury Press.

—— (1993) *Pedagogy of the Oppressed*, New York: Continuum.

—— (1999) *The Pedagogy of Freedom*, Boston: Rowman & Littlefield.

Giddens, A. (1993) *Consecuencias de la Modernidad*, Madrid: Alianza.

Giroux, H.A. (1988) *Schooling and the Struggle for Public Life: Critical Pedagogy in the Modern Age*, Minneapolis, MN: University of Minnesota Press.

Green, B. (1998) 'Aliens and others', in L. Fitzclarence, B. Green and J. Kenway (eds), *Changing Education: New Times, New Kids*, Geelong, Victoria: Deakin University.

Greenwald, J. (2000) 'School for profit', *Time*, 155(11): 56–57.

Harris, M. (1992) *La Cultura Norteamericana Contemporánea. Una Visión Antropológica*, Madrid: Alianza.

Hellison, D. (1995) *Teaching Responsibility through Physical Education*, Champaigne, IL: Human Kinetics.

Hickey, C., Fitzclarence, L. and Mathews, R. (2000) *Where the Boys Are*, Geelong, Victoria: Deakin University Press.

Hoffman, S.J. (1987) 'Dreaming the impossible dream: the decline and fall of physical education', in J.D. Massengale (ed.), *Trends Toward the Future in Physical Education*, Champaigne, IL: Human Kinetics, 121–136.

Jarvie, G. and Maguire, J. (1994) *Sport and Leisure in Social Thought*, London: Routledge.

Kirk, D. (1992) 'Physical education, schooling and the modern body', paper presented to The Postmodern Body Conference, La Trobe University (Australia), June.

Kirn, W. (2000) 'Will teenagers disappear?' *Time*, 155(7): 76–77.

Kissling, E.A. (1991) 'One size does not fit all, or how I learned to stop dieting and love the body', *Quest*, 43: 135–147.

Kozol, J. (1991) *Savage Inequalities: Children in America's Schools*, New York: Harper Perennial.

——(1995) *Amazing Grace: The Lives of Children and the Conscience of a Nation*, New York: Harper Perennial.

Laker, A. (2000) *Beyond the Boundaries of Physical Education: Educating the Young People for Citizenship and Social Responsibility*, New York: RoutledgeFalmer.

Leonard, G.B. (1968) *Education and Ecstasy*, New York: Dell Publishing.

Marina, J.A. and Válgoma, M. (2000) *La Lucha por la Dignidad*, Barcelona: Anagrama.

McKay, J., Gore, J.M. and Kirk, D. (1990) 'Beyond the limits of technocratic physical education', *Quest*, 42: 52–76.

Mercogliano, C. (1998) *Making It Up as We Go Along*, Portsmouth, NH: Heinemann.

Miller, A. (1990) *For Your Own Good: Hidden Cruelty in Child-rearing and the Roots of Violence*, New York: The Noonday Press.

Morgan, W. (1999) 'Postmodern classroom on the borders?' in J. Leach and B. Moon (eds), *Learners and Pedagogy*, London: Paul Chapman Publishing, 247–264.

Okrent, D. (1999) 'Raising kids online: what can parents do?', *Time*, 153(18): 38–49.

Pascual, C. (1996) 'Reflecting on teaching a course in physical education teacher education', paper presented to the AIESEP World Congress, Lisbon, Portugal, November.

——(1999) 'La formación inicial del profesorado de educación física: en busca del significado personal perdido', *Conceptos de Educación*, 6(2): 75–90.

Penney, D. and Chandler, T. (2000) 'Physical education: what future?', *Sport, Education and Society*, 15(1): 71–87.

Pesce, M. (2000) *The Playful World*, New York: Ballantine Books.

Pini, M.E. (2001) 'The corporatization of education: Education Management Organizations (EMOs) and public schools', doctoral dissertation, University of New Mexico.

Pizzo, S.P. (2001) 'Milken's formula', *Forbes ASAP*, September: 64–69.

Postman, N. (1992) *Technopoly*, New York: Vintage Books.

Quittner, J. (1999) 'Are video games really so bad?' *Time*, 153(18): 50–59.

Ratnesar, R. and Stein, J. (2000) 'Everyone's a star.com', *Time*, 155(12): 70–80.

Sage, G.H. (1987) 'The future and the profession of physical education', in J.D. Massengale (ed.), *Trends Toward the Future in Physical Education*, Champaigne, IL: Human Kinetics, 121–136.

——(1997) 'Physical education, sociology, and sociology of sport: points of intersection', *Sociology of Sport Journal*, 14: 317–339.

——(1998) *Power and Ideology in American Sport*, Champaigne, IL: Human Kinetics.

Savater, F. (1997) *El Valor de Educar*, Barcelona: Ariel.

Saymonds, W.C. (2000) 'For profit schools', *Business Week*, February 7: 64–76.

Scraton, S. (1990) *Gender and Physical Education*, Geelong, Victoria: Deakin University Press.

Seidman, S. (ed.) (1999) *The Postmodern Turn: New Perspectives on Social Theory*, Cambridge: Cambridge University Press.

Shilling, C. (1999) 'Towards an embodied understanding of the structure/agency relationship', *British Journal of Sociology*, 50(4): 543–562.

Sicilia, A. (1998) 'Educación física, profesorado y postmodernidad', in F. Ruíz Juan, A. García and A. Casimiro (eds), *Nuevos Horizontes en la Educación Física y el Deporte Escolar*, Málaga, Spain: Instituto Andaluz del Deporte, 123–139.

——(1999) *Las Actividades Físicas en la Naturaleza en las Sociedades Occidentales de Final de Siglo*. Lecturas: Educación Física y Deportes: available: http://www.sportquest.com/revista/efd14/postmod2.htm

Smith, R., Curtin, P. and Newman, L. (1996) 'Kids in the "kitchen." The social implication for schooling in the age of advanced computer technology', paper presented to the meeting of the Australian Association for Research in Education, Hobart, December.

Sparkes, A.C. (1990) *Curriculum Change and Physical Education*, Geelong, Victoria: Deakin University Press.

Symonds, W.C. (2000) 'For-profit schools', *Business Week*, February: 64–76.

Tapscott, D. (1998) *Growing up Digital: The Rise of the Net Generation*, New York: McGraw-Hill.

Tinning, R. (1990) *Ideology and Physical Education*, Geelong, Victoria: Deakin University Press.

——(1997) 'Performance and participation discourses in human movement: toward a socially critical physical education', in J.M. Fernández-Balboa (ed.), *Critical Postmodernism in Human Movement, Physical Education, and Sport*, Albany, NY: Suny Press, 99–120.

——(2000) 'Unsettling matters for physical education in higher education: implications of "New Times"', *Quest*, 52(1): 32–48.

Tinning, R. and Fitzclarence, L. (1998) 'Postmodern youth culture and the crisis in Australian physical education', in L. Fitzclarence, B. Green and J. Kenway (eds), *Changing Education: New Times, New Kids*, Geelong (Victoria): Deakin University Press, 103–120.

Toffler, A. (1980) *The Third Wave*, New York: Bantam Books.

——(1990) *Powershift*, New York: Bantam Books.

Villegas, A.M. and Lucas, T. (2002) *Educating Culturally Responsible Teachers: A Conceptually Coherent and Structurally Integrated Approach*, Albany, NY: SUNY Press.

Whitson, D.J. and Macintosh, D. (1990) 'The scientization of physical education: discourses of performance, *Quest*, 4: 52–76.

Woldkowsky, R.J. and Ginsberg, M.B. (1993) 'A framework for culturally responsive teaching', *Educational Leadership*, 53(1): 17–21.

9 The future of physical education

Is this the 'new pedagogy'?

Anthony Laker

Introduction

This book is based on the assumption that school physical education is failing to reach its potential for making an effective educational impact on the lives of the students who experience it. Although paved with good intentions, the road that school physical education has trodden recently has left youngsters with a subject that is largely uncontextual and culturally irrelevant to their future needs as consumers of sport, in all its manifestations. What has become known as traditional physical education is mostly games based and emphasises effort and teamwork in a variety of mostly male-oriented activities. Although Kirk (1992) provides ample evidence that traditional physical education is a fairly recent introduction to the whole school curriculum, the fact remains that the current offerings do not serve the needs of many of our school students. Additionally, our youth is faced with a powerful portrayal of physical culture in all types of media, from computer games to the popular press. Some of these portrayals are designed to promote and sell an ideal of what is desirable in terms of body and lifestyle that is attainable by only a few. Physical education has done little to equip our students to deal with this and to place such pervasive portrayals in perspective. Our students are not encouraged to be critical consumers of sport in any form. They need to be able to make rational judgements about activity choice based on knowledge, ability and inclination; and lifestyle decisions based on knowledge and the recognition of the complex realities, not the portrayal of fiction.

This problem is not only seen in the United Kingdom, but also in other countries such as the United States and Australia. Debates are continuing about what should constitute physical education, who should decide the content, how it should be delivered and what elements are important to the well-being of the youth of our nations. In essence, the debate is about who controls the curriculum and what emphasis should be placed on the physical element of that curriculum. Should we listen to the sporting establishment who would like to see a continuation of games-based education emphasising skill development and encouraging elite performance? Should we listen to the health lobby, who would be happy to see a fitness and wellness-based curriculum with encouragement for individual programmes that would inhibit the growth of health-risk factors, both personal and social? Should there be a recreational ideal behind school physical education that promotes activity choice from a wide range of offerings, hoping that youngsters will find something that they can continue after schooling is over? Or should we take the best of what is already there and reform it into a relevant curriculum that enables our children to become intelligent, yet socially critical, consumers of sport with the skills, knowledges and attitudes that will equip them to make informed and appropriate choices about future activities from the stand-point of health, cultural importance and interest? Merely posing these questions indicates that what is legitimate knowledge in physical education is a contested area. Although I have deliberately privileged my own bias, that is not to eliminate the other options presented above. I want to see a recognition of what is good and what works, thus taking the best of what exists and not allow a curriculum to be dominated by a single-interest initiative. Of course, our students need to know about healthy behaviours and health issues, but not to the exclusion of all else. In a similar way, team games have a very important legacy in most Western cultures and it would be wrong to leave them out of a curriculum, just as it would be equally wrong to have a curriculum based on team games alone.

There needs to be a reconceptualisation of what constitutes legitimate knowledge in physical education. This reconceptualisation should be based on research but played out (implemented) in the gymnasium, the playing field and the classroom. This process takes physical education knowledge from the absolute and eternal, to the specific and the local. The proposals in this book resist attempts by powerful research and political lobbies to privilege their own agendas. This postmodern emphasis requires the continual reexamination of educational practice (Pinar *et al.* 1995). In critically examining their own research and practice, the authors of this book have accepted that challenge.

The purpose of this chapter is to try to combine the essence of each of the contributory chapters into something worthwhile and forward-looking. Extended criticism of models that may not have achieved all that was claimed for them has no place here because this is a proposal for the future, not a witch hunt of the past. Each chapter explains what we know in a particular curricular issue. Some have a strong theoretical base and others are more practically oriented. Theory on its own cannot solve problems, but the way theory is interpreted into practice, i.e. praxis, can make a difference. Some deal with school physical education offerings and some are more inclined to the teacher education process. Each has a place in the analysis; if we want to change the school curriculum, we must necessarily change the way in which we educate our future teachers. However, this will not take place without a challenge. In the contested field of 'what is worth of knowing' the hegemonic powers can wield much influence. We cannot expect the teacher education institutions to instinctively know what new teachers in the field need if this is a developing and changing need. Historically, the teacher education institutions have been slow to respond to curricular initiative in existence, such as gender equity (Flintoff 1997; Laker *et al.* 2003), let alone those that are still in the proposal stage! In fact the educational establishment is an institution that has an interest in maintaining the *status quo*, so any change will tend to be resisted and slow. Nevertheless, there is a wealth of evidence detailed in the preceding chapters that indicate that the time is ripe for an attempt at proposing a better way. Even if this proposed better way does not reach fruition, the debate that I hope to stimulate will be beneficial in itself. What follows is the first proposal for this better way, for the future of physical education and for a new pedagogy.

What we know

The chapters have been written to bring the reader up to date with current thinking in a number of important curriculum areas. A brief synopsis of each one will refresh readers' memories of the details of each and pick out the salient points that can later be blended together in the following sections.

Estes (Chapter 1) argues strongly for the adoption of a postmodern justification for 21st century physical education. The whole of this book rests on his suggestion that what we offer our school students needs to be, in Toulmin's (1990) terms, oral, particular, local and timely. The transmission of what constitutes knowledge in physical education naturally has a physical narrative quality about it. Any discourse, or communication, is usually conducted with our bodies. Teachers demonstrate and students perform. Granted, there is also verbal explanation and sometimes written instruction, but these are very much secondary methods of knowledge transmission. The knowledge of the activity is in the lived, i.e. moving (as in motion), experience of the activity. We come to know movement mostly by moving. Estes is suggesting that the over scientification of the subject plays into the hands of positivist science and away from the personal and individual needs of the students. Acts of physical movement are singular and particular. They cannot be universally defined. Each is different and special to itself in that it is defined by its location in space and time and cannot be replicated exactly. Although talking here about single physical acts, the argument transfers to the bigger picture of curriculum. We can inform our practice and decisions with information that is generalisable, and universally true, but we must also realise that the social experience of education is a personal and individual process with particular contextual meanings for our students.

Sport has an important place in many cultures throughout the world. My discussion of this highlights a number of crucial issues that need to be recognised in developing a new pedagogy. Sporting culture is made up of many sub-cultures, each with its own set of behaviours and norms. These behaviours and norms, as well as physical prowess, are what leads one into acceptance into a community of sporting practice. The roles that sport plays in our society are also factors in a complete physical education. Social interaction, sporting traditions, emotional expression and cultural reproduction are all useful to students who should be able to take a knowledgeable and effective place in a sports community. There are a number of reasons for the globalisation of sport but this global nature of sport, and the commonality of the experience of sport, provide a strong platform on which to base notions of mutual communication and common, understandable discourse. Education in sport and school physical education can contribute to this acculturation and socialisation. I suggest that cultural studies and sport education are two curricular initiatives that could be employed in helping students acquire a knowledge and realisation of sport and physical activity as a cultural phenomenon, and indeed their importance as a cultural and social institution.

In my next chapter, I contend, with historical support, that citizenship has a long history as an educational aim. I use Crick's (QCA 1998) description of citizenship to identify components that could be incorporated into a physical education curriculum. These components are social and moral responsibility, community involvement and political literacy. By drawing on the work of Don Hellison, Jim Stiehl and Don Morris physical education can promote social and moral responsibility. Situated learning theory provides a supportive framework for the development of communities of practice within physical education. Last, the real life world of sport itself provides many examples and teachable moments for discussions of politics in sport and sporting politics. These suggestions match in very well with what curriculum authorities are now requiring of the subject. Citizenship is now a subject in its own right in England and Wales and the National Association for Sport and Physical Education in the United States lists one of its standards as 'Collaboration'; this includes interaction of students with communities outside school and awareness of community agencies (NASPE 2002). But regardless of these initiatives, the components of citizenship as described and used here are some of those aspects of a physically educated person that a philanthropic pedagogy would hope to promote.

Don Morris's Chapter 4 identifies and foregrounds the theme of social responsibility as one of extreme importance in considering the future education of students. Using some arresting statistics and stories, he paints a grim picture of the existence of some of today's youth. While acknowledging that not all young people are raised in desperate conditions, he asks what kind of world would we ideally like our children to live in. Much work has been done in this area by other writers (Hellison 1985; Grineski 1989; Kallusky 1996; Laker 2001 for example) and Morris draws on some of their ideas in creating a new approach that is a natural progression from his work with Jim Stiehl (Morris and Stiehl 1999). The research he cites quite clearly indicates that intervention strategies can make a difference in developing and teaching personal, social and environmental responsibility. Morris suggests that building trust and a sense of community are prerequisites for engaging in his *Becoming Responsible* programme. This three stage programme is exemplified by three activities, one for each of the stages; personal, social and environmental. These practical ideas about understanding commitments and promises, establishing agreements with others and school projects, give us a few ideas on which we can build later.

Reflective practice has become something of a mantra for teacher education programmes over the last decade. A desire to produce a reflective practitioner has been the goal of these programmes. Macdonald and Tinning in Chapter 5 question whether reflective practice has delivered its early promise. In analysing what constitutes the concept, they explore ideas of past and future reflective practice. They claim, with some justification, that contemporary teacher education has been relatively successful in producing teachers with the skills of technical reflection, i.e. the ability to analyse skill, time-on-task, give feedback, etc. However, they question whether the ability to be critically reflective, that type of reflection, dealing with such concepts as social justice, equity and sexism, has progressed at the same rate. Teacher education and professional workshops may only have raised the awareness of such issues. They further argue that reflective practice has been appropriated by the educational establishment as a means of public accountability for teachers. In many cases, reflection has been built into perform-ance standards. This represents the deprivatisation of reflection by turning a former personal responsibility into public monitoring. In their suggestions for the future of reflective practice, Macdonald and Tinning conclude that maybe teachers should be looking beyond their own subject when dealing with the reflective process. As physical education adopts health-related fitness, diet, personal development, activity choices after school, and a host of other initiatives, maybe teachers need to ask questions about the place of physical activity in the totality of a person's learning. Perhaps teachers should be helping students to become critical consumers and knowledgeable managers of their own physically active lifestyles. Additionally, we need teachers who are reflective about their practice, technically skilled at teaching, and fully aware of the social and cultural aspects of sport and physical activity.

In Chapter 6, Silverman takes a most enlightened stance to reflect critically on the pedagogy of skill learning. He contends that, as a profession, we have been too quick to criticise each other's research methods and paradigms, whereas we should be celebrating each other's successes. Beginning with misconceptions about the field, Silverman points out that quantitative research is not restrictive but evolves as a study demands, and that what we can learn from this type of research cannot be learnt from a single study, no matter how well designed or well conducted it might be. Additionally, there are concerns that it is very difficult and time consuming to do good research, that data analysis is not always appropriate for answering the research question and that the conclusions are too often generalised without considering the context of the original research. Quantitative research on teaching in physical education has provided us with a certain number of truisms. First, although time-on-task is important, the quality of practice during that time is probably more important. Second, progressive content development and selection of learning tasks based on student performance is extremely important in helping students learn. Third, Silverman suggests that long-held beliefs about the value of feedback may be wrong. Because of the complex nature of feedback and the way research had been conducted, it is not possible to say with any certainty that feedback is important for skill learning. After reviewing the evolution of his own research agenda, Silverman offers some suggestions for the future of research on teaching in physical education. What some have called performance pedagogy (Laker 2000) has provided us with a great deal of information about the teaching and learning process in physical education. Our research now needs to go beyond motor skill learning. We need to know more about attitudes, motivation and cognition (the students' and teachers' thought processes). Finally, Silverman calls for a combining of research methods and a consideration of student and teacher contexts in addressing these important issues.

Hastie's chapter on sport education begins with a brief, but useful, guide to the history of sport as a component of physical education (Chapter 7). He points out that team games and sports have a relatively short history of inclusion into educational programmes but that the place they now hold is perceived by many as being a cornerstone of the subject. Nevertheless, he recognises and elaborates on a number of concerns that have been associated with this so-called traditional physical education. The development of substantive physical skill is hindered by the units of instruction being too short, leading to lack of content mastery. The structuring of some lessons has led to discriminatory and abusive practices such as large-sided games and embarrassing student selection of teams and groups. Students have also made claims that typical content lacks authenticity and is boring and irrelevant to their home and community lives. To counter these and other concerns, sport education was developed into a curriculum and instruction model that attempts to replicate, or at least include, the defining characteristics of sport. Research has been quite supportive of the model and reports that participants tend to be more enthusiastic and work harder in sport education than in comparable physical education settings. Students also developed more knowledge about the rules, traditions and values of the sports as well as becoming more accomplished performers in game situations. In general the model is reported as being attractive to both students and teachers. Sport education models have been changed to suit local conditions, contexts and teaching objectives. For example, Hastie cites hybrid creations such as Sport for Peace and Empowering Sport, both designed to achieve specific educational outcomes. Although the data are supportive, Hastie concludes that we need more information before we can suggest that sport education overcomes the problems inherent in institutionalized sport. There is also a need for further investigations into the long-term effects of sport education. Are students continuing in physical activity after school and are they developing into citizens of the sporting community? These are the crucial questions that further research needs to answer.

The proposals that arise from 'What we know' are divided into two sections; theoretical and practical. A strong theoretical support will be constructed to provide a rigorous intellectual foundation for the subsequent practical proposals. All curriculum models need this basis and there has been ample theory reported earlier that can be accommodated into a viable structure. The practical implementation section will provide guidelines that will enable teachers and curriculum professionals to plan and develop a more relevant and contextual physical education curriculum for their students. Although suggestions will be made, the detail of implementation will be left to local and contextual levels. The following proposals are a suggested framework, not a prescription.

The 'new pedagogy'

Theoretical background

The whole of this theoretical exposition is located in the arena of situated learning (Lave and Wenger 1991). As explained earlier in Chapter 3, this theory combines the twin concepts of *legitimate peripheral participation* and *communities of practice*. Legitimate peripheral participation refers to being involved in meaningful physical activity in real or authentic settings. In the early stages of participation, practitioners are engaged at the margins and are gradually accepted into the central communities of practice as their skills, knowledge and demonstration of sub-cultural norms develop and become acceptable to the community, which in this case is the relevant sporting community. If adopted and taken seriously, this whole concept of situated learning should condition the practice of physical education, thus making it relevant, meaningful and culturally contextual to all participants; teachers, students, and their attendant communities. Additionally, situated learning theory is based on the constructivist theory of learning. As such, learning is socially constructed and cannot be separated from its social and cultural context. New learning is assimilated into a repertoire of skills and knowledges, based upon what we already know. That is, freshly presented knowledge is changed, reformed and combined with existing knowledge into a new, enlarged package of learning. In this way, new knowledge is not just added to what we already know, but is incorporated and not kept separate. Thus, the personal body of knowledge, including psychomotor skills, grows in totality not as an accumulation of bits and pieces, but as a holistic progression. This helps maintain relevance and is critical to perpetuating cultural and social contextuality.

Any new offerings in the field of curriculum must originate from a strong theoretical base located firmly in societal and cultural expectations for the educational process. Education has always had a number of purposes such as fulfilling potential, developing knowledge and skill, socialising citizens and so on. All of these are valuable components of the whole process, but physical education has a specific role to play. Our society, and most societies in the English-speaking world, want physical education to deal with a range of outcomes. These outcomes include skill learning, a healthy, active young population, personal and social responsible behaviour and positive attitudes towards physical activity. Where the emphasis is placed will be dependent upon the value that society places on each of outcomes. These value orientations are explained by Jewett *et al.* (1995). They list five value orientations: disciplinary mastery; self-actualisation; social reconstruction; learning process; and ecological integration. Each of these has varying degrees of emphasis on individual, subject or social development. It is extremely unlikely that any of these orientations alone is able to offer a complete justification for a physical education curriculum. However, when used in combination, they form a firmly rooted rationale for any curriculum proposal or development. We will take a brief look at each of these and see what they have to offer for our proposals. It will also become clear that each of the orientations can be used to incorporate some of the benefits and characteristics of the curricular initiatives explained in the preceding chapters.

Disciplinary mastery

As the name implies this orientation is predominantly about gaining expertise in the content of the subject. The content can, of course, vary from sport skills to health-related fitness to individual lifetime activities, to name but a few. Educators hope that young people will gain what they need to take a full part in their cultural heritage. In this case the heritage is what has come to be known as the traditional physical education curriculum. It is quite possible to question the worth of the content knowledge and to ask who determines what is worthwhile knowledge anyway. Indeed, traditional physical education has proved ineffective in encouraging young people to be physically active either in school or after school. But it is hard to argue against the values of skill acquisition, especially if we want to promote activity. Unskilled participants are unlikely to be participants for very long. It is also hard to argue against discipline mastery when part of the discipline is the cultural heritage of the content, i.e. the culture of sport. If we want our students to become skilled members of a community of sport then disciplinary mastery has much to recommend it.

Sport education and the pedagogy of motor skill learning are practical ways of incorporating disciplinary mastery into the curriculum. The pedagogy of motor skill learning is solely concerned with mastering the content skills of the subject. In Chapter 6, Silverman clearly outlines what we know and how it can be used to maximise skill learning. Although he acknowledges that we still need to know more about a variety of aspects of skill learning such as motivation, attitudes and cognition, our ability to teach skill, pure and simple, is adequately informed by the existing research.

If discipline mastery includes some aspects of the culture of sport, as well as learning physical skills, as Jewett *et al.* (1995) claim, then sport education can add this attractive possibility to a physical education curriculum. In Chapter 7, Hastie offers his extensive research findings to support the idea that sport education can teach more than just sport. It also allows and encourages students to become complete participants within the sports community by fulfilling a variety of authentic roles associated with the experience of sport. Sport education recognises that there is more to sport than just learning skills and taking part. This variety of roles and experiences allows participants to learn about sport as a sub-cultural, community activity, and not just as a series of motor skills to be acquired and rehearsed in an irrelevant and uncontextual way later. This fits very closely with constructivist learning and situated learning theory.

Self-actualisation

Respect for the worth and dignity of the individual is a basic aim of many educational programmes (Hellison 1985; Laker 2001; Morris and Stiehl 2002;

Stiehl 1993). Curricula that emphasise this type of value orientation concentrate on individual growth and development of self-direction. Students eventually assume responsibility for identifying their own goals and controlling their personal educational experience. Personal, social and then community responsibility form part of this ideal. By setting themselves their own goals, students are located in a task orientation situation where they measure success against their own standards not against each other. If one of the goals of physical education is to encourage socially critical, yet socially responsible citizens then a self-actualisation orientation can help in that process. But as we will see, and have already seen, although this orientation has much to commend it, on its own it is unlikely to achieve all that we require.

As Morris outlines in Chapter 4, many programmes that deal with responsibility as a major focus, begin with self-respect and self-responsibility. Individual sports and activities and the notion of merely participating are ideally suited to the promotion and development of this personal characteristic. This provides a solid foundation for a later exploration of issues of social responsibility, so important in team games and group situations. As students continue to progress chronologically, as well as in maturity, they could become exposed to a greater responsibility, community based but globally aware. This growing responsibility from individual, through social, to community and global fits well with a developing curriculum that begins with the individual skill-building blocks, later deals with sport as a social and community activity, and lastly addresses larger issues of a popular physical culture based on personal local relevance.

Social reconstruction

This orientation places society as the prime focus of the curriculum. Although education serves society, society can be changed by education. This notion of social change locates social reconstruction in the realm of critical theory. Critical theorists themselves have been criticised for being strong on criticisms and weak on solutions. Social reconstruction partially answers that criticism in that it makes real proposals for change. In some ways this mirrors what this book attempts to do and as such this orientation and this book have a natural affinity for each other. Within the context of this value orientation, a physical education curriculum would seek to develop a participatory democratic ethos, and some leadership skills as well as elements of cooperation and group problem solving. This could be done by dealing with issues of equity, gender, ethnicity, social mobility and politics (among others) as they relate to sport and physical activity. Historically, education is resistant to change, schools tend to replicate society, not reform it. However, critical pedagogy's exposure of the hidden curriculum has alerted many to the possibilities of hegemonic reproduction of invested power structures. It may be that teachers are now more receptive to ideas that challenge the *status quo* instead of supporting it.

The practice of reflection as articulated by Macdonald and Tinning in Chapter 5, has much to commend it in attempting to build a curriculum that addresses social reconstruction. Reflective practice assumes that political and social concerns are paramount in developing appropriate teaching skills. These are the same concerns that lend themselves to analysis in the social reconstruction value orientation. A true reflective practitioner wishes to improve the quality of the educational process by seeking to further his or her teaching by way of self-analysis and self-critique. A true reflective practitioner also wishes to address issues of inequity, bias and hegemony by exposing students to a fair curriculum that allows them to critically evaluate their activity choices and the popular physical cultural offerings of the popular press and media. In terms of teacher education and continuing professional development, reflective practice is crucial to building a new emancipatory pedagogy providing it is not used as a mechanism of assessment or to legitimise political action.

Learning process

There has been a call in recent years for schools to give students the skills to be lifelong learners. Whether lifelong learning is desirable or not is another debate: e.g. why should there be an unspoken compulsion for a person, content with his or her existence, to continue learning? As long as opportunity is available to learn, that should be enough. Part of that opportunity is having the necessary skills to take advantage of that lifetime of learning. The knowledge explosion and the ever increasing global availability of information mean that schools cannot possibly teach as much as we, i.e. society, would like our young people to learn and know. Physical education is no different to other subjects in this regard. More activities and sport are getting exposure on a more regular basis than ever before, and many young people would like to have opportunities to at least try those activities. Schools cannot possibly provide all these opportunities, but they could provide the foundation skills and attitudes that would allow and encourage students to take advantage of such opportunities later in life. Certain processing skills will help students engage in this increasingly data-driven society. Skills such as problem solving are very important in this value orientation, as are high-level conceptual abilities. In addition to language as a fundamental learning skill, students need to have a range of motor skills which will equip them for later learning. The ability to analyse, understand progressions, identify critical skill elements and rebuild, or construct anew, their own physical actions is desirable for these students.

How physical education deals with this is problematic. The way the subject has traditionally been presented has been direct, or command style, teaching (Mosston and Ashworth 1990). In this style a teacher presents the material, directs students in their practice and gives feedback on performance. There is very little room for variation, let alone student input. However, some styles of teaching do allow for, and encourage, student input. The more informal styles such as guided discovery, reciprocal and task teaching provide students with more opportunities for a certain amount of self-direction. This can begin very early on in the schooling process with educational gymnastics and adventure type activities. As students develop and mature they could be encouraged into elements of reflection and problem solving by implementing curricular initiatives such as Teaching Games for Understanding. What has been mentioned so far in the learning process value orientation has been directed at the psychomotor part of physical education. Students will also need to know where to go to get information, how to access opportunities, how to evaluate information (often in the form of very persuasive and sophisticated advertising) and what are the social and cultural consequences of pursuing further activity choice. This implies that part of the role of physical education in the learning process orientation is to provide acculturation opportunities for students. This would enable them to become fully functioning members of a developing and learning sporting community, not hindered by past experience, but empowered by it. Citizenship skills and cultural awareness, both in general and sporting terms, would provide a broad base and a general knowledge background in which students could locate their future participation and physical learning. Chapters 2 and 3 provide discussion and suggestions as to how this might be accommodated. The ability to be lifelong learners, as well as lifelong participants, would enhance students' possibilities of being global sporting citizens, locally active but globally aware.

Ecological integration

The final curriculum value orientation is ecological orientation. Individual self-actualisation and the celebration of personal meaning are combined with a view of education that is holistic and culturally, globally and environmentally sensitive. Individuals are viewed as integral parts of the environment; each affects the other and neither can operate in a vacuum, ignoring or ignorant of the other. It can be seen that this view combines certain elements from the other orientations but perhaps lacks the clarity of purpose of, say disciplinary mastery. It proposes a typically postmodern scenario where the curriculum moves away from the grand narratives of modernity, dominated by positivist science, to a system that requires a sociological, environmental ecology where dynamic balance is maintained by a symbiotic relationship between individuals and their surroundings. This system would use a variety of learning experiences, matching learners' needs to learning experiences while at the same time identifying connections and possibilities arising from these learning experiences. The needs of the students would be those skills and abilities required to successfully negotiate a changing, multicultural and diverse world of sporting and recreational activities and opportunities. This naturally contains aspects of social and environmental responsibility, citizenship and cultural sensitivity.

Ecological integration provides an opportunity to combine the other value orientations into a viable whole. Any curriculum that was dominated solely by a single orientation would be limited in potential and appeal. We cannot depart from the fact that the core of our subject is the psychomotor. All that we claim for physical education is supposedly achievable through participation in the activity. This being the case, there must be some element of disciplinary mastery in all physical education curricula.

Similarly, it would be an extremely irresponsible teacher who did not recognise the fact that there is an educational obligation to prepare students for later life. The learning process orientation takes account of this view and therefore must be considered in curriculum development. Physical education has always claimed to develop and improve social and personal characteristics in students so self-actualisation and social reconstruction have some relevance in helping to attain this subject goal.

As Jewett *et al.* (1995) point out, these five value orientations cover aspects of the curriculum that are individual, subject-based and society-based. Ecological integration is the only one that has elements of all three in it. The defining characteristic of any curriculum will not be that it bases its implementation on any one orientation, but how the emphasis is placed among and between the values. There are ample curriculum models, e.g. sport education, social responsibility, to construct a coherent curriculum package that takes full advantage of all the value orientations. The preceding chapters have provided many examples of how this could be done, and the descriptions of each of the value orientations have contained some hints as to which curriculum models might be best suited to each of them. However, a comprehensive curriculum package has not been proposed. What follows is a tentative suggestion of such a curriculum package. *Tentative*, because one of the purposes of this book is to provoke discussion, debate and controversy. *Suggestion*, because, as Estes points out in Chapter 1, curriculum should be oral, particular, local and timely. That is, it should be contextual and relevant to the various constituents affected by it; teachers, students, parents and communities. In terms of physical curriculum, one size does not fit all!

Before we start to talk about the practical content of a new curriculum and a new pedagogy, we must first decide what it is we want the outcomes to be. Although this will vary, simply put, most communities would want their students to become physically able, knowledgeable, socially responsible and active sports consumers. It is no longer adequate for a physical education programme/curriculum to attempt to produce only skilful performers. In spite of all that we know about teaching and learning motor skills, curricula have failed to produce such students in any large numbers in the past. Curricula must now begin to take account of the larger context and help students become what Siedentop (1994) calls literate, enthusiastic and competent sportspeople.

Practical implementation

Unusually, for a largely theoretical text, this book attempts to add some practical elements to the theoretical discussion. It provides the foundation of a curriculum that still needs to be expanded into a workable model. That will be the work of other authors, perhaps those more closely linked to the practice of physical education in the schools. In common with the rest of this book, this is meant to stimulate discussion and debate about what is the best way forward. Regardless of these disclaimers, this proposal offers the following practical extension of the preceding theoretical discussions. These suggestions are formed around three *progressive phases* which approximate to the three levels of schooling generally offered in the United States, elementary, middle and senior. Although the middle school level has virtually disappeared in the United Kingdom, it has attractions for curriculum design in that it provides the link, or bridge, between foundation and application.

Progressive phase one

In common with many other developmentally appropriate curricula, this phase will offer the physical foundations so important for later development. In a departure from most other curricula, this phase will also offer the potential for individual responsibility and self-respect, and the beginnings of social skill development and equity awareness, as well as these physical foundations.

The physical foundations should consist of the locomotor type activities such as running, walking and skipping; and twisting, turning and jumping. These simple, yet crucial movements, not only allow for later efficient movement in games and sports but can also be used to facilitate dance and gymnastic activities. Without these movements later development will be hindered, if not impossible. These skills may also serve a remedial purpose for a few students who are not as physically able as others. A second physical component is the manipulative type skills such as catching, throwing, kicking and so on. These are obviously the building blocks of future sports and games participation. All the skills in both of these physical foundation components can be taught in ways that are fun, interesting and educational instead of as isolated skills. These skills can later be used in a 'Teaching Games for Understanding' (TGfU) approach that incorporates skills into game-like activities designed to help students. The later years of this phase are an ideal place to use TGfU. Here, children will learn skills appropriate to a range of games and sports and be encouraged to make connections between activities that share common skills and strategies. Our profession is well served with knowledge that enables us to be effective teachers of physical skills. Silverman's Chapter 6 details much of what we know in this area.

This phase would also be a good place to start very simple dance. Folk dance from different countries is a good way to introduce social dance and all the social skills that are required in that activity. (It is also an excellent way of keeping alive the physical language of cultures, thus slowing the extinction of the language of marginalized communities.) In addition to the physical skills of dance, teachers will need to take account of what Macdonald and Tinning have to say in Chapter 5 about reflective practice. Issues of gender equity and gender roles can be addressed in dance but only by teachers who are sensitive to the students' perceptions. Some elements of cultural diversity can also be provided here and this would answer many of the criticisms of physical education in a monoculture, that it is Anglo, Caucasian and male-centred (Evans *et al.* 1996; Penney and Evans 1997).

Many of the activities in this phase, even dance, can be practised as individual activities, although teachers would obviously take opportunities to promote group skills. In this regard, they could provide good opportunities to try to develop the traits of self-responsibility. Hellison's (1996) first three levels of respecting the rights and feelings of others, participation, effort, and self-direction are where the teachers should be directing their efforts. The use of many of the strategies provided by Morris in Chapter 4 is appropriate here.

This section on practical implementation is being painted with broad brush strokes. There has been no mention in this phase of gymnastic activities or swimming, for example. These have not been deliberately excluded, rather, it has been left to individual teachers to decide how to incorporate them into the phase to best make use of what they have to offer. Certainly, both educational gymnastics and swimming have a great deal to contribute to skill development, individual character traits and attitudes towards physical education.

By mastering these foundation skills in small game and activity settings, and by beginning to experience the cultural diversity and social interaction provided by different types of dance, children in this phase will be able to develop the self-respect and individual responsibility that will facilitate the growing of positive attitudes towards physical activity. These skills, attitudes and knowledge can then be built upon in the next phase of the curriculum.

Progressive phase two

This second phase will see the further development of students into literate, enthusiastic and competent sportspeople. Much of what is taught here should emphasise that many physical activities are conducted in social settings and that being an effective part of that sporting community is part of being a citizen of the world of sport. In common with this ideal, it is desirable to begin to look at the promotion of social responsibility in activity environments. We should also begin welcoming students into a community of practice by ensuring good experiences in sport and activity participation.

This suggests that this phase is the best place to begin to provide the 'total' experience of sport. Sport education bases its rationale on this concept. In Chapter 7, Hastie outlines the benefits of the sport education model of curriculum. He also suggests ways that it could be improved. By utilising this model, teachers would expose participants to a variety of legitimate roles in sport. It may well be that youngsters find roles other than participant that are attractive to them. This would bode well for future involvement in physical activity in a variety of appropriate roles. While endorsing the sport education model, I do not advocate the wholesale acceptance of sport as being non-problematic. Sport has historically been presented in a gendered, elitist, stratified and exclusive environment. A reflective teacher would ensure that students were encouraged to be critically analytical of sport, as well as accepting of sport's benefits.

Not all students will be appreciative of team games or stereotypical sports. For this reason there needs to be a range of activities on offer that facilitates student experimentation with alternatives to sport education. Health-related fitness (HRF), outdoor pursuits and individual activities are important components of this phase. After initial exposure to these activities, such a programme would encourage some element of student choice to take place, in a fairly limited way.

Although it should not be the sole responsibility of physical education to teach students about health, a certain amount of HRF can readily be taught using physical education content (Almond and Harris 1997; Cale 1997; Harris 1998). This could also be a start in exposing students to a critical appraisal of what is presented as a healthy body by the media, although this element of physical culture will be dealt with in more detail in phase three. Together with the analytical requirements of the sport education part of the curriculum, this embryonic critique of popular physical culture introduces students to the notions of reasoned choices and evidence evaluation in activity settings. This is a very valuable ability to have when making choices later in their school careers and also in life.

Outdoor pursuits and its attendant incarnations of experiential education, adventure education and outdoor education can pick up the theme of self-responsibility and develop it more strongly. Problem solving, group dynamics and interdependence are things that outdoor pursuits claims to promote very well. Many lessons can be learnt 'in the outdoors' and these are just a few of them. Social responsibility should start to be emphasised and Morris (Chapter 4) has some good suggestions about how to do that in physical education. Hellison's (1996) fourth level of sensitivity and responsiveness to the well-being of others is an appropriate target for attainment in this second progressive phase. Students will be starting to look beyond themselves as they develop friendship groups and perhaps some of these groups will share some characteristics of sporting sub-cultures. It is the function of the teaching of the physical education curriculum in this phase to develop physical activity skills, knowledge and attitudes so that students can become legitimate participants within the communities of sporting practice, at the same time developing social awareness and social responsibility within those communities.

Progressive phase three

The physical education curriculum really starts to expand in its expectations, and therefore its potential, in this phase. Not only are students expected to refine their physical skills, but they are also expected to develop critical thinking skills, become globally aware of the responsibilities of choice and learn more about physical activity and sport as a cultural communication medium.

In terms of physical activities, students will be exposed to more activities of a recreational nature. They should learn the skills of these activities (remember, they should already have the foundations necessary for further development) and where they are available in the community. Some activities might only be available at locations outside the school facilities and I would agree with Fernández-Balboa

(Chapter 8) that students should be allowed and encouraged to take advantage of such availability. This is a way of making valuable connections to the outside sporting community. At the same time those that wish to continue in more traditional sports and games should have the opportunity to do so. This can be provided for in class time physical education, intramural and interschool teams and games, much as it is now.

Kirk's (1995) suggestion that we need to make students critically aware of the portrayal of the body in popular physical culture needs to be taken seriously. I would extend this critical stance to include not just the portrayal of the body, but also an analysis of what popular sports and recreational activities can offer, both the good and the bad. As he states, this connection between physical education and popular physical culture may begin to make the subject more meaningful to students. It will also allow them to make informed choices about their level and type of aspirations and participation. This would be truly educational and beneficial to students and useful in ways not commonly associated with physical education. In accord with Kirk's call, the curriculum proposed here is systematic and progressive using current theorising and current knowledge.

The final component of progressive phase three is that of extended social responsibility and awareness of a global sports community. This matches with Hellison's (1996) fifth level of responsibility; outside the gym. Morris also proposes a responsibility component in Chapter 4 that allows students to practise these social skills in surroundings other than the school gymnasium. This carry-over from school to community helps students in making connections between what they learn at school and what they can practice in the local sporting community. I suggest in Chapter 3 some possibilities for development of citizenship qualities in these community situations. However, there is a need to go beyond the local and use the global nature of sport and physical activity to engage our students. Kinchin and O'Sullivan (1999) write about a unit of work that uses physical education as cultural studies to make the subject more meaningful to students. In addition to what I have to say in Chapter 2, Clements and Kinzler (2002) write about how activities can be used in senior schools to promote an understanding of different cultures from around the world and suggest some ways in which school physical education can make a valuable contribution. The practice of sport is a pervasive force and could be used for enhancing global cultural awareness. This may be the ultimate justification for physical education in schools; i.e. the development and understanding of global cultural connections through activity; a true global language.

Conclusion

The original idea for this book was to stimulate debate and discussion regarding the future of physical education in schools. The subtitle, Building a New Pedagogy, is important but secondary. Each of the earlier chapters brings us up to date with research in important curriculum areas. For any future debate to be productive, it ought to have its basis in what we already know. Each of those chapter authors was also asked to indicate shortcomings of the research and ways in which their particular initiative could benefit from further investigation. They have done an admirable job in this regard; some have even gone as far as suggesting that their field of investigation has a problematic component.

What I have tried to do in this concluding chapter is integrate those ideas into an outline curriculum proposal for the future subject. Much of what I have written about has been commented on before. For example, the fact that physical education is seen by students as irrelevant and uncontextual. This is one of the problems I have attempted to address. However, very few people have the privilege of beginning with a clean sheet in the planning process; there is always some existing curriculum that has to be accommodated or amended or changed. I have had the luxury of that clean sheet. With the academic support of the research and the implicit support of the contributing authors, I have proposed a curriculum that takes account of what we know and also the shortcomings of current curriculum offerings. Although this may be a poor substitute for a blueprint, it is a starting point for that debate and discussion. Our subject needs it and our students deserve it. To paraphrase the Olympic opening speech: 'Let the debate begin'.

References

Almond. L. and Harris, J. (1997) 'The ABC of HRE: translating a rationale into practical guidelines', *British Journal of Physical Education*, 28(3): 14–17.

Cale, L. (1997) 'Physical activity promotion in schools: beyond the curriculum', *Pedagogy in Practice*, 3(1): 56–68.

Clements, R. and Kinzler, S. (2002) *A Multicultural Approach to Physical Education: Proven Strategies for Middle and High School*, Champaigne, IL: Human Kinetics.

Evans, J., Davies, B. and Penney, D. (1996) 'Teachers, teaching and the social construction of gender relations', *Sport, Education and Society*, 1(2): 165–184.

Flintoff, A. (1997) 'Gender relations in physical education initial teacher education', in G. Clarke and B. Humberstone (eds), *Researching Women in Sport*, London: Macmillan Press, 164–182.

Grineski, S.C. (1989) 'Children, games, and prosocial behavior: insights and connections', *Journal of Physical Education, Recreation and Dance*, 60: 20–25.

Harris, J. (1998) 'Health-related exercise: rationale and recommendations', *British Journal of Physical Education*, 29(3): 11–12.

Hellison, D. (1985) *Goals and Strategies for Teaching Physical Education*, Champaigne, IL: Human Kinetics.

——(1996) 'Teaching personal and social responsibility in physical education', in S.J. Silverman and C.D. Ennis (eds), *Student Learning in Physical Education: Applying Research to Enhance Instruction*, Champaigne, IL: Human Kinetics, 269–286.

Jewett, A.E., Bain, L.L. and Ennis, C.D. (1995) *The Curriculum Process in Physical Education*, Dubuque, IA: Brown & Benchmark.

Kallusky, J. (1996) 'This ain't English', *Teaching Secondary Physical Education*, September: 6–7.

Kinchin, G.D. and O'Sullivan, M. (1999) 'Making physical education meaningful for high school students', *Journal of Physical Education, Recreation and Dance*, 70(5): 40–44.

Kirk, D. (1992) *Defining Physical Education: The Social Construction of a School Subject in Postwar Britain*, London: Falmer.

——(1995) 'Physical education and cultural relevance: a personal statement, in A.E. Jewett, L.L. Bain and C.D. Ennis, *The Curriculum Process in Physical Education*, Boston, MA: McGraw-Hill, 2nd edn, 369–373.

Laker, A. (2000) *Beyond the Boundaries of Physical Education and Sport: Educating Young People for Citizenship and Social Responsibility*, London: RoutledgeFalmer.

——(2001) *Developing Personal, Social and Moral Education through Physical Education: A Practical Guide for Teachers*, London: RoutledgeFalmer.

Laker, A., Craig Laker, J. and Lea, S. (2003) 'School experience and the issue of gender', *Sport, Education and Society*, 8(1): 73–89.

Lave, J. and Wenger, E. (1991) *Situated Learning: Legitimate Peripheral Participation*, New York: Cambridge University Press.

Morris, G.S.D. and Stiehl, J. (1999) *Changing Kids' Games*, Champaigne, IL: Human Kinetics, 2nd edn.

Morris, G.S.D. and Stiehl, J. (2002) *Becoming Responsible*, Los Angeles: MOST Publisher.

Mosston, M. and Ashworth, S. (1990) *The Spectrum of Teaching Styles: From Command to Discovery*, New York: Longman.

National Association for Sport and Physical Education (2002) *Advanced Physical Education Program Report Manual, including 2001 NASPE/NCATE Advanced Physical Education Standards*, Reston, VA.

Penney, D. and Evans, J. (1997) 'Naming the game. Discourse and domination in physical education and sport in England and Wales', *European Physical Education Review*, 3(1): 21–32.

Pinar, W.F., Reynolds, W.E., Slattery, P. and Taubman, P.M. (1995) *Understanding Curriculum: An Introduction to the Study of Historical and Contemporary Curriculum Discourses*, New York: Peter Lang Publishing.

QCA (1998) *Final Report of the Advisory Group on Education for Citizenship and the Teaching of Democracy in Schools*, London: Qualifications and Curriculum Authority.

Siedentop, D. (1994) *Sport Education: Quality PE through Positive Sport Experiences*, Champaigne, IL: Human Kinetics.

Stiehl, J. (1993) 'Becoming responsible: theoretical and practical implications', *Journal of Physical Education, Recreation and Dance*, 64(5): 38–71.

Toulmin, S. (1990) *Cosmopolis: The Hidden Agenda of Modernity*, Chicago, IL: University of Chicago Press.

Index